EQUIPPED!
Twelve Transforming Truths
And How to Use Them

This book was previously published as
Knowing Jesus Is Enough For Joy, Period!
And
EQUIPPED! Ready for Every Day Spiritual Warfare

Living the Truth That Knowing Jesus Is Enough for Joy!

Expanded and Revised Edition,
Study Guide Questions Included

S. M. Wibberley

Edited by
Craig A. Noll

Cover by
Karen Brightbill

Illustrations by
Nat Wibberley

Edifying Services Press
www.edifyingservices.com

Copyright © 2015 by S. M. Wibberley

EQUIPPED! Twelve Empowering Truths and How to Use Them

Expanded and Revised Edition

by S. M. Wibberley

Printed in the United States of America

ISBN 978-0-9832077-2-6

All rights reserved solely by the author. The author guarantees that to his knowledge all contents are original and do not infringe upon the legal rights of any other person or work. No part of this book may be reproduced in any form without the permission of the author. The views expressed in this book are not necessarily those of the publisher.

Unless otherwise indicated, Bible quotations are taken from the HOLY BIBLE, NEW INTERNATIONAL VERSION®. Copyright © 1973, 1978, 1984 by International Bible Society. Used by permission of Zondervan. All rights reserved.

www.EdifyingServices.com

Previously published under the title
Knowing Jesus Is Enough for Joy, Period!
and
EQUIPPED! Ready for Every Day Spiritual Warfare

Order Paperbacks through http://www.edifyingservices.com.

Order Kindle version through Amazon.com.

All profits from books ordered from these two sites go directly to supporting world missions.

"This book is an honest look at what it means to really take your faith to the next level. The author's vulnerability lends it a genuineness that leaves the reader both challenged and encouraged. I would recommend this book to anyone who wants to deepen their spiritual life."
— Sarah D., a young professional and mother

"I found practical and in-depth guidance on living for Christ and resisting Satan's temptation in Steve Wibberley's book. . . . The steps to victory over Satan will be helpful to many who struggle with continual failure. The guidance in discipleship will be helpful to all who want to grow daily. It is obvious that the book represents years of experience in walking with the Lord, and that the counsel is the fruit of victorious warfare."
— Dr. Johnny V. Miller, pastor and former president of Columbia International University

"If all the books and sermons I have read and heard on spiritual life were boiled down, this book would contain the meat."
— Alicia, young teacher

"This book is my teaching tool for a church women's class — it is full of Christian principles and practical applications of familiar teachings about living the Christian life, but it has a deeper and more personal slant that opens the door in my class for sharing about problem areas, getting beneath to root problems.

"Another huge life-changer has to do with thanking God for/in every situation, as praise, as boosting belief in the character of God, as acknowledgment that He is in control and is able to use the situation for good. It is chock-full of practical ways to live the Christian Life 24/7."
— Women's class teacher

"I feel as though you have mentored me through your book. Thank you for your intentionality in getting to know our Savior, an inspirational example to me and many others.

"Also thank you for your transparency in sharing your life stories in the book. . . . All that to say, thank you! I can't wait to meet with Jesus tomorrow morning, or even tonight!"
— Amanda, young cross-cultural worker

"Today I got a phone call from my son, and we had one of the best conversations ever. He talked about how he was striving to trust God in everything and to know that, if disappointment comes, he would be able to trust God to work it out. He said he and his wife have been talking and praying together, and their relationship is better than it has been in a long, long time. My son is working toward praising God for who He is and not just thanking Him for what He has done. He said his spiritual life has been really growing, and he is spending a lot of time in prayer. And what has been the trigger for all of this amazing change? Your book! He has been reading and studying it carefully, and it has just spoken to him deeply. What a wonderful praise! And what a great answer to many years of prayer!"

— Retired English teacher

"This book has come at a PERFECT time. I totally and thoroughly love it. The book, your prayers, and God's grace (not in that order) will rehabilitate me. . . . I truly think this book is probably the best gift you have ever gotten me! The timing is just perfect. Like a brand new key in a lock!"

— Shawn, prisoner in a U.S. jail

"I am enjoying very much reading this book. What a great resource book to help in the battles we encounter in life!"

— Cathy, a veteran cross-cultural worker

"The book is challenging me just as if we were talking about one subject after another. God blessed you with all these insights over the years and has made this a treasure trove. I am slowly digging my way through it, and the Holy Spirit is nudging me constantly as I get further into it."

— Paul O., pastor

"God is blessing me each and every day since I purchased your book Equipped! I am a slow reader, so I have been using the book in my daily devotions, and what I have learned is helping me in my relationship with God. I love the way that it starts and keeps on adding and building....Thank you for listening, for obeying, and for sharing with us what you have learned. . . . I often enjoy your prayers, making them mine by changing the plurals to singular pronouns."

— Paula Baker, farmer's wife

"Recently, my wife of thirty-three years read Wibberley's book . . . and led a ladies study through it. It has noticeably impacted her as well as several of her friends. Watching her, I now become convicted when I begin to complain because, after reading the book, she virtually never does. While she has always been an encourager, with what she has learned and applied from the book, she has taken building others up to another level. And in the midst of

our very full life of ministry, she sees the positive at times when disappointment could come easily. Personally, I am ready to embark on my second reading to bring the refreshing truths back into focus."
— Chris, founder of a ministry to crack addicts

"This book is so incredibly dense with truth that I will have to read it many times throughout my life to really get it all. It is precisely the kind of truth I need in my life right now. I praise God for the timeliness and wisdom in it."
— Louis Kawood, paramedic

"Having known Steve Wibberley for many years and followed his interesting newsletters from overseas, I was delighted to see many of the practical and spiritual applications he has culled from his life experiences and years in a Middle Eastern country. His 'confessing in layers' chapter alone is worth the read, [as are his] interesting insights from his walk with the Lord through the minefields of life."
— Roland Mitcheson, pastor

"Mr. Wibberley is honest, transparent, and practical, traits that make his teaching so interesting and impressive. He has an amazing ability to make Scriptural truths/commands seem simple and doable....This is not the kind of book that one reads once; rather, it is a book to refer to over and over as we seek to grow in our walk with Christ."
— Tammy, mother of four

"Steve Wibberley shares principles and disciplines he has dug out and practiced until they have become habits. Having known Steve for many years, I know that joy characterizes his life in places where drudgery and discouragement are all too easy to succumb to....I am benefiting already from applying disciplines and practices he describes to turn the everyday circumstances and discouragements life brings into opportunities to live above them in joy."
— Chris Zeidner, computer scientist

"This is a very good book for learning how to live as a Christian and how to deal with day-to-day spiritual challenges; the author is very honest and forthright in discussing his spiritual struggles."
— Carl Rudenborg, architect

"Reading this book was a personal blessing to me. The life experience shared gives insight into how to overcome the common pitfalls of the Christian life I often get stuck in. I love the practical application of this book. Knowing that

Steve served in an overseas context for more than thirty years gave the book special weight for me. I hope to share the principles in Equipped! both with my local friends and with my own children."

— Tiffany, cross-cultural worker

"I found the book very helpful. The chapters on journaling (lifting up your soul), confessing in layers, and putting on the spiritual armor were practical and helpful. I think this is a good tool that is needed for our discipleship efforts. I also enjoyed the narratives modeling the lesson components."

— Kevin, pastor

*Dedicated to all the workers in Christar,
a faithful and committed band
carrying the Good News to difficult places.*

*And to Mark Deckard, kindred spirit, friend,
biblical counselor blessed with the gift of
discernment, and author of the insightful book*
Helpful Truth in Past Places:
The Puritan Practice of Biblical Counseling
(Christian Focus Publications, 2010)

www.edifyingservices.com

Warning!

This book is not a quick read.
It is best read slowly
taking time to digest,
understand and implement the
many lessons and insights.

Take your time and enjoy!

The Twelve Transforming Truths

1. Knowing Jesus is Enough for Joy!   Chapters 1-3…. Page 7

2. By Letting Go and Holding On, We Can Rise Above the Challenges of Life: Chapter 5…... Page 39

3. We Can Stand in Whatever Comes by Praying On and Using the Armor of God: Part 2…..Page 51, Part 7....Page 191 and A Final Word….Page 296

4. Worship Releases Power: Part 3….Page 87

5. Confession Brings Freedom: Part 4….Page 115

6. Lifting Our Souls to God Brings Insight, Direction and Joy: Part 5….Page 151

7. The Filling of the Spirit Brings Humility and Power: Part 6….Page 169

8. Forgiveness Brings Freedom: Chapter 26….Page 223

9. Offering the Sacrifice of Thanksgiving Honors God: Chapter 27….Page 237

10. Our Significance and Security Come From God: Chapter 28…Page 250

11. Biblical Meditation Transforms Us: Chapter 30….Page 269

12. Intercession is God's Invitation to Join Him in What He's Doing: Chapters 31,32….Page 285

Contents

Illustrations	xii
Foreword	xiii
Acknowledgments	xv
Introduction	1

Part 1. Living the Truth That Jesus Is Enough for Joy — 5

1. A Changed Worldview — 7
2. Living in the Context of Truth — 19
3. Total Faith — 27
4. Help for Those Who Want to Wholeheartedly Follow Jesus — 33
5. Two Concepts to Help Live in the Joy of Jesus — 39

Part 2. Spiritual Warfare: Situation Normal — 51

6. The Battle: Lies vs. Truth — 53
7. The Battle Illustrated — 58
8. Being Strong in the Lord — 62
9. On Being a Minister of Defense — 68
10. Becoming a Minister of Offense — 73
11. Other Aspects of Spiritual Warfare — 82

Part 3. Worship — 87

12. Worship = Thanksgiving + Praise — 89
13. Praise, Focused on God's Character — 93
14. Purposes of Worship — 107

Part 4. Confession — 115

15. Confessing in Layers — 117
16. Layers of Sin under Pornography — 127
17. Layers and Motives — 135
18. Confessing ahead of Time — 142

Contents

Part 5. Lifting Our Souls	**151**
19. Using Meditation and Journaling	153
20. Transparency	162
Part 6. Filling with the Holy Spirit	**169**
21. How to Be Filled	171
22. Results of Being Filled	179
Part 7. Deeper Thoughts on Putting on the Armor	**191**
23. Background	193
24. The Belt of Truth	206
25. The Breastplate of Righteousness	215
26. The Shoes of Peace	223
27. The Shield of Faith	237
28. The Helmet of Salvation	250
29. The Sword of the Spirit	263
Part 8. Essential, Lifelong Practices	**267**
30. Meditation	269
31. Prayer for Others	278
32. Prayer as Powerful — and Personal	285
A Final Word	296
Index of Subjects	299
Index of Scriptures	304

Illustrations

3.1. Intellect-based faith	27
3.2. Emotion-based faith	28
3.3. Work-based faith	29
3.4. Balanced, biblical faith	29
5.1. Let go . . . hold on . . . rise above	40
5.2. God is moving history	47
7.1. The full armor	58
7.2. Facing temptation	59
7.3. Prepared to use truth	59
7.4. Using the shield of faith	60
7.5. Agreeing with God against Satan	60
7.6. Standing against Satan in Jesus' name	61
9.1. A scale in balanced tension	69
15.1. Confession in layers: worry	120
15.2. Confession in layers: impatience	122
21.1. Out of gas!	171
21.2. The greatness of God's love	175
24.1. Proper negative-positive tension	209
26.1. The shoes of peace	223
27.1. The full armor	238
28.1. The helmet of salvation	250
28.2. The Lord crowns us	254
32.1. Prayer: like using an ax	285
32.2. Prayer: like using a ray gun	286

Foreword

The contents of the book you are holding bring to mind two small kingdom parables of Jesus, the so-called gem parables (Matt. 13:44-46):

> The kingdom of heaven is like treasure hidden in a field.
>   When a man found it, he hid it again,
>   and then in his joy went and sold all he had and bought that field.
>
> Again, the kingdom of heaven is like a merchant looking for fine pearls.
>   When he found one of great value,
>   he went away and sold everything he had and bought it.

In these words Jesus highlights the life-changing joy of one who discovers his Father's kingdom, as well as the life-denying choice to sell all in order to possess this treasure.[1]

From the very first sentence of chapter 1, you will hear author S. M. Wibberley clearly speaking as a man who shares the joy of the treasure-finder in Jesus' parables. And by the time you reach the very end of the book ("May you have great growth and joy as you walk in His way!"), you will know the author as one who couldn't be more convinced that the joy he's discovered has in fact sustained and nurtured him through an astonishing array of internal and external pressures. And that the same joy is there for the taking of any reader who will "walk in His way."

You'll meet the author also as one who is more than ready to sell everything for the sake of the kingdom-treasure, for whom no price is too high to pay that only he might fully obtain and grow in his discovery of Jesus Himself, source of the deepest joy. This zeal has led to personal insights in the areas of spiritual warfare, worship, confession, "lifting up" his soul, and being filled with the Spirit, not to mention meditation and prayer. These insights — the fruit of his steadfast, joy-based meditation and obedience, day after day,

---

1. According to commentator Frederick Dale Bruner, Jesus has a certain order in mind here in his two main points. "The main question in interpretation has always been this: what is *stressed* in the [gem] parables? Is it (1) *the joy of the discovery,* which causes the selling . . . , or is it (2) *the selling of all* in order to obtain the discovery . . . ? The best answer, I think, is 'both,' but in that order: the joy of discovery causes the zeal of the selling, grace causes good works" (*Matthew: A Commentary,* vol. 2 [Grand Rapids: Eerdmans, 2004], p. 48). Readers will quickly see that the author of this book lives by the same priority.

year after long year — show their mettle as the author relates how they have enabled him to go through and "rise above" depression, bodily injury, a host of personal sins (he lists thirty-one), a midnight arrest and week in jail for his faith, and countless other "flaming arrows" (Eph. 6:16).

My wife and I have known the author and his family for over thirty years and have had the joy of exchanging numerous visits in our homes, both in the U.S. and overseas. In the process, we have witnessed his joy and his "selling all" in very many different contexts. I can confirm that, in his daily life, these key points of Jesus' parables lack the odor of abstract theology or "ought"-driven duty. Furthermore, in my own heart I see that, as I have assisted in editing this book, the author's words have been provoking a stirring toward the worship, meditation, and spiritual alertness that the author here so convincingly describes.

Craig A. Noll
Editor, Wm. B. Eerdmans Publishing Co.
Grand Rapids, Michigan

Acknowledgments

Each of us has many people who have built into our lives, most of them doing so unknowingly. Although my father was not himself a believer, his insistence that we attend church had a huge influence in all of us five siblings coming to Christ. My mother influenced me in her example of quiet grace, a giving heart, and good works.

In my early years three Sunday School teachers in particular contributed to my growth in faith. Linwood Tracy, Alma Eastland, and Marguerite Simpson were examples and prods to help me move ahead. Linwood encouraged us students to memorize, paying us twenty-five cents for each verse learned. In her gentle, deep way Alma helped me take more seriously the things I was taught. Marguerite challenged my intellect and helped me practice what I knew.

Following graduation from college, I traveled to Alaska by motorcycle to teach in a government school in an Eskimo village. Along the way, there were some beacons pointing me to Jesus, people whose names I don't remember. One was a college professor in central Washington state who challenged me on where I was going in life. Another was a little old lady in a church in Seattle who began to pray for me every day after I attended a Sunday evening service. Her pastor also brought me up for prayer each Wednesday. Then there was the couple in Juneau who invited me for lunch after church and got me to join the Word Book Club.

In Alaska, Doug Brown, the public health nurse in an Eskimo village near where I lived, was a good example to me, demonstrating the power of Christ in his life at a time I was going through a depression. My philosophy of life (simply to help others) turned out to be inadequate for life in a tough situation, and I was forced to look for a new answer. God led me to look back on all that He had taught me in church and relationships and His Word. A clear understanding of my sinfulness, along with Christ's buying forgiveness and eternal life for me by His death and resurrection, led me to a deep surrender with the prayer, "Lord, I give you my will and take yours in its place." Then Dave and Mitzy Shinen, Wycliffe Bible translators, helped me in my newfound faith and prayed faithfully for me.

The next summer at a teacher training course in California, an older student, Jewel Joslyn, took me under her wing and mentored me in prayer. Then

ACKNOWLEDGMENTS

she and her husband, Keith, took me to a Bill Gothard seminar. Bill's teaching on the validity of Scripture and value of meditation left a bigger impact on my life than any other single factor or person.[2] All of the growth and ministry in my life have flowed from the spring of scriptural meditation that Bill explained and that I started practicing.

A year later I spent a few weeks with Francis Schaeffer at L'Abri in Switzerland, which was significant in freeing me from some baggage and providing answers to the seeming conflict of science and Scriptures.

Peter Lyons of Youth for Christ gave me good teaching on the Book of Ephesians, and Roland Mitcheson, who helped us put on coffeehouses, showed me how to share my faith in the druggy environment of the 1970s.

Then my wonderful wife, Barbara, opened up new worlds to me through her connections with Operation Mobilization. God used her to bring a desire to be part of getting the gospel to the people of the Middle East. Our faithful friend Paul Troper also played a part in this.

Some of my partners in church planting also honed aspects of my life, especially John Bell, plus others whose last names I won't mention for security reasons: Dan and Nancy, Chuck, Dick, and Ken. Fellow workers from other organizations, such as Julian and Hawoo, challenged me to think more widely.

Many of these people are probably unaware of the impact they had on me; they were just living what they believed, and it showed.

I have also profited from many books, tapes, sermons, and seminars. From some of these I have gleaned ideas that are now so embedded in my thinking and living that I have no idea where they came from, whether they are ideas arising from my immersion in Scripture or from the work of others. I have tried to give credit in this book for any such ideas when possible, but I just cannot remember all the sources. I am deeply indebted to many faithful ones who have gone before.

Who knows whom you are influencing? May this book help you "live what you believe" more effectively!

---

2. For information on Bill Gothard's Institute in Basic Life Principles, see www.iblp.org.

Introduction

My Dad as Mentor

When I was three years old, my father began to take me out to help him on his farm. I learned much from watching him in his work: how to drive a tractor, how to grease a mowing machine, and how to fix a fence. He was my first mentor, although he probably never thought of himself in that way.

As I grew older, he showed me many other practical things: how to milk a cow, how to change a tire, how to build a shed, how to cut down a tree and chop it up, how to do plumbing, and how to mow hay.

He also taught me about dealing with life: how to size up a problem, come up with a solution, and apply it; how to persevere in difficulty; and how to deal with people. He passed on to me this wisdom he lived by, distilled into proverbs:

> Always work with gravity.
> Never let politics or business get in the way of friendships.
> Money is not important at all — as long as you have enough of it.
> Customers are always right — unless it's dangerous for them.
> Never refuse legitimately offered money.

Just recently one of my father's sayings saved me from two expensive mistakes. He often said, "Listen to what's going on around you, especially when you're working with machines. What you hear could prevent a big problem." While using a tractor, I pulled the lever that controlled the scoop and heard a strange squeak. Remembering Dad's advice, I immediately stopped and got off the tractor to look at the scoop. Sure enough, there was a major problem: two bolts had fallen out of the frame supporting it. If I had continued with my work, the whole frame would have been bent and ruined. And then as I went back to shut off the tractor, I heard a strange noise coming from the transmission, so I checked the fluid level and found it below the dipstick! In the space of two minutes, heeding Dad's advice led to my being saved from two expensive disasters!

I am very thankful for this informal training; it has had a far greater impact on my life than my formal education. (Right now, I can think of only two points of knowledge from my entire college training!)

INTRODUCTION

The principles my father taught me have helped me in my life as a student, farmer, teacher, tire dealer, journalist, businessman, church planter, and pastor to missionaries.

Spiritual Lack

While I much appreciate my father's input on the practical, I regret that in my youth there was no mentor who came alongside to help me through the spiritual difficulties of life. My father did make sure we went to church, but he himself was not a follower of Jesus then, so he could not help me in these matters.

Eventually our attendance at church resulted in all five of us siblings coming to Christ. We got a good, basic education in the Bible and had some helpful input from teachers. With no one to be an actual mentor to me, however, I floundered in my inability to apply what I had learned.

I praise God that, starting in my early twenties, several men and women have taken the time to build into my spiritual life. God has used these mentors to bring to me just the input I needed at the moment. Through these mentors' teaching of the Word and modeling how to live it, God has given me insights, principles, disciplines, and spiritual weapons that have been very helpful in implementing Scripture in my life. In this book I share these with you, just as my father shared what wisdom he could with me. I hope I can be a kind of mentor in your life. In this regard, please feel free to photocopy any prayers or quotes from my journal that I share throughout the book, for your use or the use of others.

Relationship-Centered Implementation

The good tools I will pass on to you, however, can become ineffective and even destructive when used outside of a relationship with God — a vital, growing interaction with the Creator and Ruler of the universe. The Lord Jesus Christ calls us to walk with Him, to live in Him, to follow and obey Him in a relationship of love and grace.

Since we are still sinners and since what the Bible calls our "flesh" is always bent on self-centered living, when we try to apply these principles in our own natural human strength and wisdom, we will end up being disappointing, if not dangerous, to God, to ourselves, and to those around us.[3] As

---

3. The term "flesh" is an important biblical concept. It is the principle in us that continually fights against the Spirit (Gal. 5:17), even after we have repented of our sin and by grace have become children of God through faith in Jesus. Before we had this new relationship with God through Christ, we were "dead" in our "transgressions and sins" (Eph. 2:1), living out of what the Bible calls the "old self" (KJV: "old man"; see Rom. 6:6; Eph.

Introduction

Paul David Tripp puts it so well in his profound book *Instruments in the Redeemer's Hands,* "The good news of the kingdom is not freedom from hardship, suffering, and loss. It is the news of a Redeemer who has come to rescue me from *myself.*"[4]

In our own strength we cannot obey God. When by faith we invite Jesus the Savior into our lives, however, He comes with power to transform, to make us anew, to free us from the power of sin, and to indwell us with the Holy Spirit. Then, as we cooperate with Him in the process of growth, He continues the transformation. Only in this relationship with the living God can we constructively use the principles and tools I will share in this book. The result will be good, grace-filled growth in our lives and in the lives of those around us. That is my desire for you, the reader. "May the God of hope fill you with all joy and peace *as you trust in him,* so that you may overflow with hope by the power of the Holy Spirit" (Rom. 15:13).

A Word on the Format Used

The purpose of this book is to share "tools" for equipping yourself for life. It is like a toolbox of helps to be kept on hand for dealing with life. As you read it, several of the tools (i.e., disciplines, principles, or spiritual weapons) may be just what you need at the moment. The rest you can put into your "toolbox for life," to be used when the need arises. For instance, right now you may not be struggling with forgiveness, but later on when someone hurts you deeply, you can turn to the discussion of forgiveness in chapter 26 to get help.

Knowing that people learn through various methods, I have prepared this book using various styles or formats. First, listening to someone directly teach is the standard educational method, and there is much direct teaching in this book.

Second, watching someone work is another way of learning that is better for some. I've included a good number of stories of how God has led me to

---

4:22; Col. 3:9). Once we are in God's family, we discover that he has actually already crucified this old self with Jesus on the cross (Rom. 6:6), 2,000 years ago! In its place he has given us a "new self" (KJV: "new man"; see Eph. 4:24 and Col. 3:10).

Biblically, then, we thank God for what only he could do: crucify our old self (which could only be at war with our holy God) and give us a brand new self (which is made for relating with God). Regarding our "flesh," we must continually choose not to gratify it but instead to follow the Spirit (Gal. 6:7-8; Rom. 8:12-13). We aren't told to put to death the old self; God already did that in Christ. We *are* told to put to death evil deeds (Rom. 8:13; Col. 3:5), which are animated by our flesh, with its passions and desires (Gal. 5:24).

4. Paul David Tripp, *Instruments in the Redeemer's Hands: People in Need of Change Helping People in Need of Change* (Phillipsburg, N.J.: P&R Publishing, 2002), p. 16.

INTRODUCTION

apply the tools and disciplines presented here so you can see how it's done.

A third way of learning is by listening in on conversations. For readers who learn best in this manner, starting in part 3 I include some conversations between "Dave" and his mentor, "Jack," discussing the application of the material presented. Jack is a real person, while Dave is a composite of several. Their conversations are also composite: some are from real-life situations, some parts are extrapolations from real happenings plus principles, some parts are fiction. Like Jesus' parables, these conversations are designed to illustrate the application of truth. May Jack and Dave be effective demonstrators of what God has for you to learn through this book.

Fourth, I have used repetition. This is generally viewed as negative in our culture, yet Scripture often uses it to highlight important truth. The reality is that we rarely grasp something fully after one reading. We are slow to learn, slow to understand, slow to implement spiritual truths. So bear with me in the repetition, realizing I am highlighting important truths.

Finally, I wish to mention why I write about "knowing Jesus," not about "knowing God." In earlier drafts I did write "Knowing God is enough for joy, period!" On reflection, however, I decided to use "Jesus" for the following reasons:

- The word "God" is too elastic, too general in everyday speech (which God?), too easily filled with wrong meaning by the reader.
- "Jesus" makes it clearer whom we are talking about concerning salvation (Acts 4:12).
- Jesus is "the face of God"; He made God manifest to the world (2 Cor. 4:4-6).
- Jesus is the One the Holy Spirit exalts (John 16:14).
- Jesus is the One to whom we are to turn our attention, worship, and affection (Heb. 3:1; 12:2).
- Jesus is the One whose love we are to grasp (Eph. 3:18).
- Jesus is the One for whom we are to nurture our first love (Rev. 2:4).
- Jesus is the Bridegroom (Luke 5:34-35)
- Jesus is the One who intercedes for us (Rom. 8:34; Heb. 7:25; 1 John 2:1).
- Jesus is the Ruler (all things under His feet, the head of the church; Eph. 1:22)
- Jesus is the Creator (Col. 1:16).
- Jesus is over all creation (Col. 1:18).
- Jesus is the Sustainer (Heb. 1:3).
- Jesus is the Ender of history (Rev. 19).

Part 1

Living the Truth That Jesus Is Enough for Joy

CHAPTER 1

A Changed Worldview

Truth #1: Knowing Jesus Is Enough For Joy!

He opened his eyes and stared at the ceiling in the chill morning light. It was a flat, gray nothing. "Just like my life!" thought Dave.

He sighed and turned toward the wall, closing his eyes again, reluctant to get out of bed to face another disheartening day. Suddenly his eyes popped open. "Hey! Today is my first session with Jack!" Throwing off the covers, he jumped out of bed.

As he dressed, Dave let his mind run back to the meeting a fellow student had invited him to last Saturday. It had been put on by some campus group, and the man who spoke had been a most unusual presenter.

"There was something special about him…" Dave struggled to put it into words, "Something different. It was, hmmm — he kind of radiated the color of hope. That is so different from my monotone world of gray. Maybe he can help me get out of this rut that my life has become!"

Jack leaned back in his chair and looked at Dave. "Well, I think we've covered enough for our first session. You've given me a good description of what you call 'the boring and pointless life' you're leading. Now I'm going to give you some homework to do in preparation for our next meeting."

He got up and went to the large bookcase that covered one whole wall of his study. Carefully selecting a book, Jack took it down and handed it to Dave. "I want you to read the first two chapters of this book, and in our next session we'll talk about what you learned from it, OK?"

Dave took the book and looked at its cover. "And you think this will help me move ahead in life?" he asked. It was obvious that he had hoped for more to happen in this first meeting than getting a review of his life and a book to read.

Jack smiled, "If you absorb the truths in these two chapters, it will give you a foundation upon which to build the positive and meaningful life you desire. Read it, and we'll see what happens."

Dave put the book into his backpack and got up to go, but before he could move toward the door, Jack stood and put his arm around Dave's shoulder. "Let's pray," he said.

Dave bowed his head, waiting for the prayer. Jack was silent for a moment before beginning. "Lord God," he said, "you are the Almighty Creator, the Sovereign King, our Powerful Shepherd, and the Eternal Ruler. I praise you for the illogical care and concern you have for each of us rebels. I praise you that your undeserved grace flows daily into our lives, calling us into a deeper and higher walk with you, into the life of joy because we know Jesus.

"I thank you for this opportunity to work together with Dave. Open his eyes to the rich, magnificent, and transforming relationship to which you are calling him. Speak to him as he reads the assigned chapters this week that he might move toward the purposeful, powerful life you have for him, focused on giving you glory. We praise you for what you are going to do. Amen."

He gave Dave's shoulder a squeeze before turning and walking with him down the hall. He opened the door and as Dave left said, "See you next week!"

As soon as he got home, Dave took the book to his bedroom, flopped on his bed, and opened to the first chapter.

Chapter 1

"Knowing Jesus is enough for joy, period!" These words may sound to you like pop psychology or wishful, head-in-the sand thinking. Or like a simplistic theology that says "wear a plastic smile all the time and ignore how you feel!" These words, however, are just the opposite: a profound spiritual truth rooted deeply in the character of God and repeated often in Scripture.

This truth first welled up in my understanding while meditating in Psalm 62. Verse 1 says, "My soul finds rest in God alone." As I thought on this, it struck me how different this is from my own natural, innate beliefs. Here's how I would have written the verse:

> My soul finds rest in having a lot of money *or*
> — in having everything go my way *or*
> — in having a great job *or*
> — in having no opposition to my plans *or*
> — in always being on time *or*
> — in having my football team always win *or*
> — in everyone always being nice to me *or*
> — in having all of the above.

You can immediately see how tenuous each of these conditions can be for achieving my self-defined, self-serving, self-centered rest. Each is dependent on a situation that can easily and quickly change — especially having my team win!

In contrast, when my source of rest and joy is in knowing the unmovable, unshakable bedrock character of the living Yahweh (or Jehovah, written "LORD" in English Bible versions), then no matter what my circumstances are, my rest in Him will remain strong.

A Changed Worldview

Verse 5 in Psalm 62 turns this truth into a command, "*Find rest,* O my soul, in God alone." I have a choice about where I find rest — and God here clearly points us to the right one. If I look elsewhere for rest, I will only be continually disappointed.

Over a thousand years after David wrote Psalm 62, the apostle Paul expanded on the same truth in Romans 15:13, "May the God of hope fill you with all joy and peace *as you trust in him,* so that you may overflow with hope by the power of the Holy Spirit." The joy and peace Paul prays for come only *as we trust in God.* We can trust in Him only as we know Him. When we know Him, this becomes enough for joy.

Changing Your Worldview

A worldview is the means by which we make sense of all that happens around us. We develop our worldview from our culture, language, education, spiritual beliefs, family life, and experiences.

From what I have read, the most important single element in our worldview is our understanding of God. Think about how an atheist's denial of God's existence influences his or her understanding of life! A simple diagram of a worldview looks like this:

one's worldview, starts with:
    beliefs about God, from which flow:
        personal beliefs → values → behavior.

Our beliefs about God shape our personal beliefs, influence our values, and in turn dictate our behavior.

So if we want to change from our natural worldview to a biblical one, the most important thing we can do is to get a proper Scriptural view of God. And that is exactly the point of all that follows.

In his wonderful book *Knowing God,* J. I. Packer powerfully describes the profound difference between knowing *about God* and knowing *God.* He asks whether many of us could say that, because we know God, "past disappointments and present heartbreaks, as the world counts heartbreaks, *don't matter.* For the plain fact is that to most of us they do matter. We live with them as our 'crosses' (so we call them). Constantly we find ourselves slipping into bitterness and apathy and gloom as we reflect on them, which we frequently do. The attitude we show to the world is a sort of dried-up stoicism, miles removed from the 'joy unspeakable and full of glory' which Peter took for granted that his readers were displaying (1 Peter 1:8). 'Poor souls,' our friends say of us, 'how they've *suffered*' — and that is just what we feel about ourselves! But these private mock heroics have no place at all in the minds of those who really know God."[5]

Paul's experience was the opposite of those who only knew about God; he wrote, "I consider everything a loss compared to the surpassing greatness of *knowing* Christ Jesus my Lord, for whose sake I have lost all things" (Phil. 3:8).

One way we get to know God as J. I. Packer described it is by making the choice, over and over again in the small things of life, to find our rest in Him. Instead of getting upset, we flee to Him in each difficulty, disappointment, or dilemma. Primarily, we find our comfort in His Word, the Bible. We apply the Word by praising Him for what we would naturally otherwise complain about. We do this because we know His great and good character, even if we do not know His plan in detail with regard to the hard things that come to us. This is not wishful thinking. We think truth, rejecting the lies that spring so quickly and naturally from our hearts. The result is truly knowing Jesus more and more.

Knowing God through Jesus

I must hasten to add that we can find this rest in God only when we have a relationship with Him established through His Son, Jesus Christ. This means we have recognized our sin, our inability to measure up to God's standards of perfection, and are under His just wrath. We have acknowledged our need for forgiveness and have accepted the facts of Christ's sinless life, death, and resurrection, which purchased forgiveness and eternal life for all people. We have trusted Christ and bowed before our God and King, freely admitting our sin, receiving forgiveness, giving Him our will, and taking His will instead. And we have been adopted into His family. We are now sons and daughters of the Most High God, Yahweh. (See the last section of this chapter for a more thorough discussion of how to become a believer in Christ.)

Context Changes Everything

You may still be thinking, "This idea that 'Knowing Jesus is enough for joy, period!' is not a realistic viewpoint at all! My life certainly has enough difficulty that I couldn't possibly have joy all the time."

From a human point of view, you are right. In this world full of sickness, suffering, and sadness, this idea doesn't make sense. A boy gets shot in the eye and loses his sight. A teenager dives into the water, hits her head, and becomes

---

5. J. I. Packer, *Knowing God* (Downers Grove, Ill.: InterVarsity Press, 1973), pp. 20-21.

A Changed Worldview

a quadriplegic. Two girls from a Bible school ministering in a Middle East country are shot and killed by terrorists.

Humanly speaking, these are senseless tragedies. How could these people and their families have joy in such happenings? It seems to call for a rejection of reality.

A wider context, however, brings a totally new perspective. Consider a simple example. Psalm 14:1 says, "There is no God." A nice verse for atheists! Looking at the wider context, however, totally changes the meaning. "The fool says in his heart, 'There is no God.'" This larger context makes quite a difference in how we understand the claim that there is no God!

Context turns on the lights of understanding and perspective. So it is with the concept "Knowing Jesus is enough for joy, period!" When put in proper context, it makes perfect, supernatural sense to have joy in any difficult circumstance.

What, then, is the context to see when encountering suffering? The best is to focus on the three overriding themes of the Bible, of history, and of the universe: God's glory, God's greatness, and God's grace.

God's glory. Our Lord is a God of glory; for this reason He deserves to be worshipped, exalted, and obeyed. His name Yahweh is one that communicates His glory to us. "Yahweh" identifies the great I Am, "the pure and righteous God whose glory is in His holiness, who hates sin and will punish it, but who loves sinners and has provided a way of escape for them."[6]

As Moses sang in Exodus 15:11 after God had opened the Red Sea,

> Who among the gods is like you, O LORD?
>   Who is like you —
>   majestic in holiness,
>   awesome in glory,
>   working wonders?

The glory of God is revealed here in His mighty acts. Later, however, when Moses asked to see God's glory, God did not give a display of His power and majesty, of His infiniteness or holiness. Instead, the Lord replied, "I will cause all my goodness to pass in front of you, and I will proclaim my name, the LORD, in your presence. I will have mercy on whom I will have mercy, and I will have compassion on whom I will have compassion" (Exod. 33:18-19). Praise God that He has compassion and mercy on *all* His creation. (For example, 1 John 2:2 points to Jesus dying for the sins of all.)

---

6. William Allan Dean, *The Names of God* (Philadelphia: Philadelphia College of Bible, 1963), pp. 31-37.

God showcases His glory in His kindness to His creatures. Psalm 68 echoes this truth:

> Sing to God, sing praise to his name,
>   extol him who rides on the clouds —
> his name is the LORD —
>   and rejoice before him.
> A father to the fatherless, a defender of widows,
>   is God in his holy dwelling.
> God sets the lonely in families,
>   he leads forth the prisoners with singing;
>   but the rebellious live in a sun-scorched land.
>   (vv. 4-6)

Yahweh is the God of compassion who watches over the needy, helps the lonely, frees the trapped who accept His help, but deals justice to the rebellious who refuse His compassion. He will definitely judge sin, but in compassion He has made provision for every sinner who surrenders to Christ — the One whose death and resurrection made it possible for mercy to triumph over judgment (James 2:13)!

God's insistence on displaying His glory primarily by His mercy should be profoundly moving to us sinful human beings, who deserve His holy wrath but live in God's love because of His compassion shown in sending Jesus Christ as our Savior.

God's glory is the overarching reality of all creation. It is what all of existence is about: we were created to give glory to God, to focus on and live for Him — for His reputation, His honor, His name. Without this orientation on His glory, we default to self-centeredness, self-fulfillment, and self-glorification. Such a self-focus excludes God from our context and leads us to totally wrong conclusions about life.

God's greatness. Second, our Lord is a great God. This is revealed at least in part in His name "Elohim," which first appears in Genesis 1:1. This word, which is grammatically plural, can be understood to point us indirectly to the Trinity. Only a great God could be three in one; this is beyond human conception.

The meaning of Elohim is twofold. First, that He is *powerful* — unbelievably, immeasurably, incomprehensibly powerful. We can see this in all He created: a universe that is immense, beautiful, ingenious, wonderful.

Second, He is *faithful* — utterly, completely, unendingly, totally faithful.

A Changed Worldview

He showed this in providing His promised salvation, at infinite personal cost and at just the right time.[7]

In His great strength He is the Almighty One, the Most High, the undefeated One, the all-knowing One, the all-wise One, the all-present One, the Creator, the Sustainer, and the Ender of time. He is bringing history to a conclusion and taking us with Him. Nothing can hinder Him: "There is no wisdom, no insight, no plan that can succeed against the LORD" (Prov. 21:30).

The universe God created clearly shows us His greatness. It is so big we must try to measure it in light-years. In comparison to the universe, our solar system, huge as it is for us, is just a tiny speck tucked under one arm of the Milky Way. A rocket traveling at 25,000 mph (at this speed it could circle the earth in one hour) would take almost 17 years to travel from the sun to Pluto, the radius of our solar system. In comparison, if we could travel at the speed of light, 186,000 miles per second, we could circle the earth 7 times in one second. And we could get from the sun to Pluto in less than 6 hours! The God who spoke and created both the solar system and the speed of light is *great!*

God's greatness means, more importantly, that He is sovereign, He is in control. He oversees all that comes to us in every sphere of our life. It comes with His purpose and permission. Nothing catches Him by surprise.

His being sovereign does not mean that He determines every decision we make. It means that He has given us a sphere of life where we can and must make real decisions, and He commands us to do so ("seek first his kingdom!" Matt. 6:33), while He controls what comes to us ("The angel of the LORD encamps around those who fear him, and he delivers them," Ps. 34:7). Therefore whatever our state, whatever we suffer, whatever we experience, we can rest in the truth that He knows all about it, has allowed it, and in His compassion has plans to use it for good as we trust and obey Him.

Psalm 147:3-6 shows the combination of His greatness in creating the stars and His greatness in being compassionately sovereign in our lives.

> He heals the brokenhearted
>   and binds up their wounds.
> He determines the number of the stars
>   and calls them each by name.
> Great is our Lord and mighty in power;
>   his understanding has no limit.
> The LORD sustains the humble
>   but casts the wicked to the ground.

---

7. Dean, *Names of God,* pp. 1-7.

Our great God, who knows the name of every star, is also always attentive to what is happening in our lives, always involved. So when, for instance, someone slanders us, we have the context to understand that our loving God has allowed this for a reason and will use it for good. We can respond in obedience with Elohim's help, in His way and for His glory.

To those who are slandered, God says, "I am here with you; remember who you are — children of the King. Here's my desire for you when you are slandered:"

> Do not take revenge, my friends, but leave room for God's wrath, for it is written: "It is mine to avenge; I will repay," says the Lord. On the contrary:
> "If your enemy is hungry, feed him;
> if he is thirsty, give him something to drink. . . ."
> Do not be overcome with evil, but overcome evil with good.
> (Rom. 12:19-20)

When we know God's greatness, we can trust Him in what He is doing. Therefore we can have a "God-story mentality" about any event that comes into our lives, knowing that He is calling us to join Him in some important aspect of His great cosmic plan. We can respond as He desires, first and foremost with praise.

Joseph in the Old Testament is an example of how this works out. In his later life he understood some of what God had been doing in allowing all the suffering of his early years. He said to his brothers concerning their having sold him into slavery, "You intended to harm me, but God intended it for good to accomplish what is now being done, the saving of many lives" (Gen. 50:20). Joseph was referring here to the fact that he had been able to save his extended family from starvation, as well as all the Egyptians and people from surrounding countries.

This was only a small part, however, of what God was actually doing. Through Joseph, God preserved the line of Judah, His chosen seed, out of which came the Messiah. Joseph was one of the people prepared by suffering whom God could then use to bring about eternal salvation, which He offers to all. God was doing something immeasurably huge when He sent Joseph to Egypt as a slave![8] And so He is doing in our lives as He allows difficulties to come our way.

God's grace. Our Lord is a God of grace who loves to give. This comes out clearly in His names. One of these is "Adonai," which is translated "Lord" and

---

8. Some of these thoughts are due to Fran Sciacca, director and lead teacher of Hands of Hur Ministries, which many have found very valuable. See www.handsofhur.org/Site/Home.html.

A Changed Worldview

means "the ruler who has the right to demand absolute obedience and who promises to always provide completely what is needed to obey Him."[9]

Adonai knows our needs and moves to help us (Ps. 40:17; 54:4). He is our hope (Ps. 39:7). He gives grace in abundance, more than enough for us to just make it through the day. He sends enough grace so that we can be *more than* conquerors (see Rom. 8:37) — if we take it up and use it by obeying His Word for that situation.

Whatever difficulties we suffer, we can turn to Him for grace, and He will help us think and act as we are shown in Scripture, as we trust in Him and His Word.

Many of us can remember times of stress, difficulty, or crisis where we sensed the grace of God at work and certainly saw afterward how He carried us through. I remember sitting beside the road in a broken-down car on a dark, cold Sunday night in January. What came to mind almost immediately was: "Well, Lord, here we are in another adventure. Thank you for this situation. I wonder what you are going to work out with this event, where I am so weak and you are so strong!" As it turned out, He sent people to help, gave me a place to stay that night, provided someone to fix the car and a ride to get to my meetings the next day.

When we begin to focus on this invisible but rock-solid reality — the context of God's glory, God's greatness, and God's grace — then a whole different world begins to come into view. As we will discover, this world is more than full of goodness and grace.

How to Become a Believer in Christ

To have a relationship with God the Creator means we must come to Him on His terms. He explains very clearly in the Romans 3:9-18 what His terms are. In the following, the verses are in quotes, while my comments on this passage are in brackets [...].

God's *first condition* is to recognize that we are all guilty before Him. Romans 3:9b-18, quoting from Old Testament books, gives a graphic description of God's viewpoint, the viewpoint of truth:

> Jews and Gentiles alike are all under sin. As it is written:
> "There is no one righteous, not even one;
>   there is no one who understands,
>   no one who seeks God." [It is our nature to keep God at a distance,
>   to do what we think is right rather than ask Him for direction.]
> "*All* have turned away,

9. Dean, *Names of God,* pp. 61-68.

they have together become worthless; [this includes every human being]

there is no one who does good, not even one." [What good we do is tainted with our ideas, our ways, our selfishness and therefore is negated of any true goodness.]

"Their throats are open graves; [Which of us has not spoken hurtful, bitter things?]

their tongues practice deceit." [Which of us has not lied?]

"The poison of vipers is on their lips." [Which of us has not gossiped?]

"Their mouths are full of cursing and bitterness." [Which of us has not cursed in anger?]

"Their feet are swift to shed blood; [Which of us has not cut others with our tongues, if not worse?]

ruin and misery mark their ways, [How many of us are happy all the time?]

and the way of peace they do not know." [How many of us have peace all the time?]

"There is no fear of God before their eyes." [How many of us obey God without exception?]

God's *second condition* is to recognize that we are unable to save ourselves by anything we can do. You may ask, "What about keeping the Ten Commandments? Won't that save us?" God answers this directly:

> Now we know that whatever the law says [including the Ten Commandments], it says to those who are under the law, so that *every* mouth may be silenced and the *whole world* held accountable to God. Therefore *no one will be declared righteous in his sight by observing the law;* rather, *through the law we become conscious of sin.* (Rom. 3:19-20) [The purpose of the law is not to save us but to show us how we cannot possibly keep God's standard of perfection, how we cannot possibly save ourselves with good works and therefore need a Savior.]

God's *third condition* is to recognize that the only possible solution is the one that He has prepared, and that it is received by faith.

> But now a righteousness from God, apart from law [completely separate from anything we could do in trying to keep His law], has been made known, to which the Law and the Prophets testify. (Rom. 3:21) [This was God's plan from the beginning and was predicted all through the Old Testament.]

This righteousness from God comes through faith in Jesus Christ to *all who*

A Changed Worldview

believe. (3:22a) [It is through faith that we are saved, not by works, but by faith in Jesus the Savior.]

There is no difference, for *all have sinned and fall short of the glory of God* [repeating that our sins and sinfulness make it impossible for any of us to meet God's standards], and are justified freely by his grace through the redemption that came by Christ Jesus. (3:22b-24) [In believing we are justified, meaning that the record of our guilt of sin is wiped clean by Christ's buying us forgiveness.]

God presented him as a sacrifice of atonement [Jesus died to pay for our sins, taking the punishment we deserve], through faith in his blood. He did this to demonstrate his justice. . . . (3:25) [God cannot forgive without our sin being first punished; a just Judge cannot let the offender go free without the offense being paid for. Jesus paid the price of our sin, death]

He did it to demonstrate his justice at the present time, so as to be just and the one who justifies those who have faith in Jesus. (3:26) [God is able to remain just and to give us forgiveness, only because Jesus took the punishment we deserved.]

Where, then, is boasting? [We cannot boast in our accomplishments; we can do nothing to save ourselves] It is excluded. On what principle? On that of observing the law? No, but on that of faith. For we maintain that a man is justified by faith apart from observing the law. (3:27-28) [Only by faith in Christ and His finished work can we be saved from the judgment to come].[10]

This all is summarized beautifully in Titus 3:3-7:

At one time we too were foolish, disobedient, deceived and enslaved by all kinds of passions and pleasures. We lived in malice and envy, being hated and hating one another. But when the kindness and love of God our Savior appeared, he saved us, *not because of righteous things we had done,* but because of his mercy. *He saved us through the washing of rebirth and renewal by the Holy Spirit,* whom he poured out on us generously through Jesus

---

10. These truths are repeated clearly in Ephesians 2:8-10: "For it is by *grace* you have been saved, *through faith* — and this not from yourselves, *it is the gift of God* — *not by works,* so that no one can boast. [Not by our works, but by Christ's work. When we believe, we are "born again" into God's family. The results of that are now stated:] For we [who have believed] are God's workmanship, created in Christ Jesus to do good works, which God prepared in advance for us to do." [Now that we are God's children, new creations in Christ, God gives us power through the Holy Spirit to do good works as part of our obedience to Him. One of these good works is to praise Him, living in the truth that "knowing Jesus is enough for joy, period!"]

Christ our Savior, so that, *having been justified by his grace,* we might become heirs having the hope of eternal life.

You can accept God's offer of salvation right now; you can express your belief through a prayer like the following:

> Lord God of Creation, I come before you, a person in need of salvation. I agree that I cannot do anything to save myself, for my works are all tainted by my selfishness, my sinfulness, my proud independence, and my resistance to you.
>
> I believe that Jesus is God, that His death and resurrection satisfied entirely your wrath against my sin, that His death reconciles me to you and purchases my freedom from the penalty of sin. I place my confidence entirely and alone in Jesus to be my Savior. Forgive me for my sins, Lord Jesus. Come into my life, be my God, my Lord, my King. I give myself to you. Transform me, and make me your child.
>
> Thank you for the promises of eternal life, of forgiveness of sin, of adoption into your family. Thank you that I am now given the right to be the child of God. Thank you for the Holy Spirit's coming to live in me. Help me to continue to live a life that pleases you, living by faith in Christ, faith in His Word, and faith in the work of the Spirit for me and in me.

Without this relationship with the Lord Jesus Christ, there is no possibility of the joy or rest we are talking about. With Him, we can begin making the choice to trust Him in the everyday flow of life, choosing to find our rest and joy in Him.

Study Guide questions for Chapter 1: "A Changed Worldview"

1. What is the single most important element in a world view? (9)
2. How do you change a personal world view into a biblical one? (9)
3. What is the difference between knowing about Jesus and actually knowing Him? (9-10)
4. What would be the evidence in your life that you know Jesus well? (9-10)
5. What is the context that makes it possible to have joy in knowing Jesus? (10-15)
6. How are you going to apply this truth in your life?
7. What are the 3 conditions necessary to establish a relationship with Jesus? (15-18)
8. If you haven't surrendered to Jesus, what's holding you back from doing so? What will you do about it?

CHAPTER 2

Living in the Context of Truth

The context of our lives is that of having a glorious God who is great in every way and who constantly gives His creatures enough grace to be more than conquerors in whatever comes to them.

Habakkuk's Discovery

The Old Testament prophet Habakkuk gives us a picture of how this all fits together. First distressed by the evil of his own people, and then distressed by God's plan to send a brutal nation to punish them, Habakkuk goes to prayer. It is obvious in his prayer that he had grasped the glory, greatness, and grace of God. His worldview has been lined up with a biblical one. Listen to what he says, describing the Almighty, all-powerful, just, righteous Lord he served. (Please don't skip this passage — it will stir your heart!)

> LORD, I have heard of your fame;
> > I stand in awe of your deeds, O LORD.
> > . . . in wrath remember mercy. . . .
> His glory covered the heavens
> > and his praise filled the earth.
> His splendor was like the sunrise;
> > rays flashed from his hand,
> > where his power was hidden.
> Plague went before him;
> > pestilence followed his steps.
> He stood, and shook the earth;
> > he looked, and made the nations tremble.
> The ancient mountains crumbled
> > and the age-old hills collapsed.
> > His ways are eternal. . . .
> Were you angry with the rivers, O LORD?
> > Was your wrath against the streams?
> Did you rage against the sea
> > when you rode with your horses
> > and your victorious chariots?

> You uncovered your bow,
>> you called for many arrows.
> You split the earth with rivers;
>> the mountains saw you and writhed.
> Torrents of water swept by;
>> the deep roared
>> and lifted its waves on high.
> Sun and moon stood still in the heavens
>> at the glint of your flying arrows,
>> at the lightning of your flashing spear.
> In wrath you strode through the earth
>> and in anger you threshed the nations.
> You came out to deliver your people,
>> to save your anointed one.
> You crushed the leader of the land of wickedness,
>> you stripped him from head to foot.
> With his own spear you pierced his head
>> when his warriors stormed out to scatter us,
> gloating as though about to devour
>> the wretched who were in hiding.
> You trampled the sea with your horses,
>> churning the great waters.
>
> (Hab. 3:2-15)

Such a description should make us tremble before the Almighty God, and that is exactly what Habakkuk's response was:

> I heard and my heart pounded,
>> my lips quivered at the sound;
> decay crept into my bones,
>> and my legs trembled.
>
> (3:16)

Rest Demonstrated

Habakkuk went on from his description of the living God to live out this knowledge in a very uncertain world. He proclaimed his faith in describing the worst possible situation he could think of:

> Though the fig tree does not bud
>> and there are no grapes on the vines,
> though the olive crop fails
>> and the fields produce no food,

> though there are no sheep in the pen
> and no cattle in the stalls....
>
> (3:17)

Habakkuk lived six hundred years before Christ and thus had no supermarket as an alternative food source. He describes certain death by starvation — every source of food that he knows of has failed. To bring this situation into a modern setting and give us a little feeling for what Habakkuk was facing, we could update his words:

> though I lose my work, have no unemployment money, and can't get another job;
> though all my savings get used up;
> though I don't qualify for any kind of government subsidy;
> though all my family and friends abandon me;
> though my house and car get repossessed and I end up living on the street;
> though I can't even get anything by begging;
> though the economic crisis causes such a breakdown that
> all the supermarkets are empty....

This is a devastating, hopeless, and life-threatening situation. Contrary, however, to what is natural in the midst of this stressful happening, Habakkuk makes an amazing, astounding choice: "yet *I will rejoice* in the LORD!" (3:18a). This is an act of the will, based not on his situation or his feelings but on his knowledge of, and faith in, God. In fact, it is clear that he chooses to rejoice *in spite of what he's experiencing*. He knows God in the way J. I. Packer described in the quotation at the beginning of chapter 1. Habakkuk rejoices in God, and he continues with determination, whatever happens and whatever his emotions may be: "*I will be joyful* in God my Savior" (v. 18b).

Habakkuk then gives the reason he can make this decision to rejoice in God while living in dire circumstances: "The Sovereign LORD is my strength; he makes my feet like the feet of a deer, he enables me to go on the heights" (3:19).

Habakkuk knows God intimately, personally, experientially, and volitionally. He knows that God is gloriously powerful, that God is with him, and that God will give him grace to go through this time. Here there is no room for self-pity, angry talk about fairness, or blaming someone else. He knows the Most High, the Almighty One, the Sovereign Lord, the Creator and Sustainer, who is in control, and it was enough to decide for joy.

When we also see and know such a glorious, great, and gracious God, all else fades into the background. Our hurts and problems and difficulties retreat into a proper perspective where we can see them in the context of our great and loving heavenly Father.

A Modern-Day Habakkuk

Not long ago a friend wrote to us, telling us of a family whose fifteen-year-old daughter had a severe skiing accident. She suffered a traumatic brain injury and since then has had an endless round of surgeries. The mother has a Web page, where she regularly reports on the latest news concerning her daughter.[11] Despite the months of outwardly discouraging news, she is inwardly very focused on the Lord and confident — even joyful — in His goodness.

> [four months after the accident] We have had a very full week of organizing therapies in the home, going to Dr's appointments, and coordinating all kinds of care with Jessie. Our appointment with the cranio-facial plastic surgeon finally happened after months of waiting for this time. We learned that it will be another month or two before we begin the journey to have her skull replaced. It will be a staged surgery where they will replace one side then in 6-8 weeks will do the other side. They will plan to use her skull that has been stored in a bone bank in Colorado. We are so reminded to be at peace and not to look forward in fear . . . but to look forward with full hope. God, whose very own we are, will deliver Jessie from out of this. . . . Do not fear what may happen tomorrow, the same everlasting Father who cares for you today will take care of you then and every day. . . .
>
> "With skillful hands he led them" (Ps. 78:72). When you are unsure which course to take, totally submit your own judgement to that of the Spirit of God, asking Him to shut every door except the right one. So many times this week I have asked him to lead the way, shut the doors and all the windows . . . except the one He wants us to go through. . . . I believe He is guiding us each step of the way. . . .
>
> God . . . You are the Provider of our lives. We are so empty, so grief filled, so tired, so weary of this complicated confusing unwanted journey that has devastated our lives . . . yet we continue forward in hope watching You show up every day, every moment, providing what we need to care for Jessie, to take the next step, to get up every morning and face the day, to get up every night and care for Jess, to know that this season will change one day, to continue to be the receivers of such love and support from our family and friends, guiding and leading us. . . . We continue to have hope that You will make a way for Jessie to heal and begin to move and communicate. . . . We wait upon You . . . and continue to do the next "right" thing. We are so grateful we are home and Jessie is with us. . . . Thank you for loving

---

11. With the permission of this mother, I give the Web site where information is available: www.carepages.com/carepages/JessicaBoone. (Viewers must register as a CarePages member.)

and caring for us . . . amen and amen.

This woman obviously knows God deeply and intimately. She chooses to live the truth that "knowing Jesus is enough for joy, period!" She is looking primarily at His character, not her circumstances, giving God praise and glory for what others would complain bitterly about. I am sure she did not develop this attitude overnight after her daughter's accident but had been cultivating her relationship with Jesus over the years.

Joy

When we grasp the context of knowing our glorious, all-powerful, gracious God, we can have deep, solid, unshakable joy in any circumstance — joy as unshakable as His character. This joy is a powerful resting in the certainty of grace and goodness and glory flowing from God to us each moment. It is the certainty that our future beyond death is, with Jesus, sure, solid, shining, and supernatural. This joy flows from the peace that results from confessing our sins and receiving forgiveness from God, from forgiving ourselves, and from forgiving others. It is the knowledge that nothing random or meaningless comes into our lives, for He filters all in His love and wisdom. It is the deep knowing of the great, good, and grace-filled God, whose faithfulness is our shield and rampart, whose presence never leaves us, and who loves us intensely, deeply, eternally.

This is a foundational joy that can endure when tragedies, disappointments, failures, persecution, and pain enter our lives. We will feel the hurt of these events, we will weep, grieve, and mourn, for suffering and pain are part of life on earth. We must not ignore, deny or stuff pain; we must process it well with Scripture. Our weeping and grieving are necessary in painful losses; yet underneath these expressions of how we feel and process the events of our lives, the joy of knowing the triune God will remain as an unshakable rock. It will be part of what God uses to carry us through, putting into perspective what everyone else thinks is meaningless, random tragedy. And in the end we will see it from God's perspective.

Think of the three examples mentioned in chapter 1. The boy who was shot in the eye was spared from going to war in Vietnam because of his disability. The teen who was paralyzed, Joni Eareckson Tada, has become a beacon of hope for millions and the means of many coming to Christ. This was something she could never have done living as an average housewife in suburbia. Her suffering became the platform for being an effective tool in the Redeemer's hand. The two girls murdered overseas did not die in vain: the father of one responded to the example of his daughter's commitment and accepted

Christ after the funeral. And I would be surprised if there were not many more positive results in each case.

What about your life? Are you going through difficulties, disappointments, deep troubles? Is God great enough to help you? Our glorious, holy, and gracious God knows what He is doing! With such a perspective and context of truth, it is very logical that knowing Jesus is certainly enough for joy, period!

I affirm wholeheartedly that it *is* possible to live like this in our day and age of greater and greater disasters and uncertainties. This book will help you move toward adopting such a worldview yourself.

Dave's Transformation

"So, what did you glean from reading the first two chapters?" asked Jack.

Dave smiled broadly as he opened his copy of the book. "A lot! This whole idea of my worldview changing by getting a bigger view of God — well, that's proved to be a huge, powerful and positive shift in my thinking. My picture of God has been a pretty weak one: a God who was either not interested in helping me or not strong enough to be effective."

Jack smiled at his student's enthusiasm. "Those who live flat, gray, dull lives definitely have a poor view of God. They don't realize that He is the One who invites them into a rich, challenging partnership with Him."

Dave nodded enthusiastically. "Yes. I see now that one problem in my life is that I've always wanted God to help me in my plans and goals. And I've given no thought to whether my desires lined up with God's purposes or not. But I understand now that He's inviting me to join Him in His plans.

He paused to page through the book. "This business of looking at God's glory, greatness, and grace has really opened my eyes to what a pitiful understanding I had of Him. The facts about the size of the universe and how He just spoke the stars into existence —that's really awesome, far more than I can comprehend!"

Jack nodded, noting Dave's new enthusiasm, "You are right, Dave. And there's no end to this growing understanding of God's greatness. The more we spend time with Him and experience His working in our lives, the more our awe grows, and the more we are changed."

Dave was quiet for a minute, "I especially liked the quote from J. I. Packer's book about how, if we really know God, the difficulties of life lose their power over us. And then the example of Habakkuk, choosing to be joyful because he really knew God. But what struck me even more, though, was what the mother of the girl in the skiing accident wrote. That was unbelievable; such trust in God, such authentic faith! It sure showed up my faith for being nothing."

Living in the Context of Truth

Jack smiled again. "It is true that knowing the Almighty Creator and Sustainer of the universe is enough for joy. But living in the reality of this relationship is something we need to choose every day, often several times in a day."

"I'm beginning to understand that now," Dave replied. He turned to the end of the first chapter. "The biggest thing that struck me was the explanation of how to be saved. After reading that I realized how my understanding of the gospel has been pretty shallow and faulty. I'm not even sure that I was a real believer. I was probably just playing the role while doing my own thing."

"Not sure you were a believer . . . ?" queried Jack, raising an eyebrow.

"I'm sure now," said Dave, laughing. "I prayed the prayer at the end of the chapter, and I prayed it with a much better understanding of the gospel. I see now that real belief involves surrendering everything to God and His greatness. It means submission to the One who knows what is right, the One who gives direction, who loves me in spite of what I am."

"And what are you in your natural self?" asked Jack.

Dave thought for a moment, "Selfish, proud, lazy, and negative." He took a breath, "I am self-centered, thoughtless, undisciplined, and fearful of what others think. I think that's part of the reason my world has been so flat and gray."

"Soooo," said Jack, "now I understand the reason for such a big change in you. You have truly been born again! You have come across the line, out of the dominion of darkness into God's kingdom of light. You now have the Holy Spirit in you. That in itself has brought a big worldview shift!"

"Is that the reason for the great change I feel?" Dave asked.

"It sure is," replied Jack as he leaned back in his chair, looking very happy. "Reading those chapters did more than you expected, didn't it?" he asked.

"Yes! And now I am eager to read the rest of the book," Dave replied.

"That's good," said Jack, "because this step of belief and surrender that you've taken is going to plunge you right into spiritual warfare, into the adventure that Jesus is calling you to. So I don't have to tell you your assignment for this week."

Dave laughed. "No, just how many chapters you want me to read and process."

"Try the next two, chapters 3 and 4," said Jack. "But more importantly, I want you to begin reading the Bible regularly. Try starting in Matthew, reading a chapter a day. That will take you between seven and ten minutes. You probably have that much time in a day, don't you?"

Dave laughed, "Certainly! I can see that this book emphasizes the importance of Scripture, so your suggestion fits right in. I'll begin that today."

Study Guide questions for Chapter 2: "Living in the Context of Truth"

1. What was Habakkuk's view of God? (19-20)
2. What was Habakkuk's response to tragedy? (20-21)
3. Why could he respond as he did? (21)
4. What do you think the devotional life of the mother of the injured skier was like? (22-23)
5. Describe "Jesus-based" joy. (23)
6. How can you move towards having such a joy in your life? (23-24)

CHAPTER 3

Total Faith

Habakkuk was able to make the choice to rejoice in the face of fear and famine because he had a true faith, or we could say, a "total faith." This is something each one of us can cultivate. He did not have just an intellectual grasp of the facts of God. Habakkuk did know God intellectually, but he also knew Him with his will and his emotions.

A biblical faith involves all three aspects of our soul, our "inner being": mind, will, and emotions. Such a faith grows out of a knowledge of God gleaned first from the Bible; second from a heart-based surrender to Him, allowing us to see Him more; then from the experience of seeing Him work in our lives; and finally from following through on a commitment of the will to obey whatever He commands us.

The problem is that all of us, depending on our personality, naturally tend to major on only one of these: intellectual faith, emotional faith, or volitional faith. The result is that we tend to become imbalanced.

For many of us Christians, faith is primarily intellectual. We have a pretty good knowledge of the Bible, we know what it means to be born again, and we have an idea of how we are to act, at least at church. But there is little heart, little passion in our belief. Our implementation of the Word is often legalistic, passionless, and self-centered duty, missing the sweet spirit of obedience. This is what I was like in my teen years. As modern-day Pharisees, with heads stuffed full of knowledge and eyes closed to the needs around us, we tend to look like the person in figure 3.1.

Fig. 3.1. Intellect-based faith

James in his letter has a message for believers like this: "Do not merely listen to the word, and so deceive yourselves. Do what it says" (1:22). He gave this advice because those of us with only intellectual faith tend to compartmentalize our lives. We may be nice at church, but at home or work or play, we tend to live like the unbelievers around us. Our knowledge is more in our heads than in our lives. Notice in figure 3.1 that there is no connection between the head and the body!

Others of us have a faith that is primarily emotional. At times we sense we are close to God and therefore conclude that we are spiritual. Other times we feel far away and are despondent. Everything is measured by our feelings. If the worship time at church didn't move us, then it "wasn't good." If we didn't have some great insight in our daily quiet time of Bible reading and prayer, it "wasn't worth it." If the message on Sunday didn't stir me, the pastor "failed." The result is a yoyo life, up and down, being blown about by whatever emotion happens to prevail. We tend to look like the person in figure 3.2.

Fig. 3.2. Emotion-based faith

James had a word for such a person too. He wrote about the prayers of a person with an emotion-based faith, "When he asks, he must believe and not doubt, because he who doubts is like a wave of the sea, blown and tossed by the wind. That man should not think he will receive anything from the Lord; he is a double-minded man, unstable in all he does" (James 1:6-8). Faith based on emotions is by definition unstable; having such faith is a prescription for doubt. Emotions are not to be the basis of faith or the master of faith, but the servant of faith.

Others of us have primarily a volitional faith. We are decisive! We like action and enjoy the sense of accomplishment when we help out with things at the church or with neighbors. Knowledge is not very important ("doctrine is so stuffy!"), being decisive is ("let's get with it!").

Total Faith

Such believers are diligent and dependable, serving whether they feel like it or not, for they are committed to help. Their help, however, is not necessarily based on the Word, nor does it flow primarily from a desire to obey God but from their desire to be fulfilled. With their overdeveloped "help muscles" they tend to look like the person in figure 3.3.

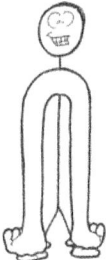

Fig. 3.3. Work-based faith

Here's what James has to say to these hard workers who act from their own understanding: "Anyone who listens to the word but does not do what it says [doing instead what he or she thinks is best] is like a man who looks at his face in a mirror and, after looking at himself, goes away and immediately forgets what he looks like" [that is, he or she is operating without biblical knowledge] (1:23-24). This person ends up acting out of his own wisdom, not God's. An example of this is the fellow who rushes in to help a man who can't make his monthly payment on his huge entertainment center, short-circuiting God's attempt to help this person be wiser and more disciplined in his finances.

Each of these three types of faith is a caricature of biblical faith; each one is weak, lopsided, and very human. In contrast, God wants us to have a strong, balanced, biblical faith, which looks like the person in figure 3.4.

Fig. 3.4. Balanced, biblical faith

James has a description of this person also: "The man who looks intently into the perfect law [intellectual faith, valuing and reading the Word of God] that gives freedom and continues to do this [volitional faith, consistently doing what is right], not forgetting what he has heard, but doing it [volitional faith, acting in accord with what the Word has to say, not his own ideas] — he will be blessed ["fortunate" or "happy" — emotional faith flowing from obedience] in what he does" (1:25).

Habakkuk's Balance

Biblical intellectual faith should result in biblical volitional faith, which should lead to wise emotional faith. Habakkuk's faith was balanced like this because his knowing God involved his mind, his will, and his emotions. His priorities were right: with his intellect he believed the Word, with his will he acted upon what he knew, and with his emotions he committed himself to trust what he knew of God. Thus, he trusted God for the emotions to come around as a result of obeying God's Word. We can trust that our emotions will, with time, follow in support of what God has said is right and good.

It is important to note that to have a balance, there must be a tension. Think of an old-fashioned scale with a pan on either side. When the weight in one pan and the produce in the other are equal, the scale is balanced. The tension on the arms, with a weight on either end, brings it into balance. So with faith there will often be a discernable tension, especially between what we know and what we feel, or between what we decide on and what we feel. This is not bad; it is part of being balanced. It is natural to want to get rid of tension, as it makes us uncomfortable — we want to give in to one side or the other, not keep the two in tension — but such creative, positive tension is what helps us move ahead in our lives. As we grow spiritually, this tension will become less noticeable because we will become accustomed to it.

Habakkuk's emotions were not his leader but were trained through obedience to follow truth. We could say that his emotions were both the color of his life and the lights blinking on the dashboard of life that warned him when something was wrong (anger, jealousy, impatience, etc.) so he could properly deal with it.

The result of Habakkuk's balanced intellectual/volitional/emotional faith was that, whatever came, he was able to make the right choice with a strong will based on knowledge and then to rejoice in God, the proper source of joy.

Total Faith

Praying with the Intellect, the Will, and the Emotions

Consider another example of total faith. In his book *Disciplines of a Godly Man* (Wheaton, Ill.: Crossway Books, 1991), R. Kent Hughes discusses the pastor and author Dr. J. Sidlow Baxter, quoting at length from a colorful letter that Baxter sent him in 1987 on the matter of praying with the intellect, the will, and the emotions.

One morning Baxter "stood over his work-strewn desk and looked at his watch. The voice of the Spirit was calling him to pray. At the same time another velvety little voice was telling him to be practical and get his letters answered, and that he ought to face up to the fact that he was not one of the 'spiritual sort' — only a few people could be like that. . . . He was horrified by his ability to rationalize away [prayer] the very ground of his ministerial vitality and power.

"That morning Sidlow Baxter took a good look into his heart, and found there was a part of him which did not want to pray and a part which did. The part which did not was his emotions; the part which did was his intellect and will. This analysis paved the way to victory. In Dr. Baxter's own inimitable words:

> As never before, my will and I stood face to face. I asked my will the straight question, "Will, are you ready for an hour of prayer?" Will answered, "Here I am, and I'm quite ready, if you are." So Will and I linked arms and turned to go for our time of prayer. At once all the emotions began pulling the other way and protesting, "We are not coming." I saw Will stagger just a bit, so I asked, "Can you stick it out, Will?" and Will replied, "Yes, if you can." So Will went, and we got down to prayer, dragging those wriggling, obstreperous emotions with us. It was a struggle all the way through. At one point, when Will and I were in the middle of an earnest intercession, I suddenly found one of those traitorous emotions had snared my imagination and had run off to the golf course; and it was all I could do to drag the wicked rascal back. A bit later I found another of the emotions had sneaked away with some off-guard thoughts and was in the pulpit, two days ahead of schedule, preaching a sermon that I had not yet finished preparing!
>
> At the end of that hour, if you had asked me, "Have you had a 'good time'?" I would have had to reply, "No, it was a wearying wrestle with contrary emotions and a truant imagination from beginning to end." What is more, that battle with the emotions continued for between two and three weeks, and if you had asked me at the end of that period, "Have you had a 'good time' in your daily praying?" I would have had to confess, "No, at times it has seemed as though the heavens were brass, and God too distant to hear, and the Lord Jesus strangely aloof, and prayer accomplished nothing."

Yet something *was* happening. For one thing, Will and I really taught the emotions that we were completely independent of them. Also, one morning, about two weeks after the contest began, just when Will and I were going for another time of prayer, I overheard one of the emotions whisper to the other, "Come on, you guys, it is no use wasting any more time resisting: they'll go just the same." That morning, for the first time, even though the emotions were still sullenly uncooperative, they were at least quiescent, which allowed Will and me to get on with prayer undistractedly.

Then, another couple of weeks later, what do you think happened? During one of our prayer times, when Will and I were no more thinking of the emotions than of the man in the moon, one of the most vigorous of the emotions unexpectedly sprang up and shouted, "Hallelujah!" at which all the other emotions exclaimed, "Amen!" And for the first time the whole of my being — intellect, will, and emotions — was united in one coordinated prayer-operation. (Pp. 105-6)

Habakkuk and J. Sidlow Baxter both demonstrate a biblical faith that comes from knowing God. Such a faith must be developed, and God is waiting to work with us hand in hand to nurture such a vibrant, balanced faith in our lives. The question is, Are we willing to deny self, get beyond our comfort zone, and move out with God in this journey of growth?

Study Guide questions for Chapter 3: "Total Faith"

1. Describe the three unbalanced kinds of faith and the shortcomings of each. (27-29)
2. Describe a balanced, biblical faith (29-30)
3. What can you do to have such a balanced faith? How will you apply this?
4. Why was Habakkuk's faith balanced? (30)
5. How can we train our emotions to follow truth so we have a total faith? (30-32)

CHAPTER 4

Help for Those Who Want to Wholeheartedly Follow Jesus

This book, *Knowing Jesus Is Enough for Joy, Period! Lessons from the Battle Lines,* has been written out of the crucible of ministry in the Middle East. While things for me were not as bleak as Habakkuk's situation, the everyday battle was real enough. There was the constant threat of arrest, expulsion, betrayal, and failure — and over the years, all of these things did happen. During that time the Lord began to teach us the truths leading to the conclusion that knowing Jesus is indeed enough for joy — period!

What about you and your daily battle? The events that you experience on a regular basis are different from what we went through. The truth, though, is that wherever we are, whatever our work, if we are seeking to live for the Lord Jesus, we are in the front line of the battle, because "everyone who wants to live a godly life in Christ Jesus will be persecuted" (2 Tim. 3:12).

Satan will attack. Difficulties will come. But Jesus is enough. Whatever enters our lives cannot take away the deep, positive, abiding rest and joy we can have in Christ — *if we are making the decision to find them in Him.*

Jesus' Character, Creation, and Commitments

There are many reasons to find our rest and joy in Jesus alone — in fact there are countless ones as we look at Jesus' character, His creation, and His commitments to His creatures.

As we get to know the character of Jesus from spending time in the Word, in prayer, in worship, and in obedience, we will begin to see all our experiences in the cosmic framework of His glory, greatness, and grace. This is so important that I would like to briefly review these points here.

The glory of God is the reason for our existence. In comparison, anything else we may live for is microscopic in significance. All the things that human beings value so highly — our comfort, our fulfillment, our success, our honor — are not even on the radar screen. They are actually potential by-products of our real call, namely, to live out the privilege of glorifying the eternal, all-powerful, all-knowing, all-good Creator of the universe.

The greatness of God speaks of God's sovereignty. He is in control, so all that comes into our lives is filtered through His goodness and wisdom. Therefore whatever happens, we can rest in the knowledge that it will be a demonstration of His love and goodness directing His power.

The grace of God speaks of how He provides whatever we need at each moment. His loving, wise, and gracious heart is ever at work helping us. We can trust that if we reach out to Him, we will be able to take up and use whatever grace we need.

Jesus' character is a rich mine for our faith. He is the holy One, the mighty One, the wise One, the all-present One, the all-knowing One, the sovereign One. He is the God of perfect balance, the combiner of what to us are opposites: justice and mercy, truth and love, righteousness and forgiveness, judgment and grace, power and tenderness, greatness and intimacy. He is able to hate sin and love the sinner, to punish sin and save the sinner. God is the triune One, perfectly balancing unity and diversity. He is the creator, the sustainer, the ender of all. He breathed the stars, He spun the earth, He holds the atoms together. He has no beginning, no end, no limit on goodness, no ability to sin. He is glorious, great, gracious, and good. What a privilege it is to know Him!

In Jesus' creation we see the outworking of His wonderful power, from the subatomic world to the huge galaxies made up of billions of stars. Just think about the earth: hung in space, its axis tilted at just the right angle to make the seasons, spun at just the right speed so things don't get too cold at night or too hot in the day, put in orbit just the right distance from the sun so we neither freeze nor bake, moving in orbit at just the right speed so the seasons aren't too long (so we won't starve) or too short (so crops have time to mature), accompanied by a moon of just the right size to provide for tides and to help protect the earth from meteorites. God thought of everything! We will talk more about the wonders of God's creation when we discuss worship.

Then we have Jesus' commitments to us, which give us further ground for joy. Jesus has given us:

- unconditional love
- full forgiveness
- eternal life
- meaning in life
- a new heart
- a relationship with the Ruler of the universe
- continual access to His full attention

Help for Those Who Want to Wholeheartedly Follow Jesus

- the Holy Spirit to live within us
- His unceasing love, grace, guidance, and goodness every day.

Furthermore, Jesus has given us the privileges of:

- being a child of God
- being watched over every moment
- being equipped for meaningful, significant service
- having all events filtered through God's loving hands
- having every event designed for our growth and maturity
- having an endless supply of grace, significance, and security.

In this book we will explore these and a number of other reasons for choosing joy through Him. I will also mention keys for finding many more on your own. May you begin today to tap into the truths that will lead you to live the reality that knowing Jesus is enough for joy, period!

A Test

While working on this book, I received a test from God to see if I really believed that knowing Jesus is enough for joy. News came of a significant turmoil in my circle of friends, news that meant the possibility of great personal loss to me, both physical and relational. I lay awake at night, my mind racing, my emotions churning. I had no joy or peace at the moment — but I knew it would come because of what God has shown me of Himself. And I knew that, before the joy could come, I had to process this news.

Dealing with news such as I received is like having to cross a raging river. There is no way to move from the safe bank on one side to the safe bank on the other without facing a struggle in between. For every such river, though, God will give us the help we need to deal with the struggle, a rope to hold onto as we struggle through the waters.

In my personal test, God was helping me to lay down one desire (the things in jeopardy) to give me something better — but as I write this, I don't yet know what that "better" is! Laying something down is loss, and as a human being, when we lose something significant, we have to go through a grief cycle, no matter how brief. In this case my "processing" and grief cycle lasted about four days — it can take longer or shorter, depending on the seriousness of the issues being dealt with, and how much I am willing to cooperate with God in the process. I first had to let go of the old before being able to grasp the new.

In this process, in the midst of the turmoil and uncertainty, the voice of the Spirit spoke to me, "Remember Psalm 62:1, 'My soul finds rest in God alone.'

Remember, knowing Jesus *is* enough for joy, even in the midst of this pain. Choose to live it!"

I said, "Yes, Lord, this is true. I choose to live it. Help me to live it!"

As I lay awake in the night, I fled to His Word, meditating on the rich passages I had memorized. Psalm 34: "I will bless the Lord at *all times*. His praise shall *continually* be in my mouth." There were no positive feelings in this struggle, but there was faith, and I chose to praise, "Heavenly Father, I praise you for this challenge to my faith, this opportunity to trust you instead of my sight. You are wise in what you allow, and I praise you for it."

Psalm 46: "God is our refuge and strength, an ever-present help in trouble. . . . God is within me. I shall not fall; he will help me, at break of day [personalized]." Prayer welled up within me, "I praise you, O Lord Jesus, for your presence which I cannot sense, your protection which I cannot feel, your provision which I cannot yet see! You have proved yourself trustable in the past, so you will be in this!"

Psalm 86: "Bow down and hear me, O Lord, for I am poor and needy. [And I certainly did feel weak and needy, unable to make any progress in my own strength!] Preserve my soul, for I am holy. O my God, save your servant who trusts in you."

God was calling me to look away from the present to the eternal, to rise above and have His view of things. I tend to hold a new problem close up before my eyes, with the result that the problem then fills my whole vision.

Try putting your thumb up close to one eye and then close the other eye; all you can see is that big thumb. When we let our problems fill our vision as this thumb does, we are practicing what I call "thumb theology." (Notice that it rhymes with "dumb theology"!) However, if we hold our thumb (our problem) out at arm's length, we can see the bigger picture and are able to look away to God to get His perspective on this problem.

I know that one thing God is doing in this present situation of misunderstanding and conflict with friends is burning out the dross from my character and helping me to let go of the inadequate sources of joy (idols) I've been trying to draw on. He is helping me to plug into the inexhaustible supply of joy in knowing Jesus Christ.

Working it through, poring over the truth, lifting my soul, writing in my journal, cooperating with Him — all these steps (which we will further consider in this book) led me through the raging waters to the other side of this river. I don't have a solution yet, but I do have joy in Jesus, knowing that He will do what is best.

So, I do not write out of unrealistic optimism or out of pitiful positive

Help for Those Who Want to Wholeheartedly Follow Jesus

thinking. I write from the crucible of fiery experience that God is sufficient, always. I can assure you that whatever spiritual battle you face — and each believer is in a spiritual war every day — whatever valley you walk through, knowing Jesus is enough for joy.

Dave and Faith

He sat in Jack's office, his book open on his lap. "This third chapter was awesome," Dave said. "I had never heard of such distinctions of faith, but they sure ring true in my life. I think the faith I've had was mostly the second kind, emotional faith. My emotions tend to sway me easily."

"You're not alone," answered Jack. "Most people in our society are more strongly influenced by what they feel than by what they know. That's why intelligent people make foolish mistakes over and over again, even though their intellect tells them they are wrong."

Dave nodded, "And I've been one of those. Now that I understand the need for an integrated faith and what that means, I think following God's Word and His truth will be easier. That is, I will be better able to discern when my emotions or intellect or desire for action pull me away from God."

"That's a good start, Dave. It will require a lot of practice in applying this, though; it's a battle," replied Jack.

Dave nodded, "That story of the pastor being willing to pray even though his emotions fought against it was helpful. I want to be able to lead my emotions, not be controlled by them."

Jack laughed. "Yes, that was a good and true story. With God's help we can grow into having a full-orbed faith like that pastor. As you saw, though, it requires self-denial and obedience to truth, a difficult task, possible only with the power of the Spirit."

"Speaking of that, chapter 4 was helpful in focusing me on Christ's help," replied Dave. "Let's see, yes, here it is — 'Jesus' Character, Creation, and Commitments.' I think the author is right on with my need to nurture my faith in God by looking at these aspects of Him regularly."

"Very true," replied Jack, smiling at the enthusiasm and joy he saw in Dave — quite a contrast from their first meeting.

Dave went on, "And I liked the example the author gave of how he had to struggle with his own faith — and that 'Thumb Theology,' I could really identify with that. I tend to blow things out of proportion, which can certainly block my view of God.

Jack smiled. "As you now realize, Dave, this book is an equipping book," he said. "It gives you perspective, encouragement, and understanding. You will need to come back and review it periodically to refresh your grasp of its truth. Right now, your part is learning to focus on God in worship and prayer, and then obeying Him in the Spirit's power.

"This week's assignment is shorter, just chapter 5, but it's one that will make you think, hopefully bringing further worldview shifts for you!"

Study Guide questions for Chapter 4: "Help for Those Who Want To Wholeheartedly Follow Jesus"

1. What basic decision do we need to make in the everyday battle of life? (33)
2. Describe the reasons we have for Joy in Jesus because of His character. (34)
3. …because of His creation. (34)
4. …because of His commitments. (34-35)
5. How will these realities change your life?
6. What enabled the author to pass the test God gave him? (35-36)

CHAPTER 5

Two Concepts to Help Live in the Joy of Jesus

Truth # 2: By Letting Go and Holding On, We Can Rise Above the Challenges of Life

In order to help you, the reader, get a better handle on living in the joy of knowing Jesus, I share here two phrases that have helped me put this into practice: "Let go, hold on, rise above" and "God is moving history to a conclusion and taking us with Him."

Let Go, Hold On, Rise Above

At one point while meditating on Colossians 3:1-2, I saw part of a movie. The hero, who had his hands full of heavily loaded shopping bags, was being chased by a gang of thugs. He was running hard, but since he was weighed down by all his possessions, he was losing ground, with the thugs gaining on him. Just then he looked up. Right there above him was a hot-air balloon with a rope hanging down within reach. He looked back at the thugs, then down at all his bags. He dropped all but one important item, grabbed the rope, and was lifted off to safety.

Colossians 3:1-2 describes this situation in spiritual terms:

Since, then, you have been raised with Christ,
    set your hearts on things above [that is, hold on to eternal reality],
        where Christ is seated at the right hand of God.
    Set your minds on things above [hold on to what is above], not on
        earthly things [let go of earthly things].

Combining these two ideas, this phrase came to mind: "let go, hold on, rise above." That is, let go of what is temporal, hold on to what is eternal, rise above the everyday events of life.

Let go of earthly things, hold on to things above, rise above the attacks of the enemy. The help we need is always there. We just have to let go of what is occupying us, grab hold of the help, and God will carry us up and over. Here's the concept in pictures. (See fig. 5.1.)

When chased by the world, the flesh, and the devil . . .

Fig. 5.1. Let go . . . hold on . . . rise above

As an example of how this works, I share this story. My wife and I were discussing how to do a project; I was sure my way was better, but I was also aware that she really wanted to do it her way. The world, the flesh, and the devil were all encouraging me to hold on to my perspective and to fight her on it. However, the Spirit brought to mind the phrase "let go, hold on, rise above," and with His help I decided to go that route rather than fight for my petty ambitions.

So I:

> *let go* [what does it really matter? I actually only wanted to win to make myself feel good],

Two Concepts to Help Live in the Joy of Jesus

held on [my significance comes from God, not from getting my way; He tells me to nurture my wife, and here's my chance to do it. Knowing Jesus is enough for joy; I don't need to win], and

rose above [I can be free from my petty desires, can escape the push of the world, the flesh, and the devil, and can look at the situation from God's point of view; and I could be glad in my wife's pleasure at doing this her way].

I relaxed, my wife was happy, and we both enjoyed the rest of the day, instead of having to pick up the pieces of a damaged relationship.

I tell you, this approach makes life easier. There are times to hold your ground, but those are far fewer than we might think. Most of the time we are living out of wrong motives rather than righteous principles.

In another situation, in a public gathering, a friend of mine had a chance to give me a nice compliment, but instead he made a joke that cut me down. I was hurt, angry, and insulted. But the Holy Spirit immediately brought to mind our phrase: *let go* (of my pride, selfishness, and hurt, as well as my desire to defend myself), *hold on* (to the truth that my significance and security come from the character of God, not from people, that knowing Jesus is enough for joy), and *rise above* (leaving behind the hurt, as well as the desire for revenge and justification).

I went home, thanked the Lord for the opportunity to live in truth, forgave my friend as I have been forgiven (I was reminded by the Spirit that I've done the same thing myself at times), and asked God, for my friend's sake, to convict my friend of his wrong action. My friend later came and apologized for his hurtful words. I, of course, could only forgive him, considering how much God has forgiven me in Christ!

Let's look at this saying in more detail. *What does it mean to "let go"?* It means to keep things in an open hand, to surrender all that we have to God. It means to trust God, to believe that He is good — all the time! It means to obey what I know to be true, rejecting the temptation to take shortcuts, to compromise, to do things the way the world does. It means giving God permission to take and give as He sees best.

It does not mean, however, being irresponsible, letting go of our obligations, failing in our relationships because of laziness, or not following through on our promises. It does not mean letting people walk over me, nor does it mean ignoring my responsibility to confront those who may sin against me. It does mean to practice Psalm 37:4, "Delight yourself in the LORD" instead of delighting in getting my way, knowing that in the long run, "he will give you the desires of your heart."

> Let go of the world, hold on to the Word, rise above the flesh.
> Let go of the flesh, hold on to truth, rise above the devil's attacks.
> Let go of the devil's advice, hold onto Christ, rise above temptation.

What should we let go of? Everything temporary. That includes most tangibles, much of what we have in life, giving them back to God. Why? Because we will lose them anyway — that's the definition of temporary!

In letting go, we will gain new freedom; holding on to things weighs us down, binds us, keeps us from better things. Surrendering ownership of all we have to God puts them in safer hands. He can take much better care of what we have than we can; we need to entrust all to Him.

Letting go protects us from idol worship: when I demand to have something to be happy, that thing or event or desire becomes an idol to me. When we let go, surrendering it to God, He can protect that for us, or He can take it, or He can give us something better, whatever in His wisdom He decides.

If we are holding on tightly to the things we have, we are hampering God from giving other things He desires for us. It's like giving my little boy a dime; he is very pleased and clasps it tightly in his little hand. Later I say, "Give me back the dime, I have something better for you." But maybe he values that dime too much to give it up! Finally, I pry open his little hand, take the dime, and give him a bright silver dollar in its place. Now he's happier, even though his hand hurts from being pried open — and I am happier too.

It's much better to hold things with an open hand so God doesn't have to pry it open. Then God can take and give as He sees fit. What He has for us is always better from the eternal perspective. When you let go, God can both protect and, if it is best, give you more!

> Let go of my selfish ambitions, hold on to Jesus' vision, rise above the disappointments of life.
> Let go of the negative comments of other people, hold on to Jesus' love for me, rise above the conflicts of life.
> Let go of my anger, hold onto Jesus' power to protect, rise above the hurtful events of life.

Here are some examples of things we can let go of. (Some of these things need to be "processed" in order to let go of them; we will talk more about processing in the coming chapters.)

Two Concepts to Help Live in the Joy of Jesus

Wrong attitudes/reactions
    anger
    selfishness
    pride
    impatience
    scorn
    impure thoughts
    worry

Things or intangibles
    my relationships (family, friends)
    my success
    my future
    my money
    my clothes
    my possessions

Wrong goals
    trying to achieve significance and security in my own strength
    looking to position, power, and success to bring meaning
    trying to protect myself by being controlling
    seeking fulfillment in what I do
    seeking happiness in what I have

As a side comment, I would say that it is possible you could be in bondage to some habit or sin that you cannot so easily let go of. It will require work in confession, in using the sword of the Spirit, and perhaps in getting someone to help you work it through. The end result, however, is that, with Christ's help, you will be able to let go.

    Let go of my negative emotions, hold on to joy in Jesus, rise above my sinful desires.
    Let go of my fears, hold on to the Lord God Almighty, rise above the unknown future.
    Let go of my disappointments, hold on to Jesus' wisdom, rise above the failures of others.

What does it mean to "hold on"? It means that we are committed to something, that we value, live by, obey something. We as believers value God, His Word, and being His children. It is in the light of these truths and relationships that we make decisions.

What should we hold on to? The primary answer is truth. A significant truth is, "Knowing Jesus is enough for joy, period!" Jesus Himself is the truth. More specifically, God's Word is the most important single item to cling to; we need to go to it for comfort, encouragement, guidance, and perspective. We need to let go of the lies that surround us and those we tell ourselves so we can hold on to what God says is true.

As a simple example of this, when the weather is difficult, people often say, "What a terrible day!" A more accurate statement would be, "I don't like rain." I would save "terrible day" for when you have an accident and cut off your leg! Speaking truth to yourself is letting go of all the inaccurate, negative statements that weigh us down.

My relationship with God should always be a factor in deciding what to let go of and what to hold on to. It is important to hold on to good character based on the Word and integrity, leading us to obey what we know to be true.

> Let go of my desire to defeat others, hold on to my position in Christ, rise above competitiveness.
> Let go of my feeling like a fool, hold on to my being a child of God, rise above angry responses.
> Let go of my natural thoughts, hold on to praise, rise above every circumstance.

When we let go and hold on, what can we rise above? The simplest answer is, the petty things that weigh us down. Most of our conflicts flow from minor issues, which are magnified by the sins that hold us down. Our ungodly attitudes bind us, as do the values, thoughts, and words of those around us. We can rise above all of these.

> Let go of my desire to dominate others, hold on to my significance in Christ, rise above conflict.
> Let go of my possessions, hold on to the Great Provider, rise above the need to protect things.
> Let go of my failures, hold on to forgiveness, rise above self-condemnation.

The next time you are feeling pressure, are in conflict, or are upset, unhappy, or negative, think of this phrase: "Let go, hold on, rise above." Look at what the world, the flesh, and the devil are encouraging you to hang on to; drop them, hold on to truth, and relax as God pulls you up above the turmoil of everyday life.

> Let go of self-pity, hold on to praise, rise above difficult situations.
> Let go of feelings of rejection, hold on to Jesus' rich love for you, rise above negatives, past and present.
> Let go of pride, hold on to humility, rise above the power of the flesh.

God Is Moving History to a Conclusion and Taking Us with Him

The media are full of disturbing headlines. The flood of bad news can be over-

Two Concepts to Help Live in the Joy of Jesus

whelming.

In 1999 there were great, violent earthquakes in the Middle East, with at least 18,000 people killed. As I saw pictures of the collapsed buildings, frantic relatives, and devastated families, my heart was pierced. The natural question rose up from within, "Why, Lord? Why all this suffering?"

At the time I was reading in Revelation for my daily quiet time and had come to chapter 9. At the end are these verses:

> The rest of mankind that were not killed by these plagues *still* did not repent of the work of their hands; they did not stop worshiping demons, and idols. . . . Nor did they repent of their murders, their magic arts, their sexual immorality or their thefts. (vv. 20-21)

It struck me that the intentions of God in sending these plagues included the desire to bring people to their knees in repentance. God was working to open the stubborn eyes of rebellious people so they can be saved from their headlong plunge into the abyss. And that is one of major things God is doing in all of the tragedies that occur in the world!

He would much rather win people by their seeing His goodness, but if they reject that, He loves them so much that He will do what it takes to open their eyes. Psalm 107 gives four scenarios of God doing just that. And this psalm begins with the statement "Give thanks to the LORD, for he is good; his love endures forever." He is forever seeking to bring people into His kingdom, if they will only listen.

One event that shook much of the Western world in 1979 was Ayatollah Khomeini's takeover of Iran, which led to violence, oppression, regression to sixth-century thinking, and expulsion of all foreigners. The country was closed to mission work. We all were sad about it. However, God knew what He was doing. In the 100 years leading up to 1979, in spite of much efforts to spread of the gospel, less than 1,000 Iranians had come to Christ. Since 1979, however, tens of thousands have come to Christ, with estimates of believers ranging up to several hundred thousand — some say maybe up to a million.

Why? In the oppressive regime of the Iranian Revolution people saw the true face of Islam and began looking elsewhere! What looked like a tragedy turned out to be God's plan for reaching this people.

There was a similar story with China in 1949, when it was closed down to mission work as the Communists took over. But God was using this to plow the hearts of people and to open the way to many millions coming to Christ, as they now have, with many more coming each year.

In Psalm 81 God enunciates this principle of His using tragedy, especially self-made difficulties, to open the hearts of people:

> I am the LORD your God,
>> who brought you up out of Egypt.
>> Open wide your mouth and I will fill it.
> But my people would not listen to me;
>> Israel would not submit to me.
> *So I gave them over to their stubborn hearts*
>> *to follow their own devices.*
>
> (vv. 10-12)

When we refuse to go God's way, He says, "OK, you think your way is the right one? Go ahead and try it." "So you think Communism is the way? Try it for seventy years." "So you think qur'anic thinking is the way? Try it!" And after we try our way and find it woefully, tragically lacking, then we are often ready to listen to what God has to say. Witness the great spiritual openness that came to light in the early 1990s after the Communist system collapsed.

A second passage of Scripture reinforces this perspective. The author of Psalm 73, Asaph, struggled unsuccessfully to understand the evil of his day, the prosperity of the wicked, and the injustice to the poor and defenseless. He said, "When I tried to understand all this, *it was oppressive to me*" (v. 16). I can identify with this feeling. In our human understanding, all the evil, tragedy, terror, and problems that come from Satan's work and men's corrupt hearts are overwhelming and incomprehensible.

But Asaph looked to God and found an answer: ". . . it was oppressive to me, *till* I entered the sanctuary of God; then I understood their final destiny." When Asaph looked away to God in worship, then he got the big picture of what God was doing.

This is an important key: When we look away to God, spending time in worship, we get His perspective. We can better understand how God is using the outworking of sin and Satan's plans, all the tragedy, suffering, and turmoil in the world to work out His plan to:

- sweep millions into His kingdom
- bring believers to maturity
- make their testimonies more powerful
- bring judgment on evil
- bring history to a conclusion
- and, in the end, wipe out evil.

Two Concepts to Help Live in the Joy of Jesus

Now when I hear of all the terrible things happening in the world, when events threaten to overwhelm me, I do grieve for those suffering. I do pray for them (we should be using the news as part of our prayer matter). But I no longer let this weigh on me because I now see it in the larger framework of God using these events to bring many into His kingdom and to bring history to His desired conclusion.

I no longer carry the burden of the world on my shoulders; I do not get worked up about "the wrong person being elected" or "the wrong bill being passed." I pray about it, perhaps write to my senator, and certainly vote when the opportunity comes, as well as give, help, and get involved in any other way the Lord may direct me to. But I know that God has His plans in allowing and sometimes sending such things. I can trust Him to do what is right and good, even though I can't understand it now.

I flee to the eternal perspective of Colossians 3:3-4, "For you died, and your life is now hidden with Christ in God. When Christ, who is your life, appears, then you also will appear with him in glory." God is moving things to an end and will appear! He has things in hand! He's fitting everything into His plan! He is moving history to a conclusion and taking us with Him!

Our part is to worship, pray, and trust our great God — and to be involved as He directs. (In no way do I believe we should try to avoid taking responsibility!). We need to find our joy in Jesus, not in having things go well in the world!

Fig. 5.2. God is moving history

Learning to Let Go

"Come in, Dave," said Jack's wife, Barbara as she opened the door for him. "Jack's waiting for you."

"Thanks," Dave said and walked down the hall to the study.

"Good morning, Dave," Jack greeted him, getting up from his chair and warmly grasping Dave's hand. "Good to see you again. Have a seat and we'll start our time with some prayer."

Dave sat down in his usual seat and waited for Jack to pray, but instead Jack said, "Why don't you pray for us this time?"

Dave looked a bit taken aback. "Well, OK, if you want," he said. He bowed his head and was quiet for a minute before beginning.

"Lord Jesus, we praise you as the Great and Mighty One. You breathed the stars into existence, you put them each in their place. You created the earth, you placed us on it. We praise you for your wisdom as we see it in creation. And I praise you for the privilege of being your child, of being carried by you to the conclusion of history. You are worthy of worship and honor and praise. May your Spirit speak to us today, may you be exalted in our conversation. Reveal yourself for your glory. Amen."

Jack looked at Dave with a very pleased smile on his face. "Well, that was one good prayer!" he said.

"I've been listening to a master," Dave replied.

"And you are incorporating some of what you've learned from the book we're reading."

"Yes, that has been helpful in getting my eyes up on God and focusing more on worship," said Dave.

"So what have you gleaned from this past week's reading?" asked Jack.

Dave opened his book to chapter 5. "Well, this concept of 'let go, hold on, and rise above' is a very helpful one. I liked that it comes right out of Scripture. Where was it? Colossians 3, I think.

"I'd never realized how easy it is to be held down in my thinking and feelings by things that are really trivial. This week when I went shopping, I greeted a person working in the supermarket, but he ignored me. I felt foolish — and then angry. But the Spirit brought this chapter to mind, and I was able to recognize how unimportant being ignored is. Maybe the guy was having a hard day; maybe he was deaf! I could let go of my anger, let go of the slight, hold on to the truth that the Lord is my Shepherd, and rise above my tangle of emotions. It really was helpful!"

Jack nodded, "I certainly find it so. It is especially helpful in relationships, where we can be so touchy and easily hurt and then slip into self-pity. Being able to let go and rise above is part of the freedom that Jesus bought for us on the cross. He enables us to live in the realm of truth rather than be caught in the net of lies and bad feelings Satan spreads for us."

Two Concepts to Help Live in the Joy of Jesus

Dave smiled, "When I read about letting go, it was like the lights come on for me. Now I can see how often I have fallen into these traps, getting caught in my own weaknesses, self-pity, and anger. And this concept is so easy to remember, 'Let go, hold on, rise above!' I want to practice this more."

"Don't worry, you'll have plenty of opportunity to use it!" Jack commented. He paused, "In your prayer you mentioned the second aspect of the chapter, that is, having God's perspective on happenings on the world."

"Yes, I liked that too," replied Dave. "I liked the summary statement, 'God is moving history to a conclusion and is taking us with Him.' Hearing this idea was like looking up and getting a glimpse of the big picture, of God's perspective. It is wonderful to know that He's in control, that He knows what He's doing. I tend to worry quite a bit about where things are going in the country and the world, but this helps me to have a better perspective. I see now that my job is to pray and trust God whatever He brings."

"Exactly," replied Jack. "This makes the daily news an impetus for praise and prayer rather than one for worry, fear, and apprehension."
"That's certainly a worldview shift, isn't it?" commented Dave.

Jack laughed. "You're catching on fast! The next few chapters are going to bring more worldview shifts for you. This week I'd like you to begin the section on spiritual warfare, reading chapters 6 through 8."

"OK," said Dave, "I'm glad you are having me read the book slowly. There's a lot to absorb and apply."

"That's true, and will be especially true for this next section," replied Jack.

Study Guide questions for Chapter 5: "Two Concepts to Help Live in the Joy of Jesus"

1. What should we let go of? (42-43)
2. What should we hold on to? (43-44)
3. What can we then rise above? (44)
4. How is Colossians 3:1,2 one source for "let go, hold on, rise above?" (39-40)
5. What are some of the things you need to let go of? Hold on to? Rise above?
6. Give some examples of how you have "let go, held on , risen above."
7. How will you use this concept in your life?
8. What does it mean that "God is moving history to a conclusion and taking us with Him?" (46-47)
9. How does applying the truth of this statement help us deal with the disturbing events of this world?
10. Give some examples of how you have used this statement, or will use it.

Part 2

Spiritual Warfare: Situation Normal

Truth #3: We Can Stand In Whatever Comes by Praying On and Using the Armor of God

CHAPTER 6

The Battle: Lies vs. Truth

"Spiritual warfare"! When you hear that phrase, what comes to your mind? Often the first thing we think of is casting out demons, or Satan attacking through violence. These are definitely a part of it, but spiritual warfare covers a much broader span of our lives than these narrow slices of experience.

Spiritual warfare is actually an everyday happening for believers. It is what I call "situation normal" for Christians. This warfare is the ongoing struggle between Satan's kingdom of darkness and Jesus' kingdom of light.

Satan is a defeated foe, seemingly still strong, but actually *infinitely* less powerful than God. In His wisdom, God allows Satan to attack in certain areas, while at the same time He equips us to stand in this daily battle. He makes it possible to live the truth that knowing Jesus is enough for joy, even in the midst of this battle — *especially* in the midst of this battle.

It is human to question the wisdom of God in allowing this strong opposition in our lives, but He has many positive purposes for our struggles. James 1:2-4 gives us four of them: "Consider it pure joy [there's that word again!], my brothers, whenever you face trials of many kinds, because you know that the *testing of your faith* develops *perseverance.* Perseverance must finish its work so that you may be *mature* and *complete,* not lacking anything." The four purposes for suffering that James here points out are:

- to test or prove our faith so it can be purified and strengthened
- to develop our perseverance
- to lead us to maturity
- to provide completeness in our character and life.

Without the difficulties of the daily battle, we could not, and we would not, have these qualities fully develop in our spiritual lives.

As we get to know God, it becomes clear that everything He does has multiple purposes for us in this warfare. His purposes include developing the fruit of the Spirit in our lives, giving us opportunity to demonstrate His grace to the world, and providing us with chances to be a more effective witness to those around us. In the midst of our difficulties, our joy will actually grow as we run to Jesus for help and get to know Him better.

Satan's Attacks

Spiritual warfare can be described as a spectrum of possible attacks, ranging from the forms in the left below to the more extreme forms on the right:

> from the temptation to grumble — to suicidal urges
> from having sullen neighbors — to being arrested by the government for being a Christian
> from daily tensions in marriage — to divorce
> from anger — to murder
> from mild depression — to demonic possession of unbelievers.

The spiritual-warfare happenings in the left column above are common events in our lives — temptations and situations that come to us either from our flesh or from the world (1 John 2:15-16). Satan then seeks to escalate them toward the situations on the right.

We must never forget that Satan's goal in attacking us is to *destroy:* he wants to destroy believers' testimonies, lives, families, and churches. In order to do this, Satan tries to insert at least four items into our lives:

> delusion (concerning what is good)
> doubt (usually about God's goodness)
> diversions (from what is good)
> division (among believers).

Notice that in each of these four items, Satan desires to make us think the opposite of truth or to separate us from what is good.

Satan's Three Main Weapons

In order to activate delusion, doubt, diversions, and division in our lives, Satan uses lies, fear, and violence as weapons against us. He always begins with lies and has three that are his favorites.

Satan's first big lie is that *God certainly did not mean what He said.* This is Satan's use of delusion. We see his use of this lie in the very first incident in the Bible involving Satan's interaction with human beings. In Genesis 3 notice how Satan tempted and deluded Eve, getting her to doubt God's Word.

The Battle Lies vs. Truth

I have emphasized certain words in the following texts to help bring this out.

> He [Satan] said to the woman, "Did God *really* say, 'You must not eat from any tree in the garden'?" (Gen. 3:1)

Do you see the insinuation in that statement, the encouragement to doubt God's Word? Did God *really* say . . . ?

> The woman said to the serpent, "We may eat fruit from the trees in the garden, but God did say, 'You must not eat fruit from the tree that is in the middle of the garden, and you must not touch it, or you will die.'"[12]
> "You will *not* surely die," the serpent said to the woman. (vv. 2-4)

Satan flat-out denies what God said. Sometimes Satan will attack so brazenly that it takes us off guard — and we believe it! Certainly Eve believed it!

Satan continues with his second big lie, which is that *God is not always good.* Satan works hard to convince us to doubt that God has our best interests at heart. Notice Satan's words to Eve:

> For God knows that when you eat of it your eyes will be opened . . . (v. 5a)

The clear implication is that God is withholding something good — her eyes were closed, but now they could be opened. This lie brought doubt of God's goodness.

Then Satan finishes with his third lie, that *you can be more fulfilled and happy if you disobey God.* This is the use of diversion, getting us to look away from God to something else.

> . . . and *you will be like God,* knowing good and evil." (v. 5b)

This is the final blow, bringing Eve to her decision to sin.

Look at this progression again. First Satan flatly denied God's word that disobedience would bring death. Then he insinuated that God was not good in giving His command not to eat this fruit. Then he implied that God was keeping something very good from Eve. And finally he declared that by disobeying God, Eve could reach a higher plane — that she could actually be like God, and even be independent from God. Eve took the bait. She got her eyes off God and onto the attraction of the temptation.

---

12. Note that Eve knew what God had commanded, but she added something to God's command: not to touch the fruit. I see here the human tendency to bring legalism into the picture, to overstress conformity to rules.

> When the woman *saw* that the fruit of the tree was good for food and pleasing to the eye, and also desirable for gaining wisdom [note that she was looking away from God to the circumstances], she took some and ate it. (v. 6)

Eve actually believed that God was withholding some good from her and that it was up to her to get it![13]

Every one of us has heard these lies multiple times in various ways. I remember once when I was ten or eleven years old, I stole a small flashlight from a store. At the time I did not recognize what was happening, but now I realize that I was listening to Satan's lie that obeying God's will ("Do not steal!") would keep me from getting something good, something better than what God offered, and would make me happier than if I obeyed God and denied myself. I believed Satan and became a thief, and Satan stole my joy.

In reality, God's will is exactly what we would desire *if we had all the facts*. We, of course, don't have all the facts and never will in this life, but we do have a trustworthy God who does have all the facts and will both give us direction and bring to us what is truly best. We can obey in faith because we know His character.

After Satan uses lies, he follows up with his other weapons of *fear* and *violence* to try to force us in wrong directions and, ultimately, destroy us. In the garden, the seed of fear sprouted as a consequence of sin; it is immediately evident in Adam and Eve's lives after they ate the fruit, causing them to hide from God and from each other. And the bud of violence formed immediately in them as they accused each other before God. Later, it bloomed in their firstborn son, Cain, who murdered his brother Abel. Satan continues to use these same three powerful weapons of lies, fear, and violence against us on a daily basis.

God's Provision

Our heavenly Father, however, has not left us defenseless in this battle. He has given us means to counteract each of Satan's weapons:

---

13. Notice that verse 6 adds, "She also gave some to her husband, who was with her, and he ate it." Although Adam was right there with Eve, he didn't defend her or contradict Satan's lies or resist his wife's encouragement. Eve, we are told, was deceived, but Adam made a clear, knowing decision to disobey God. This is a sad example of a husband failing to lead his wife; instead, he followed her lead without checking in with God's Word. The result? He brought great, unnecessary suffering on all who came after him. This is defeat in the spiritual battle, not just for himself, but for all who followed. It is a reminder that if we fail in the battle, we negatively affect many people around us and after us. But likewise if we win in the battle, we affect many people positively, potentially for generations to come.

The Battle Lies vs. Truth

Lies are defeated by *truth.*
Fear is overcome by *faith.*
Violence is conquered by *love.*

From a human standpoint, the spiritual weapons of truth, faith, and love appear to be much weaker than Satan's. In reality, though, they are far more effective because they tap into the great power of God.

Life is hard; it is a struggle and a battle. Therefore we need this help. Our first line of offense and defense is always truth. Jesus, who is Himself Truth, said in John 8:32, "You will know the truth, and the truth will set you free." We therefore need to immerse ourselves in truth each day. The best way to do this is to have a daily quiet time where we read and meditate on the Bible; this is a necessary preparation for the spiritual battle we face every day.

Study Guide questions for Chapter 6: "The Battle: Lies vs Truth"

1. Why does God allow spiritual warfare in our lives? (53-54)
2. What is spiritual warfare? Give some examples. (53-54)
3. What are the three lies Satan uses? (54-55)
4. Give an example of each from your own life.
5. What are Satan's other two weapons? (56)
6. What are God's answers to each of Satan's weapons? (57)
7. How does a daily quiet time tie in with spiritual warfare? (57)
8. How will this chapter change your approach to life?

CHAPTER 7

The Battle Illustrated

Throughout this book, we will be discussing the tools that God has provided for us to overcome the lies, fear, and violence that Satan uses against us in his effort to destroy us. The clearest single passage that mentions these tools is Ephesians 6:10-18. Here Paul uses the image of a Roman warrior in full armor to teach us how to stand up against and defeat Satan and all his forces. Each part of the armor is an element of truth we are told to take up, put on, and use.

As Dr. Johnny V Miller comments, "Almost all of these items are cited from Isaiah, in which they apply to the Messiah. I think that this is important for people to understand in spiritual warfare: we are putting on Christ, and He is our victor."

Before we look at this passage, consider the following pictures, which deal with the dynamics of the spiritual battle we all face every day. When my younger son was in high school, facing the sexual temptations every male deals with, we taught him about spiritual warfare, and he drew this series of pictures to illustrate his own struggles.

As he went to school, he had to have the full armor on.

Fig. 7.1. The full armor

The Battle Illustrated

He needed all the armor because, as soon as he entered the door, he knew he would be faced with the temptation to think lustful thoughts, stimulated by the way the female students dressed and acted.

Fig. 7.2. Facing temptation

He realized from Scripture, however, that his enemies weren't the girls but his own desires used by Satan and Satan's evil principalities and powers, who were setting a trap for him. While turning away or running from the temptation, he needed to use his armor against the attack, primarily thinking and speaking truth.

Fig. 7.3. Prepared to use truth

He would pray something like this, "Thank you, Lord, for this temptation, which reminds me how weak I am in myself and how much I need your help. I praise you that you made women so attractive and that you give us godly and constructive guidelines of how to interact with them." Note that he is using the shield of faith, thanking and praising God, as his first offensive weapon; this puts the enemy off balance.

Fig. 7.4. Using the shield of faith

"I agree with you, Lord, that lustful thoughts are selfish, for when I think such things, I'm using others for my own self-centered ends. I agree that these thoughts are destructive, caustic to my soul, that they are pleasing to Satan, and that they are grievous to you." In praying this way, he picks up and uses Satan's own weapon against him.

Fig. 7.5. Agreeing with God against Satan

The Battle Illustrated

"I reject these thoughts and desires in the name of the Lord Jesus Christ. I thank you that I am living for eternity — and what's this girl going to look like in eighty years anyway?!"

Fig. 7.6. Standing against Satan in Jesus' name

"I'm going to follow your Word, which says, "It is God's will that I should be sanctified: that I should avoid sexual immorality. . . . For God did not call me to be impure, but to live a holy life" (1 Thess. 4:3, 7).

This type of warfare is what I call "spiritual judo," using the attack of the enemy against him. What looks like an irresistible temptation becomes the key to defeating Satan's intent. What would seem a negative — temptation — becomes a way to know Jesus more, and thereby to live more in the joy He gives. These pictures show the basics of what we will cover on spiritual warfare as we progress through Ephesians 6:10-18.

Study Guide Questions for Chapter 7: "The Battle Illustrated"

1. Why do we need to keep on the armor of Ephesians 6:10-18? (58-59)
2. What is spiritual judo? (61)
3. How have you experienced such spiritual fights in your life?
4. What did you do, or could you do to win?

CHAPTER 8

Being Strong in the Lord

Now let's take a look at Ephesians 6:10-18. Verse 10 says, "Finally, be strong in the Lord and in his mighty power." Note that this is not a suggestion but a command. The question is, How can we obey it?

As I meditated on this verse, three means of being strong in the Lord came into focus. First is *engaging in personal worship,* which I would define as "giving God glory and honor for who He is, without thinking about how that benefits me." Such worship happens when we spend time using Scripture to exalt God because of His character, giving Him esteem, lifting up His name, glorifying Him for who He is. This kind of worship transforms us. (See part 3 for an extended discussion of worship.)

This kind of worship also leads to the second way we can cooperate with God in being strong in Him: *being filled with the Spirit.* This first involves confession of known sin, which we will consider more fully in part 4. In worship the Holy Spirit is able to point out sins we have not noticed (for example, attitudes, tendencies, culturally acceptable but biblically wrong things) so we can confess them. Then we need to ask for the Spirit to fill us. (See part 6 for a more extensive treatment of this topic.)

At the beginning of each day we need to make this initial surrender, then through the day commit to obey Him. This means that we agree to avoid grieving the Spirit with sin or quenching Him with disobedience when He seeks to lead us. This attitude on our part allows Him to continue to fill us.

The third way of being strong in the Lord is by *praying through your day* in your quiet time. God's calling us to participate in intercessory prayer is His invitation for us to join Him in what He is doing (as opposed to asking God to join me in my plans). Each morning I must submit myself and my plans to His guidance and therefore go forth in His power.

Perhaps you, like me, have struggled with distractions in your quiet time, especially in worship and reading the Bible, thinking instead about what is coming in your day. I utilize this tendency by keeping a pad with me during my quiet time and jotting down these "distractions," then making them part of my praying. This is another part of "spiritual judo," using Satan's attempts to distract me as a help in writing my to-do list for the day.

Being Strong in the Lord

I have found, especially when living overseas, that praying about each thing I am planning to do makes a big difference in the way my day goes. For instance, receiving a package via international mail is quite a process in the country where I work, one fraught with bureaucratic pitfalls. One time before I learned the value of praying through my day, I went to the post office to get a package that a friend had sent. The inspector opened it and pulled out two jars of peanut butter and two of grape jelly. At the time neither were available in our country, so I was very happy to get this "comfort food."

"You can have only one of each of these," said the inspector and set aside a jar of jelly and one of peanut butter. I objected, but to no avail. I'm sure he took them for himself, but there was nothing I could do — further objecting would probably have resulted in the other two being taken also! I could only take the remaining jars and go home.

However, after beginning the practice of praying through my day each morning, things went differently. When I had to go get a package, I would pray something like this: "Lord, today I have to go to the post office to get a package. I pray that the people who will wait on me will have had a good night's sleep, a nice breakfast, will have gotten a seat on the bus going to work, and will have had a nice cup of tea before I get to them. Guide them in making good decisions, and help me to get the package without unnecessary hassle."

I found that praying like that made a huge difference in what happened in the post office. It did not necessarily eliminate troubles, but it certainly made things easier and helped me to work through any difficulties that came up.[14]

Three Things We Need to Know

In preparing ourselves for daily spiritual warfare and in taking specific steps to be strong in the Lord, there are three things we need to know.

---

14. A further illustration of how the Lord answered such prayer came in another visit to the post office to pick up a package. A woman looked at my passport and asked if I had a wife and if she had a passport. When I said "Yes," she told me to bring my wife's passport to her before she would give me the package. I felt anger rising at this unnecessary request, especially since it was a hassle to get to this post office, but the Holy Spirit reminded me to praise God for this development (putting up the shield of faith) and to obey. So I rode the bus home, then back, arriving an hour and a half later. The woman looked at my wife's passport and said with a smile, "You entered the country more than six months ago, so I can't give you this package custom free, but since your wife entered the country less than six months ago, I can write it in her passport, and you won't have to pay customs!"

What if I had complained about the woman's unreasonable request and expressed my "righteous anger?" She would not have helped me, and I would have had to pay an exorbitant customs fee. Prayer not only prepared this woman to help me, it also made *me* different as God answered through this woman.

1. *Know yourself!* Ephesians 6:11 says: "Put on the full armor of God so that you can take your stand against the devil's schemes." Note again that this is not a suggestion, but a command: "Put on!" Some people have questioned whether we really need to put on the armor of God every day. They've asked, "When did I ever take it off?" In my own life, I find myself without defense many times, having unknowingly laid aside the armor. How? By preferring my own ideas, ways, methods, or values instead of God's (see Ps. 81:11-16; 84:11-12). That's why I need to put on the armor every morning. So each day I meditate and pray through this passage, consciously putting on each piece, reminding myself of what God has provided, and committing myself to using it in living for God and sharing His Word with those around me.

Note also that it says, "Put on the *full* armor of God." Picking and choosing parts is not an option. (In part 7 we consider in detail how to put on each piece.)

This verse says we are to put on the armor for a purpose: ". . . so that you can take your stand against the devil's schemes." The King James Version speaks colorfully of standing against "the wiles of the devil."

We need to ask ourselves, What are the wiles, or schemes, that the devil uses against us? Satan will attack us where we are weak, as he did my son in high school. He tempts us where we are prone to sin. Satan has never tempted me to rob a bank because I have no inclination or need to do that. But he often tempts me to think negatively of others, to compete in unhealthy ways, and to think lustful thoughts. He knows me well! The better I know myself, the more prepared I can be to stand against his wiles.

You need to know your weaknesses, to sit down and list them out. Then prepare yourself with the sword, with a verse or passage memorized to use specifically against temptation in each area. This is part of putting on the whole armor.

My prayer from this verse is, "Lord, help me to put on your whole armor and to use it through the day; help me to recognize the tricks and traps the devil is using against me and avoid them — or if I fall into one, to immediately recognize it and get out."

You can be sure God will answer that prayer because it is His will. When we pray God's Word to Him, He is highly pleased and promises to answer. We must remember, though, that He will do it in His time and in His way.

2. *Know your enemy!* Verse 12 goes on to say, "For our struggle is not against flesh and blood, but against the rulers, against the authorities, against the powers of this dark world and against the spiritual forces of evil in the heavenly realms." These words make it clear that our enemies are *not* governments, big

corporations, and powerful people — or any people at all. Our enemies are Satan and his spiritual forces, the rulers and authorities under him. This is a spiritual battle against spiritual, not human, powers. That's why we need spiritual armor.

Satan, however, wants us to fight people. The people who are acting like our enemies are actually pawns in his hands; we should be feeling sorry for them, not fighting them. When we understand this, we can use God's weapons against Satan, not against the people who appear to be our enemies, who may even be acting cruelly against us.

3. *Know your future!* The next verse, Ephesians 6:13, looks to the future: "Therefore put on the full armor of God, so that when the day of evil comes, you may be able to stand your ground, and after you have done everything, to stand."

According to this verse, what is our future going to include? Evil days! They will come to each of us: an accident, a broken relationship, a sickness, a robbery, an unexpected death, a failure. There may be worse things, like arrests, torture, or expulsion from the country where you are working. But *no matter how evil the day is,* we can remain standing if we put on the whole armor! This is why it is important to put on the armor, all of it, every day, so we become good at using it and are always ready when tough times come.

Note that the verse also says that we *will* be able to do everything and still stand.[15] The teaching here is that, if we have the armor on and are using it in God's power, we will be able to stand in any circumstance He allows and to accomplish all He intends for us to do. No event can take from us the joy we can have in knowing Jesus — unless we give it permission!

The stirring verses at the end of Romans 8 echo this truth:

Who shall separate us from the love of Christ? Shall trouble or hardship or persecution or famine or nakedness or danger or sword? As it is written:
"For your sake we face death all day long;
we are considered as sheep to be slaughtered."
No, in all these things we are *more than conquerors* through him who loved us. (vv. 35-37)

---

15. God's idea of "everything" may often be very different from ours. I think he expects a lot less "doing" than we would like, and much more "becoming holy" than we'd like. Sometimes being patient and waiting is more on God's mind than, for example, finishing a project at the expense of a relationship. We need to make sure we are doing God's "everything," not just our

Dave's Insight Into Spiritual Warfare

Dave was visibly energized, sitting on the edge of his seat in Jack's den. "Talk about worldview shift! Those chapters took me into a whole new realm!" he said enthusiastically. "It helped me to understand a lot of what's going in life."

"God's truth certainly is different from the illusions and shadows of this world," replied Jack.

Dave nodded. "I see now that I've been fighting people all these years, not even being aware of how Satan was using them against me! I remember poor old Mr. Bennett, our neighbor. He gave me a hard time about a lot of things, including playing too loudly in our yard. I saw him as the enemy, but now I see him as a poor, unhappy person that Satan used to push me away from older folks."

"Good insight," Jack commented. "Understanding our true enemy is a foundational shift we need in our thinking, Dave. Then we can begin to fight the right enemy, Satan, in the right way, with the armor on. It saves us a lot of grief and messy relational issues."

"I also really liked the pictures illustrating spiritual warfare and the description of 'spiritual judo,'" commented Dave.

"Using spiritual judo is a great concept; it is part of living smart," said Jack. "Using the strength of the enemy against him means we have more strength for the tasks God gives."

Dave nodded. "That's something I have to think more about. I also noticed that personal worship came up again in the chapter on being strong in the Lord. That seems to be foundational to everything in our spiritual lives."

"Absolutely," replied Jack, "worship is the wellspring from which flows most growth in our lives. That's because it involves the whole person — mind, will, and emotion — not just the intellect. And that's why Satan will work hard to keep us from personal worship."

"Hmm," said Dave, "that's a good warning about anticipating an attack there."

Jack nodded, "And personal worship leads us into being filled with the Spirit. There will be another, longer section on this later in the book."

Dave went on, "I also liked the idea of praying through my day, joining God in what He wants to do. I've already begun doing that."

"Excellent," Jack said. "That's what I want to see happen, you beginning to practice the truths in this book. If you do, you will be able to stand against Satan's attacks, no matter what."

"I sure want to. And I'm eager to get the next chapters to see the rest of the armor."

"Well, that's your assignment, Dave. Read chapters 9 through 11."

"OK!" Dave stood up to go.

Jack held up his hand and said, "Just a minute, let's pray before you dash

Being Strong in the Lord

out the door!" As they both bowed their heads, Jack began, "Lord God, the Triumphant Savior, Undefeated Lord, Conquering King. I praise you that you have equipped us for the battle of life in this sin-warped world, where Satan is allowed to roam. Help us, Lord God, each day to take up and put on the armor you have provided so that we can join you in your victories over Satan, sin, and self. We praise you for how you will help us in this. In the powerful name of Jesus, Amen."

Study Guide questions for Chapter 8: "Being Strong in the Lord"

1. What are the three things we can do to be "strong in the Lord?" (62)
2. Describe how you do, or will do each of these.
3. There are three things we should know (64-65)
    a. "Know yourself" What does this mean?
    What are some of your weakness that Satan tries to use?
    b. "Know your enemy" Who is your enemy? Who is not?
    How does this change your behavior?
    c. "Know your future" What two things does this tell you about your future? How should this influence your response to difficulty? (65)

CHAPTER 9

On Being a Minister of Defense

In this chapter we look at the first three pieces of the spiritual armor mentioned in Ephesians 6 — the belt of truth, the breastplate of righteousness, and the shoes of peace. These are basically defensive tools, each one representing relationships.

The Belt of Truth

Ephesians 6:14 says, "Stand firm then, with the belt of truth buckled around your waist."

Think about the basic truths of the Bible — most foundationally, the story of salvation. God created man as good, man rebelled, Christ brought redemption and eternal life, and those who accept these truths, confessing their sin and asking for forgiveness, believing on His name, become the children of God. This is all about our relationship with Jesus. This is the gospel.

So how do we put on the belt? We do it by looking at, and affirming, the whole gospel, the "two sides of truth" — one negative, one positive. On the negative side is what we were before we believed, and what our flesh continues to be; on the positive side is what we are in Christ.

Negatives	*Positives*
We were sinners.	We are a new creature in Christ.
We were God's enemies.	We are God's friends, forgiven and transformed.
We were separated from God.	We are reconciled with Him.
We were children of wrath.	We are forgiven children of the King.
All our righteousness is like filthy rags.	We are declared righteous by faith in Christ.
What we deserve is hell.	We have been given heaven.
We deserve punishment.	We are blessed by God every day.

Now think about an old-fashioned scale with a pan on each side. Such scales are common in the markets of the country where I work. A weight is put on one side, and produce on the other. When the two pans are equal in weight, the scale is balanced, as in figure 9.1. It is the tension on each end of the scale that keeps it in balance; remove the tension, and it is out of balance.

Fig. 9.1. A scale in balanced tension

In putting on the belt of truth, it is helpful to have such a scale in mind, with the negatives on one side and the positives on the other. There is a tension here, as we would like to focus on one side or the other, but we must maintain the tension, for that is what brings balance. Each morning as I pray through this passage, I say something like this:

> Thank you, Lord God, that although I deserved punishment, you
>   gave me pardon;
> although I deserved separation from you, you made me your beloved son;
> although I deserved condemnation, you commend me and commission me
>   to do good works;
> although I deserved nothing good, you blessed me with all spiritual
>   blessings in the heavenly places.

I use Ephesians 1:3-8 as a source for many of these thoughts. What we are doing in speaking these thoughts in prayer is proclaiming the gospel to ourselves, speaking the truth that sets us free: what we are in the flesh and what we are as children of God.[16]

This concept of contrasting what we deserve and what we get does three important things. *First,* it gives us a balance in our understanding. Some people tend to look only at what they were and what their flesh is, tipping their mental scale toward the negative, and therefore have gloomy thoughts leading to depression. They have a false, negative view of God and an unhealthy focus on their spiritual weakness.

Others look only at what we have in Christ, unbalancing their mental scale toward the positive, which can lead to spiritual pride and, like the Pharisees,

---

16. Jerry Bridges develops these thoughts in his excellent book *Respectable Sins: Confronting the Sins We Tolerate* (Colorado Springs, Colo.: NavPress, 2007).

a dependence on self rather than God. Both have removed the tension needed to keep both sides in a healthy view.

In contrast, when we are balanced in our grasp of both the positive and negative, we maintain the necessary tension, and we have a biblical view of ourselves. This leads to humility, which can be defined as seeing ourselves as God sees us, in both the positives and the negatives

Second, it helps us to face, embrace, and leave behind the shame we may feel from our actions, from others' comments and actions toward us, or from an understanding of our innate sinfulness.[17] We can adopt God's attitude toward us, one of unreserved love and acceptance.

Third, when we remember how much we have been forgiven and see the great grace God has bestowed on us, we will be "grace receivers." Then we are much more likely to be "grace givers," that is, to extend to others the grace that we have been given and to be merciful to others as God has been merciful to us.

I usually finish up putting on the belt of truth by quoting Colossians 3:12a, "Therefore, as God's chosen people, holy and dearly loved...." I pray, "Lord, I praise you that I am chosen in Christ before the foundation of the world, that I am called to be your son, that I am cleansed of my sin and transformed, that I am commissioned to special work, and that I am completely and unconditionally loved by you." This is truth to delight in, to revel in, and to rejoice in.

This approach of having a balanced view of truth gives a balanced mental and emotional perspective. Satan is constantly seeking to knock us off balance in our thoughts and emotions. If he can dislodge the belt of truth, then the rest of the armor won't be very effective for us. (See chapter 24 for an expanded exposition of the belt of truth.)

I am learning to think, feel, and act on these truths, cooperating with the Spirit's work of transforming me. This is putting on the belt of truth, thinking the truth about my relationship with God, accepting His wonderful forgiveness, and living it out moment by moment. Living in this truth allows us to take the next step.

The Breastplate of Righteousness

While the belt of truth speaks of our relationship with God, the breastplate of righteousness speaks of our relationship with ourselves. The breastplate covers our most vital organs — including our heart, what is very much "us."

---

17. This concept is developed in the book *The Shame Exchange: Trading Shame for God's Mercy and Freedom,* by Steve and Sally Breedlove and Ralph and Jennifer Ennis (Colorado Springs, Colo.: NavPress, 2009).

Becoming a Minister of Defense

God demonstrates His love, forgiveness, and acceptance of us by giving us *His* righteousness to carry into the day, even though He knows we will fail Him and stands ready to forgive us. In like manner, we, after confessing and receiving forgiveness from God, must apply the work of Christ by forgiving ourselves in the light of His forgiveness (Col. 3:13).

Let me hasten to explain that in forgiving ourselves, we are not trying to act in God's place; we are simply applying the forgiveness that Christ bought in His death and resurrection. Just as we are told to forgive others, so we must be willing to forgive ourselves — we must agree with Him that Christ's death and resurrection were enough to secure forgiveness. (Mark 12:31 teaches, "Love your neighbor as yourself"; if we don't forgive ourselves, we probably won't forgive our neighbors!)

For more perfectionistic people like myself, this is both hard and very important. After confessing and receiving God's forgiveness, I still tend to berate myself ("you idiot!"), even to punish myself for my sins ("no more ice cream for a week!").

For instance, in a thoughtless moment I have said something that was really hurtful to a friend. My natural response is to say to myself something like, "How could I have done that?! I am such a fool!" Then I berate myself for hurting others and embarrassing myself. This is, in a perverted way, a fleshly attempt to deal with my sin and the guilt it produces.

A biblical response, however, is to pray something like this, "Lord, I just thoughtlessly hurt my friend. This shows that your Word is true, namely: I do still have an active flesh and naturally sin. Thank you for this reminder of my need for your guidance and ongoing transforming power in my life. Forgive me for my thoughtlessness. I thank you for your forgiveness. And as you have forgiven and accepted me, so I forgive and accept myself." Then, of course, I must go and ask forgiveness from my friend.

Most mornings as I pray through this section, I find that there is an unhealthy tension within me. It comes from not processing my mistakes, failures, and sins from the day before. As I confess, receive forgiveness, and then forgive myself, the tension drains away. This prepares me for the next piece of armor.

The Shoes of Peace

The third defensive piece of the spiritual armor is the shoes of peace. According to Ephesians 6:15, we are to stand firm "with our feet fitted with the readiness that comes from the gospel of peace."

As we have said, the belt of truth and the breastplate of righteousness deal with our relationships with God and ourselves. Now this portion talks about our relationships with others, especially as it speaks about the gospel of peace and our readiness to apply it.

As God has forgiven us, so we are to forgive ourselves and must forgive others. Colossians 3:13 is very clear: "Forgive as the Lord has forgiven you." We must be willing to implement the "readiness" to live out the gospel of peace first through forgiving.

Forgiveness is very important in God's eyes. It is the only aspect of the Lord's Prayer that Jesus elaborated on (". . . as we also have forgiven our debtors. . . . But if you do not forgive men their sins, your Father will not forgive your sins," Matt 6:12, 15).

He also told a significant parable about this point in Matthew 18:23-35, the parable of the unforgiving servant. And there are many commands in the letters about forgiveness. (See chapter 26 for a fuller discussion of forgiveness.)

There is a second aspect to these shoes of peace, which is going to others to share the gospel with them. If, however, we are unforgiving, harboring grudges and anger against others, our sharing of the gospel will only be theoretical, not a rich reality into which we can lead others. First we must forgive, and only then we can teach others about God's proffered forgiveness and the joy that comes from knowing Jesus.

Study Guide questions for Chapter 9: "On Being a Minister of Defense"

1. What does the belt of truth represent? (68)
2. What are the two sides of truth in this relationship? (68-69)
3. What are three benefits of putting on the belt? (69-70)
4. What does the breastplate represent? (70-71)
5. How do we put it on and what's the result? (71)
6. What do the shoes of peace represent? (71-72)
7. How do we put them on and what is the result? (72)
8. How will you now go about putting these three parts of the armor on?

CHAPTER 10

Becoming a Minister of Offense

After putting on the first three defensive pieces of armor, we can go on to put on the parts of the armor that are used both offensively and defensively.

The Shield of Faith

Ephesians 6:16 says, "In addition to all this, take up the shield of faith, with which you can extinguish all the flaming arrows of the evil one."

Notice carefully that first phrase: "In addition to all this. . . ." These words give us the condition for being able to take up the shield of faith: before proceeding with the shield, we need to have the first three parts of the armor on. As we have pointed out, these three refer to our relationship with God (receiving His forgiveness), with ourselves (forgiving ourselves), and with others (forgiving them), and each part needs to be in place. If we are struggling with resentment, anger, or bitterness, being unwilling to forgive in any area, then it will be very difficult to lift up the shield of faith.

When Paul wrote this passage, he was thinking of a Roman soldier's outfit. (See fig. 7.1 in chapter 7 above.) A Roman soldier's shield was a large one, usually four feet high, held in the left hand and covering about three-quarters of the body. This left him somewhat exposed. When a Roman soldier was in formation, though, his shield overlapped with the shield of his neighbor, covering the exposed part of his body.

If a soldier moved his shield aside so he could use his sword against an enemy, he would expose both himself and his neighbor to danger. So the Romans often attacked in a row, with each soldier's shield held to cover part of himself and part of his neighbor. Running into their enemies, they tried to knock them down and then stab them on the ground. In this way, the shield was both an offensive and a defensive weapon.

Now, let's say we have our relationships in place. How do we lift up this shield? How do we express our faith in God when things are difficult, when the air is filled with fiery arrows meant to destroy us? God gives us a clue in Psalm 34:1, "I will bless the Lord at all times" (ESV). We raise and hold up the shield of faith with praise — praising especially when things are difficult, expressing our faith in God's power, wisdom, and love.

Praising in the face of difficulties does three things. First, it gives God great honor because we are operating by faith, not by sight (see 2 Cor. 5:7). Second, Satan is allergic to praise; when we lift the shield, we are on the attack against him. Third, as verse 16 says, when we hold up the shield of faith, we can quench *all* the flaming arrows of the evil one. These arrows can be hurtful things that others do to us or say to us, or things we do or say to ourselves. Any of these can incapacitate us if the arrow gets through.

Each of us is vulnerable to different "arrows." For me, one powerful flaming arrow is self-pity. Another is anger at people for making me look foolish or for not meeting my expectations. Another is worry, as is fear of man. Each one, though, can be countered and quenched with praise, which lifts up the shield of faith.

Here's an example of how this works. I was responsible for the organization of three overlapping conferences, all of which were held in the same hotel. At the end of the first week, the hotel owner called me in and told me that, because of problems with another customer, he was going to close down our conferences and throw us out.

That threat was certainly a flaming arrow! And it was quickly followed by other fiery arrows of fear, worry, and fear of man. ("What will people think of me when the plans I made for their conferences all crumble before their eyes?")

In the midst of this turmoil the Holy Spirit spoke to me, "In this situation, can you believe and live the truth that 'knowing Jesus is enough for joy'?" (This sentence, in fact, was the very theme of one of our three conferences!)

This question jolted me out of my natural responses and refocused me on truth. "With you, Lord Jesus, I can!" I replied and immediately began praising Him for this situation, which seemed headed for disaster, with no way out.

The story with the hotel owner had no totally happy ending, for in order to complete the conferences, we ended up having to pay far more than we had agreed on. However, praise turned the situation around spiritually and brought a whole different perspective to those in the conferences. The Spirit moved, bringing a beginning of revival, deepening, and change. The main conference I was involved in was the best conference I've ever attended because of what the Spirit was doing. All this was in the midst of great unresolved conflict with the hotel owner, which I held at bay by putting up the shield of faith.

It is helpful to note that there are often three stages in giving a response of faith. First a purely obedient, clenched-teeth praise that goes against everything we are feeling, wanting, or thinking. Second is biblical praise, using Scripture to strengthen our resolve. Third is a processed praise, given after we've had time to work through our emotions and thoughts and bring them in line with Scripture.

Here's an example of how this works. One time I backed up and knocked down a scooter parked out of my line of sight behind my car. I was angry with myself, upset that this had happened, fearful of the financial consequences. But with clenched teeth I thanked God for allowing it to happen.

The owner of the scooter was there and came right over with his friend. He quickly pointed out damage on the fiberglass fairing. Some of it obviously was not from this accident, but after a quick prayer, I offered him $20 for the damage, and he accepted it. I walked away with my emotions in turmoil but turned to Psalm 23 in my thoughts, "Lord, you are my shepherd. You allowed this situation for a reason, you will use it for good, and I praise you for it."

Then as time went on and I had opportunity to reflect on the whole event by journaling, I could praise Him wholeheartedly for protecting me from worse, for having the owner accept the small payment, and for giving me another opportunity to praise Him by faith.

Here's an example of what happens when I don't hold up the shield of faith. Recently, as I went down the ramp to board the first plane on a trip to Germany, I heard the stewardess say, "There is no more room in the overhead bins, so you will all have to check your carry-ons."

I was not happy with that news! My carry-on was packed with personal things, many of which I wanted to use on the trip. Fortunately, most of these were in my backpack in my carry-on. It was pretty heavy, and I was glad to have it on wheels — and now it was being taken from me. I asked if I would get it back when I changed planes. "No," was the answer. So I got out my backpack, surrendered my carry-on case, and made my way back to my seat, all the while complaining in my heart about this injustice.

This event and my response to it colored the whole rest of the trip. On my next plane, the transatlantic flight, I was able to have three seats across so I could lie down to sleep. Instead of being thankful for this, however, I complained inwardly about not having the fourth seat so I could stretch out my legs all the way. I was aware that I was not responding correctly, not "letting go, holding on, rising above," and tried to do so, but it was so hard because I was staggering along, wounded by the arrows of the enemy, having dropped down my shield.

Later, in praying about the whole situation, the Spirit pointed out to me that, at a crucial moment, I had failed to hold up the shield of faith: I chose to complain instead of praising God for what He was doing in allowing my carry-on to be taken away. In that split second of failing to praise, failing to hold up the shield of faith, I got hit with the fiery arrow of self-pity, followed by one of anger. I was angry at the stewardess for taking my bag. I was, without thinking it, angry at God for allowing this trivial event to happen. My relationships were not in place, and I was now wounded by the arrows and weakened by their poison. It was very hard, basically impossible, to get that shield of faith up in order to ward of further arrows. Without confession and repentance, I was defenseless. I was down, and Satan just kept shooting me with other fiery arrows of fear, frustration, selfishness, and more complaining. Satan has no mercy and is quick to follow up on an advantage.

It was several joyless days before the Spirit broke through in my journaling and helped me see where I had committed my initial, tactical sin of choosing to grumble instead of praising. Then I could confess, surrender, and be healed. Then I could again easily raise the shield of faith. Then joy could flow again. But first I had to choose to live the truth that knowing Jesus is enough for joy, period!

How easily I fall, how significant a seemingly small decision can be, how dangerous is the innocuous sin of complaining! Complaining arises from unbelief, rebellion against what God has brought, as well as from pride, from fear, from selfishness, and from listening to self, not the Spirit.

To God, complaining is a serious, destructive, and deadly sin. That's why He reacted so strongly to the Israelites' complaining and grumbling: "And the people complained in the hearing of the LORD about their misfortunes, and when the LORD heard it, his anger was kindled, and the fire of the LORD burned among them and consumed some outlying parts of the camp" (Num. 11:1 ESV). It was important enough that this is repeated in the Psalms:

> They murmured in their tents,
>   and did not obey the voice of the LORD.
> Therefore he raised his hand and swore to them
>   that he would make them fall in the wilderness.
>   (106:25-26 ESV)

It is important also to note that my temptation to complain came after an intense, very full three weeks of successful work and ministry. I was tired, worn down, and not watchful; I chose to sin without even realizing it. I need to remember that after victory often comes significant temptation.

But praise God that He is faithful, that He is at work, and that He brings us back to Himself into the light so we can be healed, restored, strengthened, and again put on the armor He has provided. "Put on the whole armor of God so that you can take your stand against the devil's schemes. . . . Take up the shield of faith, with which you can extinguish all the flaming arrows of the evil one" (Eph. 6:11, 16).

The Helmet of Salvation

The next piece of armor is in verse 17: "Take the helmet of salvation." The helmet is to protect our head, especially our thoughts. God knows how mixed up we can be in our thinking, especially when it comes to the natural tendency to want to earn our salvation or to secure His love by our performance.

As you know, our salvation depends entirely on the finished work of Christ. We need to think clearly on this. Our salvation is secure in what Christ has done and in the character of God, so we don't have to worry about performing to earn or keep it — even though our natural tendency is to do so. We are free to obey because we love Him and are new creatures with a new heart; we do not have to earn His approval. We are called to holy lives in His power and to do the good works He has prepared for us (Eph. 2:10). So now we can perform, not to earn anything, but to bring joy and honor to our King.

Many benefits flow out of the salvation Jesus bought for us. Two of these are things for which people will kill, both literally and figuratively: the desire for significance and the hunger for security. For men, significance is generally more important, and for women, security, but both are necessary for a healthy life.

The wonderful truth is that God has given us both of these as part of our salvation in Christ. Ephesians 1 says a lot about these topics — we were chosen "before the creation of the world" and are "holy and blameless in his sight" (v. 4); we are equipped to serve Him. This significance is a gift from Him, and we have a whole warehouse full of it, so to speak.

The same is true of security: in Him we are secure. A quote I have often used is, "Security is not the absence of danger, but the presence of Jesus." I have been in some uncomfortable situations: arrested, expelled from the country, and slandered in national newspapers. But the truth of Psalm 62:1 has been my security in each case, "My soul finds rest in God alone." And in each case God guided me through the problems, protecting me in them.

Each day as I put on the helmet of salvation through prayer, I thank God that my significance and security come from Him and that they cannot be taken away by any person or circumstance.

An interesting and powerful result of drawing our significance and security from God (rather than from our performance and others' opinion of us) is that we can then minister out of these gifts of God rather than competing with others for scraps of significance or security on the streets of life. It is sad how much ministry is done to gain significance or security, a point we consider further in chapter 28.

The Sword of the Spirit

The last piece of armor is "the sword of the Spirit, which is the word of God" (Eph. 6:17). We need to know the Word well. And beyond knowing it, we need to internalize it so we can apply it from within. As I have mentioned, Western Christianity is often very cerebral, focused on what we know. We need to go beyond this and involve the whole person in our walk with God, including our mind, our will, and our emotions.

Reading the Word regularly is important. Studying it is also important. However, both of these are basically cerebral activities. In my opinion, biblical meditation is the most potent way of internalizing Scripture, the most effective in bringing transformation, for it can move us beyond just the psychological, involving the whole person. Chapter 30 gives a full explanation of meditation, so I will describe it here only very briefly.

Meditation, as I am using the concept, means three things. First, we *memorize* portions of Scripture. This is cooperating with the Holy Spirit in the transformation of our mind; we begin to think God's thoughts after Him.

Second, we *personalize* the passage, quoting it with personal pronouns where possible ("you chose *me* before the creation of the world!"). This is cooperating with the Spirit in the transformation of our emotions.

Third, we *pray through* the personalized passage ("Help me to remember through the day that you chose *me* before the creation of the world!"), which is cooperating with the Spirit in the transformation of our will.[18] Thus the Word is active in our whole being: mind, will, and emotions.

The Word must be a part of us. We need to know passages so well that we can quickly bring up an appropriate one to use against the enemy when he attacks. This is why we need consistent quiet times to equip us. I trust that you have one. We need to have some plan, some strategy for getting into the Word.

Personally, I read a chapter in the New Testament every morning and at least one in the Old Testament every evening. This means I read through the New Testament every nine months and through the Old Testament in about twenty-six months (not counting the Psalms, which I use for worship

---

18. In chapter 22 I mention several interesting examples of how the Lord used meditation in my life to free me from serious depression, anger, and selfishness.

in the morning), getting a bird's-eye view of it all, having a continual review of truth, seeing new connections, and collecting verses on various topics (for example, the deity of Christ). In addition to this reading is study in preparation for messages.

Whatever plan you use, it should include reading, studying, and meditating.

The passage in Ephesians 6 ends in verse 18 and gives us these instructions: "And pray in the Spirit on *all* occasions with *all* kinds of prayers and requests. With this in mind, be alert and *always* keep on praying for *all* the saints."

After putting on the whole armor, the first thing we are to do is pray! Note in this verse how often Paul uses the word "all." This is a high calling. Prayer is basically God's invitation to join Him in His great work. See chapters 31 and 32 for much further discussion of prayer.

Putting It All Together

To summarize, the first three parts of the armor refer to our relationships: with God, with ourselves, and with others. When these are in place, then we can raise the shield of faith, by praising God in and for all things; put on the helmet of salvation, drawing our significance and security from Him; and take up the sword of the Spirit, the Word of God. Then with these powerful weapons we can go to prayer, able to pull down Satan's strongholds, able to overcome adversity, and able to live a life of power and grace.

Here's an example of how you can pray to put on the armor each day. I have memorized Ephesians 6:10-18, which I use in praying this prayer.

> Lord Jesus, help me today to be strong in you and the power of your might. I confess to you my sinful tendencies [you can add your own list here]:
>
> - to be selfish (help me to be Christ-centered instead)
> - to be critical (help me to reject such thoughts and words before speaking)
> - to be unloving (help me to be a channel of your love)
> - to think lustful thoughts (help me to flee from them to you immediately)
> - to rely on myself rather than praying to you about all things (help me to pray even in the midst of conversations so I may be joining you in what you are doing).
>
> Forgive me for these tendencies. Fill me with your Spirit in a way that He overflows my life, so that those who meet me today will meet Him too.

SPIRITUAL WARFARE: SITUATION NORMAL

I make you my Captain and Navigator. Fill me with your Spirit so I will follow your direction throughout the day. Here are the things that are on the docket for me today: help me to.... [list out what you have planned for the day]

Help me, Lord, to put on the whole armor of God that I may be able to stand against the wiles and evil schemes of the devil. May I be aware of his traps before I fall into them, may I fight them with the whole armor on.

Help me, Lord, to remember that I am not fighting against flesh and blood but against powerful spiritual forces of evil. Help me to fight them with praise, prayer, and persistence in obedience to you.

Help me, Lord, to put on the whole armor of God so I can stand in the evil day, whenever it comes — and to be able to do all your will, whatever that may be.

Help me, Lord, to stand having on the belt of truth, remembering that in my flesh I am a child of wrath, deserving only hell, that in my flesh there dwells no good thing. But you, in your great love, chose me before the foundation of the world, you called me to yourself, cleansing and transforming me, claiming me as your son, and I stand before you now in Christ, delighted in and dearly loved.

Help me, Lord, to put on the breastplate of righteousness, forgiving myself as you have forgiven me. (Some specifics may come to mind here.)

Help me, Lord, to put on the shoes of peace, forgiving others as you have forgiven me. (Some people to forgive may come to mind.)

Help me to, above all these things, having my relationships in place, to lift up the shield of faith, with which I can quench all the flaming arrows of the evil one. Help me to praise you in and for all things, trusting you to be ordering my life and all that is in it. Help me to give you honor before all the unseen hosts by trusting you through praise.

Help me to put on the helmet of salvation, believing that you have given me all the security and significance I need, and to minister out of them with your grace.

Help me to take up the sword of the Spirit, reading, thinking, and acting out of what your Word has to say.

And help me to pray with all prayer and supplication for all saints. Guide me as I intercede for those you have given me responsibility for. Praise be to you, Lord Jesus, for this equipping you have given me!

Study Guide questions for Chapter 10: "Becoming a Minster of Offense"

1. What do we need to have in place before we can use the shield? (73)
2. How do we lift up the shield of faith? (73-74)
3. What three things does this accomplish? (74)
4. What are the flaming arrows of the evil one? (74)
5. What arrows does he use on you?

Becoming a Minister of Offense

6. What are the three stages of giving a response of praise? (74-75)
7. What happens if we don't get up the shield of faith? (75-76)
8. What does the helmet of salvation represent? (77)
9. How does God give us significance? (77)
10. How does He give us security? (77)
11. What is the result of drawing our significance and security from God? (77-78)
12. What is the sword of the Spirit? (78)
13. Why is biblical meditation the most potent way to internalize Scripture? (78)
14. What are the three parts of this type of meditation? (78)
15. Why do so few believers practice this type of meditation?
16. What is our first task after putting on the whole armor? (79)
17. What are you going to do with the suggestion/example to pray through Eph 6:10-18 each morning? (79-80)

CHAPTER 11

Other Aspects of Spiritual Warfare

We've talked about "everyday spiritual warfare." But what about the other facets of spiritual warfare, more dramatic ones like casting out demons or so-called power encounters? Such things are definitely a part of spiritual warfare, but less common for most of us.

As we look at this, I want to emphasize that, unless you are practicing spiritual warfare on the basic, daily level we've just talked about, you are not going to be prepared to deal with these other aspects. When we have on the armor and are adept at using it, then we are ready to deal with power encounters and demons.

Let me tell you a personal story that shows how Satan works to overcome truth. It shows what power Satan has to blind minds if we give him an opening.

Believing a Spiritual Lie

In my early twenties, shortly after I surrendered my life to God, a Jehovah's Witness came to my door. He proposed that we have a Bible study together, and, being curious, I accepted. We set Sunday afternoon as the time.

Saturday night a girl who was an old high school friend called. She said that she was thinking of committing suicide, and would I come over and talk with her? So I went and spent the whole night talking to her.

After being up all night, I went to Sunday School and church and then returned home. When the time for our Bible study came, I was ripe material for Satan to work on: really tired, defenses down, and my mind not working well.

The Jehovah's Witness began with themes we agreed on and then proceeded to show me that Jesus was an angel. He read from Hebrews 1, and sure enough, it seemed to say that Jesus was an angel. I was astounded — it had never said that before when I read it!

After he left, I got down on my knees and prayed, "Lord, I don't know what's going on here, but I do know that you, Jesus, are not an angel; you are God Himself. Yet here as I read Scripture, it looks like it says you are an angel. Show me what to do!"

The next day I got hold of a book on Jehovah's Witness doctrine and saw their errors. I again got down on my knees, confessed my sin of opening my mind to a spiritual lie, rejected this lie, and asked again for the filling of the Spirit. Then I opened my Bible to Hebrews chapter 1. This time I found that it no longer said that Jesus was an angel, but that He was God Himself.

Bringing Sight

This was a very important experience for me, preparing me to work with others who have accepted a big spiritual lie such as other major religions and who are blind to truth. We are told in 2 Corinthians 4:4, "The god of this age has blinded the minds of unbelievers, so that they cannot see the light of the gospel of the glory of Christ, who is the image of God."

Satan's desire is to deceive us about who Christ is. After this experience, I now believe that, beyond the initial blindness all unbelievers have, when someone accepts a spiritual lie, it brings additional and deeper blindness. So when we deal with Jehovah's Witnesses, Mormons, Muslims, Hindus, Buddhists, people in cults, or even those stuck in and defending a dead Christianity, we must realize that this level of spiritual warfare is beyond our normal strength. Only as we work primarily through prayer and use God's armor can this blindness be penetrated.

Our three main weapons must be brought to bear on the forces at work in the person — truth, faith, and love. We've looked at these as the belt of *truth,* the shield of *faith,* and the helmet of salvation, which speaks of the *love* we receive from God in being forgiven and adopted into His family. We are to share these in relationships using the breastplate of righteousness and the shoes of preparation of the gospel of peace. Our goal is to get the person we are sharing with into the Word, praying for them consistently and showing them godly love, which can break down the barriers as the Spirit works in response to our prayers.

Satan's Attempts to Control

Now about some other aspects of spiritual warfare. There are people who are demon possessed, as we see clearly in the Gospels. And there are times when it would be necessary to cast out a demon, that is, when the will is so overridden that they can't act themselves, and you have to step in for them, as Jesus and Paul did with some. However, if the person is able to exercise his or her will, another approach is to help that person deal with the sin that has given entrance to Satan. Then, instead of that one feeling like a victim and always feeling the need of help from others, you have equipped him or her to deal with future spiritual attacks.

I must hasten to add that I do not believe a Christian can be demon possessed (he or she belongs to Christ), but a believer can give ground to Satan so that there is a stronghold within from which Satan can attack. Remember Ephesians 4:27: "Do not give the devil a foothold."

At one point I had to face the fact that I had given the devil a foothold. Because I had given an opening to Satan through certain sins, I had serious emotional instability and could make it through the day only by having three or four hours of quiet time. I was also seriously depressed and constantly tired.

Gaining My Freedom

The Lord led me to a pastor who helped me through several steps to freedom. This was a process of confession, cleansing, reclaiming of ground given to Satan, and then surrendering to the Spirit, which freed me from Satan's control.

The pastor took me to Galatians 5:19-21 and pointed out the four major areas or categories of sin listed there:

> sexual sins, sins in thought, action, and habit (v. 19)
> sins of the occult (v. 20a)
> interpersonal sins (v. 20b)
> sins of appetite (v. 21).

He helped me examine my life in light of each of these general areas of sin. Then he led me to take the following steps in prayer, taking the four different areas of sin, one at a time, starting with sexual sins.

1. *Confession: agreeing with God.* He had me pray a prayer like this: "I confess to you, Lord, my sin in the area of _____ sins. The specific sins in this area that come to my mind are _____. Lord God, I agree with you that these attitudes, thoughts, words, and actions are sin; they are wrong, destructive, ungodly, and against your character."

2. *Asking and receiving forgiveness.* He then led me in praying, "Being your child, heavenly Father, I ask in the name of the Lord Jesus Christ for you to forgive me for these sins and to cleanse me from all unrighteousness in this area of _____ sins. I thank you that you have forgiven me as promised in 1 John 1:9, and I praise you, Lord Jesus, for providing forgiveness through your death and resurrection."

Other Aspects of Spiritual Warfare

3. *Reclaiming any ground given over to Satan.* Then he guided me in standing in the authority of Christ: "In the name of the Lord Jesus Christ, I reclaim any ground I've given to Satan in this area of _____ sins."

4. *Ask for filling of the Spirit in this area.* Finally, he had me give this area to God. "I ask, Holy Spirit, that you would fill the _____ part of my life. I surrender all in this area to you. I give you my will and take your will in its place. Fill me, use me, glorify yourself in me."

Then the pastor led me into the area of sins of the occult, and then the next two areas. For each area, he had me thoughtfully pray through these four steps. He interspersed these prayers with praise and Scripture reading.

There were some immediate results, such as an end to an antagonistic attitude toward my father, plus freedom to stand against some compulsive behavior. However, this was followed by an intense battle for the next month as Satan tried to reclaim the ground I'd taken back.

During this battle, the pastor coached me in using two things against Satan's attacks: the armor of God we've talked about, and the four prayer steps listed here when tempted to commit the sins I'd confessed earlier.

Standing firm in God's truth brought victory in the end, but it was a difficult time. When things got really bad, I would call the pastor, and he would give me good advice and then pray for me. By the end of the month the victory was won, and Satan withdrew to wait for new opportunities to attack me. The spiritual battle goes on, but in Christ we can be victors.

Let's finish with a word of prayer:

Lord God, Creator of heaven and earth, Ruler of all eternity, the all-powerful and all-wise One, we glorify you, for you have set us free, you have given us love, you have given us freedom from sin, and you have given us spiritual weapons to fight the battle before us. Help us to learn to take up and use the whole armor every day. In your powerful name, Lord Jesus, Amen.

Dave Learns to Use the Armor

Jack opened the door for Dave. "Welcome! It's good to see you! How was your week?"

"Good and bad," replied Dave as they walked down the hall. "You were right that I needed to be prepared for spiritual attack. It certainly came this week!"

"Tell me about it," said Jack.

"Well, to start with, I got a stomach flu after our last meeting. I'm always grumpy when I'm sick, but this time instead of sliding into self-pity, I used the time to read the chapters you assigned. It wasn't hard to see my old self at work— my sinful, impatient and grouchy self was obvious-- so putting on the belt of truth was pretty easy. And that also made asking and receiving forgiveness easier because I could see my sin!

This also emphasized the breastplate of righteousness, my need to forgive myself. Then there was opportunity to put on the shoes of peace, as there are always people who aggravate me at school, so I could forgive them as Jesus has forgiven me.

"After that came the shield of faith. Being sick, throwing up, not being able to eat, missing a fun evening with my friends — these were not things I wanted to thank God for. But with the new worldview taking hold in me, I decided to act in faith and give thanks for each one, trusting that God knows what He's doing."

"Very good," Jack commented, nodding.

"And I found that, after a bit of thanking and praising, my mood was better, even though my body was still hurting."

Jack smiled. "Yes, that's part of entering into the joy of knowing Jesus. He has a higher plane in the midst of our misery, and we can trust Him to work it out," he explained.

"I'm beginning to see that," Dave replied. "The helmet of salvation aspect, the struggle with significance and security, didn't show up for me this week, but I'm sure it will come. Being sick gave me more time to be in the Word and practice some with the Sword of the Spirit. I read in the Psalms, and that was helpful in getting a better perspective."

"And what about the last chapter?" asked Jack.

"I found that to be a whole new subject." replied Dave. "I think I should go through those steps to freedom that pastor mentioned. Perhaps we could do that sometime together?"

"Certainly, Dave, I'd be glad to do that with you. When the right time comes, we'll get together for a session just on that; it will take longer than our usual one hour, though, so be prepared!"

"I will," said Dave. "So what's my assignment for this coming week?"

"Part 3, chapters 12 and 13 on worship," replied Jack.

"Didn't we already cover worship?" asked Dave.

"Yes, we've had an introduction, but this will take you more in depth and give you more practical advice. You'll enjoy it, and so will I!"

Study Guide questions for Chapter 11: "Other Aspects of Spiritual Warfare"

1. How does Satan seek to blind us? (82-83)
2. Have you experienced such a blindness at some time in your life? What happened?
3. What does this tell you about witnessing to people in cults or other religions?
4. How can we deal with any ground we (or another person) have inadvertently given to Satan? (83-84)

Part 3

Worship

Truth #4 Worship Releases Power

CHAPTER 12

Worship = Thanksgiving + Praise

Now that we've covered the basics of spiritual warfare in part 2, we are going to look at some deeper aspects of these things. In parts 3-6, we consider four personal disciplines that are crucial for being strong in the Lord's might so we can wage spiritual warfare successfully: worship, confession, lifting our souls, and being filled with the Spirit.

None of these disciplines is new to you, but I trust that the guidance given here in applying them, including the practical examples, will help you move on to new levels of growth and effectiveness for God. These means of implementation are effective because they are essentially cooperating with the Holy Spirit in the transformation of our lives.

Worship as a Discipline

> Worship is a personal thing before it goes public. It is an individual thing before it is part of a community. It is a disciplined thing before it is natural.
> — Ravi Zacharias, *Recapture the Wonder*

Ephesians 6:10-18 begins with the command "be strong in the Lord and in his mighty power." I believe that in following this command, the foremost discipline we can practice is worship. Essentially everything we do can be worship, which, at its core, is *giving God glory*. No matter what activities we are engaged in — washing dishes, changing diapers, building a stone wall, driving a truck, or preparing a sermon — each is an opportunity to act in a way that gives God glory.

Doing a task wholeheartedly and well is both pleasing to God and honoring to Him, depending on our motives. As we'll see later, motives are very important: doing the right thing in the right way for the wrong motive can negate the opportunity for worship through our work.

One potential high point for worship is when everything goes wrong! For instance, recently while trying to pay my rent online, I realized I'd forgotten my internet password for my bank account. I went to the bank and got a new one, but when I tried to use it, I couldn't even get to the place to put the password in! And I needed to pay my rent online that day — it was due within the next hour!

My response to this impasse could be one of worship of God or disgrace for God. I could choose to praise God for an opportunity to trust Him, or I could choose to fret, worry, and complain.

If we react in such situations with praise to God for His greatness and power, for His wisdom and love demonstrated in allowing this difficulty, then we have participated in high-level, "costly," and powerful worship, one based on faith, not on sight. This, however, is a very unnatural response — we could say, a "supernatural" response. Who lives that way?

Answer: *the one who practices personal worship on a daily basis, and who therefore responds with worship in the everyday crises of life.* Such a person has learned to live the truth that knowing Jesus is enough for joy, period!

The Essence of Worship

At its core, worship is giving God glory. Great worship happens when I give Him glory, especially when there is no discernable reason to do so! Why is this great worship? Because then we must offer such praise strictly by faith — and faith is very important to God. He declares that faith is "of greater worth than gold" (1 Peter 1:7), and that "without faith it is impossible to please God" (Heb. 11:6).

In the example above of the bank password, there was no outward reason to praise, and lots of reasons to complain. However, going by what I know of God's character, there were at least three reasons for me to praise in worship.

First was praising Him *for the incident itself,* knowing that my sovereign God is going to somehow use it positively — He is in control, and He is good; He is wise, and He is powerful. We can praise by faith because of what we know of God's character, not because of what we can see and understand of the situation.

Second is giving praise *for what I can't do*: not being able to pay the rent today, even though it is going to bring some potential problems. I can praise God for this, knowing that He is also going to use these problems for good. He has the long-term view in mind and is doing much more than I can possibly understand. Accepting this and praising Him in it is again by faith.

Third is to give thanks *for the outcomes*: the face-to-face interactions I will have with bank employees, my landlord, and others because of this problem, knowing that each will be an opportunity to be a witness. By faith we can affirm the unseen positives rather than focus on the potential negatives, because we know how great and faithful and wise our God really is.

Worship = Thanksgiving + Praise

One reason that we don't respond naturally with such faith is that we don't practice worshipping God regularly in private, so we are not ready when the outward challenges come. In the following sections we will explore this private, personal worship and how we can use our words and thoughts to exalt Him. When we practice this in our quiet times, then it can overflow into our daily life.

Worship as Thanksgiving and Praise

There are two basic aspects of verbal worship: thanksgiving and praise. Both are important and necessary. Most Christians are more familiar with thanksgiving than with genuine praise.

Thanksgiving, as it is usually practiced, focuses on God's work in our lives, including sending answers to our prayer.

Thank you, Lord Jesus, that you saved me.
Thank you for healing Aunt Josie.
Thank you for this beautiful day.

Thanksgiving usually has to do with what we can see and touch. It generally does not require much faith except in giving God credit for what could also appear to be a natural happening.

The second aspect of worship — praise — is on a higher level because, instead of focusing on what we can see or what benefits us, it focuses on God's character as revealed by His Word and His acts. We could define such praise-worship as

giving God glory for who He is,
without thinking of how that benefits me.

An example of this is to pray, "You, Lord God, are worthy of exaltation because you are wise, for you know all things and how they are to work together. All you do is guided by your wisdom, You never do anything foolish or unwise. You are worthy of worship because of your great understanding."

What Is Your Focus?

Think about your church's worship services. What is primary, thanksgiving or praise? Unless your church is very unusual, most of what occurs is thanksgiving. And we *should* give thanks. However, if the primary emphasis of our private or corporate worship is thanksgiving, three dangers await us.

First, we can, and usually do, end up focusing on ourselves or on the answers to prayer God has given, not on Him:

> Thank you, Lord, that you saved ME.
> Thank you that you answered MY prayer and gave ME this.

Think about what usually gets prayed for in church prayer meetings, and you'll notice this tendency. Too often it is us-centered and answer-centered, not Christ-centered. It certainly is possible to thank Him for His answers and end up focused on Him, but this perspective best flows out of practicing praise and requires work and discipline, as we will see.

The *second* danger of emphasizing thanksgiving over praise arises out of the first: when the focus is on the answer, we fail to see who God is because we are absorbed merely in what He's given and how it benefits us. When thanksgiving is primary, He tends to fade into the background. It becomes easy to think of God as the great vending machine in the sky who gives us what we want. Such "worship" requires little or no faith.

Third, and as an outcome of the first two points, when difficulties and disappointments come, we will tend to complain. We will not give thanks because we can see nothing to give thanks for — we will continue to operate by sight. All too easily, we become grumblers, unthankful and unpleasant. God didn't give us what we wanted, so we begin to doubt His goodness.

We fail to realize that such times of difficulty are the greatest opportunities to exalt God before the unseen hosts. As we go through our day, it is easy to forget that, along with the people who watch us, there are also angels and demons observing what we do (see Eph. 3:10); before them we can either give God glory by praising Him in faith or bring shame to His name by grumbling, and thereby grieving Him.

Study Guide questions for Chapter 12: "Worship = Thanksgiving + Praise"

1. What prepares us to respond to difficulties in life with praise? (89-90)
2. Define worship. (90)
3. What are three reasons for praising God when things go wrong? (90)
4. Why is praise generally a higher level of worship than thanksgiving? (91)
5. What are the three dangers of only giving thanks for what we can see? (92)
6. How will these truths influence your personal worship?

CHAPTER 13

Praise, Focused on God's Character

Praise, in contrast to thanksgiving, helps keep us focused on God's character, which is the fundamental reason for worship — He is worthy of worship because of who He is. We have joy in Him simply because of who He is.

When praise trains our thanksgiving, we learn to exalt God for His character rather than focusing only on what He did or does. The things we thank Him for are reflections of His character:

> His power and desire to help His creatures
> His faithfulness in protection
> His wisdom in guiding and His grace is giving things to us.

What's the key to growing in worship? Look up from the reflection of God's good character that we see in His blessings to praise the full image of His glory. We can do this by giving God glory for who He is, without thinking of how that benefits me.

Personally, I find it difficult to praise God like this, to keep my thoughts "up there," only exalting Him. There is always the pull to think about how God's character benefits me. There certainly is a time for that, but not when we are seeking to glorify God in praise.

For instance, it is easy to pray like this: "I lift you up, Lord, and worship you because of your faithfulness" — but all the while to be thinking, "because I know I can trust you, and that makes me comfortable!" We probably wouldn't actually say that last phrase in our prayer, but we often tend to think that way!

An example of pure, genuine praise is found in Revelation 4:8, 11. Notice the focus:

> Holy, holy, holy
> is the Lord God Almighty,
> who was, and is, and is to come. . . .
> You are worthy, our Lord and God,
> to receive glory and honor and power,
> for you created all things,

and by your will they were created
and have their being.

Here there is no focus on self; the Lord God is at center stage, right where He should be, and all attention flows to Him. It is here that we are fully worshipping in praise.

Let me repeat that after we learn to praise well, there are times to give thanks, rejoicing in how His character is revealed in what He has given to others, to the church, and to us. This is because when we grow in our discipline of praise, our thanksgiving will also be on a higher level.

As an example of this, in the expanded section below on putting on the belt of truth, we will talk about how we should thank Him for, bask in, exalt in, and revel in the love and acceptance that the Lord God has poured out on us — and continues to do so every day. This deepening grasp of who Christ is in us and who we are in Christ is possible, though, only when we first learn to worship Him in biblical praise.

I'd like to suggest five helps I've found effective for growing in the ability to praise God, to give Him glory for who He is, without thinking of how that benefits me.

Praise Help No. 1: Scripture.

The first help is the Bible itself.

The Psalms are my favorite help in praise. I am constantly reading through them, using the revelations of God's character to praise Him. For instance, let's look at Psalm 50:1.

> The Mighty One, God, the LORD,
> speaks and summons the earth
> from the rising of the sun to the place where it sets.

This verse is loaded with information about God's character — but are we interested in digging it out? As I was memorizing verses from this psalm, I wondered why this verse uses three names for God in a row: "the Mighty One," "God," and "the LORD." So I did some research.

One book that was helpful is *The Names of God,* by William Allen Dean.[19] It has long been out of print, but you can easily find other books or Bible dictionaries that explain the names of God and how each one reveals something about His character. Let's look at the names in this verse.

---

19. Dean, *Names of God.*

Praise, Focused on God's Character

First is *the Mighty One* (El). This is the One of great power and strength. There is no good deed He cannot do; there is no one greater than Him. He will never be defeated, for all might is His. His power is truly awesome: He is able to speak and create, to fling the stars across space and spin the planets in their orbits. He is mighty in every aspect: love, wisdom, knowledge, patience, and grace. He is worthy of worship!

Second is the name *God.* This is a translation of the Hebrew word "Elohim," which is used to speak of God's power and faithfulness. He displayed His power in creation and His faithfulness in providing salvation. Both of those give a lot of material for praising Him. For instance, one verse describes how God "made the heavens and the earth, the sea, and all that is in them" (Exod. 20:11). We can praise God for His wisdom and power in how He designed the universe so the earth could support carbon-based life, how He made the seasons, how He put atoms together to form molecules, made the elements, spoke all creatures into existence.

We can praise Him for His creativity seen in the myriad of creatures, for the variety of bodies of all shapes and sizes (from fleas to flamingos, amoebas to aardvarks) for the many means of movement He has made His creatures capable of (walking, hopping, crawling, flying, swimming). We can praise Him for the way He has made it possible for life to reproduce, and for living things to heal when injured.

Did you know that there are about 300,000 types of beetles?[20] Wouldn't you think that just one or two types, or maybe a hundred, would have been enough? Apparently God did not! God delights in variety and shows His great creative powers in playing thousands of variations on one theme.

God is powerful in creation, and He is faithful in how He planned the way of salvation even before the world was formed, then brought it to pass at just the right time and at great cost to Himself. His love, wisdom, strength, and grace are all powerfully displayed in the salvation story.

Elohim, the powerful and faithful one, is worthy of worship!

Third is the term LORD. This is the Hebrew word "Yahweh," meaning "I Am." It refers to God's self-existence — that He always was, always is, and always will be (see Exod. 3:13-14.) It is the covenant name of God, who "is" what the people need Him to be — a covenant God who will fulfill His covenant promises. And it refers to His holiness. His glory is in His holiness: His being is completely pure, without sin, evil, or darkness. In His holiness He hates sin and will punish it, but in His perfect

---

20. See http://hypertextbook.com/facts/2001/KeithSingh.shtml,

mercy He loves sinners and has made a way of escape for them from His wrath. He is worthy of worship! Only He could so unite justice and mercy, truth and grace.

Worship Now!

Let's offer some verbal worship right here based on Psalm 50:1. "The Mighty One, God, the LORD, speaks and summons the earth from the rising of the sun to the place where it sets."

> *O Lord God, we exalt you as the Mighty One, for you are the Most High, the strongest One in the universe. No one comes even close to you in power, not within a billion miles. There is no good thing that is too hard for you to do. There is no enemy you cannot defeat. You are worthy of worship because of your might.*
>
> *We lift you up because you are Elohim, the powerful and faithful One. You, Lord Jesus, showed your power in creation. As we think of the incredible variety of creatures you have made, the size of the earth and of our galaxy, we must bow before you, stand in awe of you, and exalt you in our hearts, our minds, our lives.*
>
> *Not only that, but you, Father in heaven, are the ultimate in faithfulness: you promise and you do it, no matter what the cost. You are faithful to your character; you never stray from what is right, good, pure, and lovely. You, Lord Jesus, did not shrink back from providing salvation at the right time, in spite of the great physical, emotional, psychological, and spiritual suffering you had to endure. You are worthy of worship because of your great faithfulness.*
>
> *You, Triune God, are Yahweh, the Holy One. Your glory is in your holiness. There is no sin, no darkness, no hidden evil in you. You are never tempted to sin, you are incapable of sin, praise be to your name! You are completely "other," completely different from your creation. You hate sin and will judge it in righteousness. Yet you love the sinner and have provided a way of escape. No one could do this but you, maintaining your justice while at the same time having mercy triumph over justice. You are worthy of glory and honor and obedience. You are great, You are awesome, You are the eternal Lovely One, and we worship you.*

I don't know about you, but such a look at our great God takes my breath away! I feel cleansed, lifted up, and enlightened. Worship is such a joy! When we look away to Him, He gives back to us! But worship is also hard work, for we need to be thinking through what we are praying as we savor, contemplate, and meditate on these massive truths. The more we worship God in

Praise, Focused on God's Character

praise, the more praise is generated. But we have to work at it and not let ourselves slip into old patterns and clichés, into mindless repetition of words, or into dropping down to focus on how this benefits me.

Praise Help No. 2: Words of Worship

Expanding our vocabulary helps to deepen our ability to stay up in the realm of praise. In everyday speech we don't use phrases like, "I exalt you" or "I lift you up" or "I glorify you." But these are proper words of worship that convey the grandeur of our God. Learn to use such words:

I glorify your name.
I honor you.
I lift up your name.
You are worthy of great esteem.
You are the Glorious One.
I bow before you.
I enthrone you with praise.
I revere you.
I magnify you.
I proclaim your goodness [or some other characteristic].
I fear you because you are the Almighty [and other qualities].
I give you honor and praise and glory.

These phrases are means of lifting our thoughts and eyes to the Lord Jesus Christ. At the same time, it is important to recognize that repetition of a few familiar phrases can bring mindless prayer. Good worship involves creativity and whole-hearted engagement.

These words and phrases I've just mentioned are biblical ones we need to work at inserting into our prayer vocabulary — and collecting more that are appropriate in worship.

How should a person implement this discipline of exaltation? Personally, I am committed to spending at least five minutes each morning in pure praise at the beginning of my quiet time. The Psalms are a prolific source for praise and are my primary source of inspiration and information for worship. Starting with Psalm 1, I work my way through them, focusing on one psalm every day. It usually takes many months for me to go through them all, for I often get "stuck" on one for a few days, or perhaps even for several weeks when I find it especially rich, memorizing and meditating on it so I can use it better in worship.

Often in this time of worship I will write out my praise in my journal. Then later, when I am having a dry time, I like to go back and use these entries to aid my worship.

I would encourage you to begin by committing yourself to *five minutes of praise* each morning, staying up there in worship, not thinking about how your Father benefits you. Then watch how God uses it to change you and your perspective.

Praise Help No. 3: Journaling

Writing our worship in a journal is a wonderful way to discipline ourselves to stay "up there" in praise. This means writing out some worship paragraphs in our quiet times.

Here is an example from my journal:

> Lord God, Creator of heaven and earth, we praise you for your wisdom, which permeates all you do. Your power is limitless, stretching over the billions of light-years of the universe. You know each star and call it by name. You are the One who holds together the atoms. You are the One who is carrying the world to the conclusion of history. You are patient, waiting for the right time to do each thing. You are gracious, ever giving, always loving.

Note the lack of thinking how these qualities of God benefit me — as they certainly do, very positively. There is a time to think of and thank Him for the benefits that flow into our lives from His great character, but not when glorifying God in worship.

Here's another example:

> O Lord Jesus, I praise you for your goodness. Whatever you do is good, whether it appears so to me or not. I praise you for your love, which permeates everything you do. I praise you for your wisdom. You know how everything fits together, You know what is appropriate now and what should wait. I praise your name because you are holy, without sin, untemptable, and high above your creation. You are worthy of honor, and I praise you for this.[21]

---

21. For further discussion of journaling, see chapter 19. Here are four other examples of worship taken from my journal:

Praise be to you, O Lord, that you are perfect, that your work is flawless, that you are trustworthy, right, radiant, clean, enduring forever, and altogether righteous. We glorify you because you are the superlative of everything positive. Lord, you are glorious, you are great, you are good. You are worthy of praise. We can and must praise you in and for all things, thus walking by faith. I praise you for the problems with my computer and car [both were not functioning properly]. You

Praise, Focused on God's Character

Praise Help No. 4: Poetry and Music

Poetry, often a higher expression of truth and adoration, can serve to lift our thoughts to God in new ways. Poems about creation, about God's work, and about the positive qualities of God's character are all useful. Personally, I like poems that focus on the character of God, like this one I recently wrote:

> Praise be to you
> O Triune One,
> Creator of the sun,
> Spinner of the earth,
> Bringer of the dawn.

---

have allowed these problems, you are using them, and you will use them for a specific purpose in my life, and I give you honor for that, though I do not know yet what these purposes are.

Praise be to you, Lord God, my Creator, my Shepherd, my King, my God. I give you honor, glory, and praise for your wonderful character as seen in your creation, in your Word, in history. You are the One who turns the disasters of men into the triumphs of heaven. You are able to weave all the free acts of people into your tapestry of eternity, bringing as many as possible into the kingdom. Glory be to you, glory be to your name. Honor and praise be to you forever and ever.

Praise be to you, O Mighty One, mighty in wisdom, in love, in justice, in mercy, in goodness, in grace, in righteousness, in truth. Exalted be your name, glorified be your person, magnified be your honor. You are Elohim, the One whose power is seen in creation — the centipede, the eagle, the cell, the whale, the ant, the giraffe, the kangaroo, the elephant — your ideas are astounding, marvelous, ingenious. Put a potato in the ground, get out twenty! You are the Faithful One, promising a Savior in the garden, following though in selecting Seth on through Abraham, preserving Jacob in spite of his rebellion, saving David from Saul, protecting Ruth and Naomi, shielding Jesus from Herod, then sacrificing Him at the right time. You are faithful, no matter what the cost to yourself. You are Jehovah, the wholly other One, completely different and independent of your creation. The triune God completely complete in yourself: Father, Son, and Holy Spirit — unity and diversity, fellowship, leadership, submission, diversity of roles, perfect harmony. And you are pure, without sin, unable to sin, unwilling to sin. There is no darkness, no evil, no imbalance, no impurity, no lack in you. You hate sin; in your righteousness you will punish it. Yet you love sinners and have provided a way of escape from your just wrath, from righteous punishment of sin. You are good!

Praise you, Lord God, that I awoke and found you waiting for me to join you in today's relationships and activities. You, O triune God, are worthy of worship today, for you are the Mighty One; you never lack strength, you always are ready, you will never be defeated. You are moving history to a conclusion and taking us with you! You are Elohim, the powerfully creative One who always has a better way than ours, who is faithful to your Word and faithful to provide what is needed. You are Yahweh, the Holy God, in whom there is no darkness, no sin, no evil, no unrighteousness, no ignorance, no ability to sin; you are perfect in character, in wisdom, in balance, in action. There is no end to the delights of your person, for you are infinite. I give you glory and honor by trusting you, by praising you in the midst of trouble, by offering the sacrifice of thanksgiving, by boasting in my weakness so the power of Christ can rest on me and on the situations before me.

WORSHIP

We glorify your name
O Holy One,
Sparkling in purity,
Spreading light into every heart,
Shining truth into our lives.

We honor you,
O Mighty One,
Towering far above all creation,
Powerful in every good work,
Filling the universe with your presence.

We exalt you,
O Good One,
Raining grace upon creation,
Planting seeds of good desire,
Watering our souls with love.

We lift up your name,
O Heavenly One,
Father, Son, and Holy Spirit
Worthy of all honor, all worship, all glory.
All creation points to you, all will bow before you.

We extol you,
O Majestic One,
High and lifted up,
Wrapped in light,
Ruling for eternity.

We worship you,
The only One
Deserving full adoration,
glorification,
exaltation.

To you
It is right to bow down in worship,
It is right to rise up to obedience,
Praise be to you for ever and ever.

Praise, Focused on God's Character

Such poems, loaded with biblical truth, are useful as springboards to stimulate praise.

The lyrics of hymns and songs are another source of inspiration for verbal worship. It is helpful to pick songs that focus on God's character and on what true surrender means, like Matt Redman's song "Blessed Be Your Name":

> Blessed be your name
> In the land that is plentiful. . . .
> And blessed be your name
> When I'm found in the desert places.

Many songs, though, focus more on us and what God does for us than on Him. As you grow in your ability to exalt God for who He is, you will become more aware of the self-centeredness in many popular praise songs and may want to replace such words with higher ones. An example is the wonderful song "Above All" — wonderful, that is, until the last lines: "Like a rose trampled on the ground / You took the fall and thought of me above all." Not true, for while on the cross, Jesus did not think of me above all. He was thinking primarily of giving the Father glory, of finishing the task given Him to bring an end to sin and suffering, to bring salvation to all. Yes, He thought of you and me, but not above all. Some have suggested ending this song instead "You took the fall and honored God above all."

In contrast, Jack Hayford's song "Majesty" clearly focuses throughout on God's character and gives Him glory for it: "Majesty, worship His majesty, / Unto Jesus be all glory, honor, and praise. . . ." Majestic music with such words truly lifts our thoughts to Him and releases our spirits to worship with our whole being.

Other forms of art (pictures, stories, photography, sculpture, etc.), insofar as they accurately portray God's creation, can also be used to stimulate praise-worship for the creative God, who makes us creative.

Praise Help No. 5: Science

Think huge. I like to gather facts about the creation and the way it reveals truths concerning God's character. For instance, consider the speed of light: 186,000 miles (300,000 kilometers) *every second.* At that speed, light could circle the globe seven and a half times in one second!

Just to give some perspective on this speed, try to imagine how long it would take you to walk 100 miles. At a doable pace of four miles an hour, it would take twenty-five hours to make the trip. Then compare that to light, which makes that same trip in a little over 5/10,000ths of a second! This shows us how small and feeble and slow we are — but also how great and powerful our God is. He made light; He made it travel that fast. And the universe He created is so large that we have to measure it in light-years. According to one estimate, the most distant known galaxies are 12 billion light-years away. Some estimates say the universe is 28 billion light-years in diameter.[22]

How far is a light-year? We can calculate it by multiplying the distance light goes in one second by the number of seconds in a year: 186,000 miles × 60 (seconds) × 60 (minutes) × 24 (hours) × 365 (days), which is roughly 5.9 trillion miles, or 9.5 trillion kilometers.

But how big is a trillion? This number comes up fairly often in the financial news, but it really is beyond our comprehension. In his book about building "margin" in our lives,[23] Richard Swenson gives us a way to grasp at least a bit of how big this number is. He asks, If you count from one to a million, saying one number every second, day and night, how long would it take to complete this task? The quick answer — a million seconds. That is 278 hours, or about 11½ days.

Now, what about counting to a billion? That would take 32 years of day-and-night counting!

Finally, how long would it take to count to a trillion? The answer? 32,000 years, counting one number every second.

Even this example doesn't go very far toward helping us comprehend such a large number as a trillion. It does, however, give us some perspective of how majestic our God is, for He was able to create a universe trillions and trillions and trillions of miles in size.

Moody Science Films has a wonderful DVD on the universe entitled *Journeys to the Edge of Creation*.[24] In it the viewer takes an imaginary trip starting at the sun and traveling at the speed of light, 186,000 miles a second. In the first eight minutes and twenty seconds we reach our earth; within seven hours we have passed out of our solar system and are heading toward the nearest star, Alpha Centauri. We travel one week, then one month, then one year, two years, three years; finally, after four and a half years of traveling 186,000

---

22. For example, see www.pbs.org/wgbh/nova/universe/howbig.html. This Web site is fairly accessible in describing the vast unknowns of our universe, all of which certainly magnify our Creator — at least, once we turn in His direction!

23. Richard A. Swenson, M.D., *Margin: Restoring Emotional, Physical, Financial, and Time Reserve to Overloaded Lives* (Colorado Springs: NavPress, 1995).

24. Available from Moody Publishers at www.moodypublishers.com/Publishers/default.asp?SectionID=86DE745783B8435ABFF5832DD9E4C78A&action=details&subid=D7C57CA0677F3ABEF3B3ADB7EA502277.

Praise, Focused on God's Character

miles per second, we arrive at this "neighborhood" star!

Then we turn and go upward out of the Milky Way, up and up until we can see across the whole width of it. This part of the trip would take us 100,000 light-years, which is also the diameter of the Milky Way Galaxy. Just think, our "home" galaxy is 100,000 times 5.9 trillion miles across!

Now we head out further into space, speeding toward what scientists tell us is the outer known reaches of the universe. Our galaxy is just one of *billions* of galaxies, each made up of *billions* of stars. We travel another 100,000 light-years, then:

500,000 light-years,
    then a million,
        then 500 million,
            a billion,
                five billion,
                      ten billion.

Finally, at 14 billion light-years from home, we arrive at the furthest known galaxies of the universe.

Our God is the One who spoke and created all this. It took only His Word. He knows every star by name and has determined their number (see Ps. 147:4; Isa. 40:26). And He fills the whole universe (see Eph. 1:23). This is the God we are called to worship. This is the One whom we can know and walk with in joy.

Think tiny. God's hugeness is only half of creation's story. On the other end of the scale, the micro universe is just as astounding. The average cell, which was considered just a lump of protoplasm before the invention of the electron microscope, is now known to be an extremely complex unit. The DVD *Unlocking the Mystery of Life*, produced by Illustra Media,[25] gives a wonderful explanation of the cell with great graphics. I mention here a few of the complexities of a cell that this DVD explains.

The inside of the cell is like a small city, complete with factories, a communication system, and tiny railroads for delivery of goods and garbage pickup. The membrane of the nucleus is equipped with sensors that control ports, or doorways, into it. When something wants to get in (bacteria, virus, food, supplies), the sensors determine whether this substance is good or negative and accordingly open the portal or keep it closed.

As supplies come in through the portals, they are loaded onto the train, given a chemical address label, and shipped off to the appropriate factory,

---

25. See www.illustramedia.com/productions.htm.

where they are processed. The waste is loaded onto another train to be taken away and disposed of.

This analogy is a very simplified explanation, but it shows how marvelously God designed things, right down to the level of molecular and atomic detail.

DNA gives us another glimpse of God's creativity and the way He orders things. The DNA molecule in each cell contains the instructions for the development of the whole body, but only the parts relevant to that cell are operative. Using just four chemical letters, the complex instructions in one DNA molecule, if written out in book form, would more than fill an entire encyclopedia set — and all of this is stored in just one molecule! Another testimony to God's greatness, wisdom, creativity, and power.

I encourage you, too, to collect facts about the universe, our world, and the microcosm so that you can use them in your private worship time to remind yourself and all you speak with of how incredible God is. They are great to stimulate faith in others as you share them.

What Does This Mean to Me?

These facts about the universe and the cell are especially important to remember when we get a flat tire! If our God is big enough to create and run this universe, and if He has the knowledge and skill to design the tiny atomic and subatomic worlds, He certainly can deal with a problem in our lives as trivial as a flat tire!

We can be sure that He allows or sends flat tires into our lives for a reason. Therefore we can praise Him both for the situation and for what He will do with it. He is the Almighty One, whose power knows no limits. If we have focused on Him in worship, then we will know enough of His character to praise Him in our hardships. We can remember the fact that *knowing this God who has created and controls all is enough for joy.* He watches over us, guides us, and leads us through the valleys and to the mountaintops. We can rejoice in Him alone.

I have mentioned that, during my time in the Middle East, many difficulties came into my life: false accusations in national newspapers, court cases against me, being fired from my job, and attempts to evict us from our apartment. In each of these God was teaching us to trust Him, to praise Him for His character, to thank Him for the unseen things He was accomplishing through these traumatic events. A lot of my worship knowledge came out of what He taught me through these incidents by getting me into Scripture and looking to Him, not circumstances.

Praise, Focused on God's Character

In some problems we had no idea what God was doing — and probably will not know until eternity what His purposes were. In other hard situations, it seemed that we could see what He was doing. For example, one thing we know God did through these difficulties was to expand our freedom as Christians in that country. Every time the police arrested us and brought us to trial, the courts would more widely define our freedom to practice our faith and propagate the gospel. In the end, the police stopped bothering us, seeing that they were only helping our cause.

Knowing God through worship helps us trust Him so that when unpleasant or dangerous things come, we can continue to praise.

Now, dear reader, it's up to you to put this knowledge to work in your life, worshipping God in praise in your quiet time, praising Him when you have a problem, and trusting Him to give you what is needed in the situation.

Let's finish this section with some prayer.

O God of the heavens, creator of the billions and billions of galaxies, keeper of every atom, the One who is bringing all history to a planned conclusion — praise and glory be yours! We praise you for these insights. Help us to be more faithful and effective in our worship of you. Amen.

Jack and Dave on Worship

Friday morning dawned cool and clear after a night of rain. Dave finished his quiet time early, eager to be on time with his mentor. He arrived a few minutes before his appointment and knocked on the door. Jack's wife, Barbara, opened it. "Hello, Dave," she said. "Please come in, Jack's in the den."

As Dave entered, Jack looked up from reading his Bible. "Welcome, Dave, good to see you. How was your week?"

Dave smiled. "I had a chance to practice what you talked about on Tuesday concerning praise and worship."

"Have a seat and tell me about it," said Jack.

Dave took his usual seat. "On Thursday night, just when I was heading out for an evening class at the university, I couldn't find my keys. Instead of getting upset and complaining as I normally do, I thought of this as a chance to worship and praise God for the problem, then praised Him because he knew where the keys were. Then I asked Him for help.

"Right when I finished praying, I remembered that I was not wearing the same jacket I had in the morning. I looked in the pocket of the other jacket, and there they were!"

"So, what was your response to that, Dave?"

Dave laughed. "Just what you'd expect, Jack, more worship — praising God for His wisdom and knowledge and guidance, and thanking Him that he showed me where the keys were!"

"You're catching on, Dave. What you experienced is God's formula for spiritual growth: Worship based on His Word + daily difficulties + more praise = the experience of His care, which leads to more worship and thanksgiving!"

"Right," replied Dave. "That's exactly what happened! I can see that practicing worship is going to make a huge difference in my life."

Jack looked thoughtful. "My guess is that you also did some worship in your quiet time on Wednesday and Thursday morning."

"How did you know?" asked Dave.

"Your response to the lost keys shows that you've been practicing worship, focusing on God's character, goodness, power, and love. That helped change your response from a natural one to a supernatural one when the disappointment came. You were "primed" to respond with an explosion of praise, rather than an explosion of anger and impatience."

Dave laughed, "It's much better to explode with praise. There's no mess to clean up like when I react with anger! As I said, praise and worship are going to make a big difference in my life!"

"I'm sure than that you'll enjoy chapter 14, which will give you a greater understanding of what God is doing through worship," said Jack.

Study Guide questions for Chapter 13: "Praise, Focused on God's Character"

1. What is the key to growing in worship? (93)
2. Why is doing this difficult? (93)
3. How does Scripture help us with praise-focused worship? (94-95)
4. What do words of worship do for us? How can you use them? (97-98)
5. How does journaling help in praise worship? (98 and footnote on 99)
6. How can you use music and poetry to help in praise worship? (99-101)
7. What can you do to use science as a springboard for worship? (101-104)
8. How do these scientific facts help us in daily difficulties to trust more? (104-105)
9. After reading this chapter, how will your personal worship change/grow?

CHAPTER 14

Purposes of Worship

We've been emphasizing how the praise part of worship should be focusing on God and not ourselves. There is an interesting, paradoxical aspect to this truth. When we look away to Him in worship, not only does He receive glory, but *we also* profit, for we are changed.

This is an illustration of what I call the "right-side-upness" of God's kingdom. In the world's kingdom we get by taking, but in God's kingdom we get by giving. In the world we are "blessed" by watching out for ourselves, but in God's kingdom we are blessed by taking care of others. In the world we win by defeating others, but in God's kingdom we win by helping others (the last shall be first). In the world we save ourselves by protecting what we have, but in God's kingdom we are saved by dying to self.[26]

This principle works out in worship, too. When we offer God-centered praise and thanksgiving, exalting the Lord Jesus, He uses this worship to bring changes in our lives and to benefit us in several other ways as well. Here we look at five specific purposes God has for us in worship.

26. We can easily give more illustrations of the surprising, seemingly contradictory principles of God's kingdom:
  when we give up, we receive
  when we are weak, we are strong
  when we die, we live
  when we give, we get
  when we suffer, we can rejoice
  when we confess our sins, we are cleansed
  when we forgive, we are set free
  when we believe, the unseen comes to pass
  when we humble ourselves, God exalts us
  when we forgive, God deals with those who hurt us
  when we deny self, we are given more
  when we suffer, God's glory rests on us
  when we are chastened, this proves God loves us
  when we are a leader, we serve
  when we give God glory in worship, we are transformed
  when we are transparent, we are more loved
  when we overlook an insult, we are wise
  when we delight in God, he gives us the desires of our hearts
  what we are is more important than what we do.

We are transformed.

Second Corinthians 3:18 says, "And we, who with unveiled faces all reflect the Lord's glory, *are being transformed* into his likeness with ever-increasing glory, which comes from the Lord, who is the Spirit." As we worship in praise, we are gazing on Him, reflecting His glory, and, without our realizing or seeing it, are being transformed by the Spirit to be more like Christ.

Second Peter 1:6 expands on this theme, telling us to add to our perseverance godliness. According to Vine's *Expository Dictionary of New Testament Words,* the Greek word *eusebeia,* here translated "godliness," denotes a piety that is "characterized by a Godward attitude."[27] It is a turning toward God, a gazing on Him, that leads to becoming like Him, being transformed into the image of Christ.

One person compared this transformation process to taking a picture: God is the light, worship is the lens, and we are the film. As we spend time in worship in the presence of His light, His character is burned into us. We are transformed from darkness to light.

This is an inner change that we don't see, but over time others see it in us. Like Moses when he met with God on the mountain, there will be a "shine" about us — and like Moses' shine, ours will increase or decrease, depending on how much time we spend with God. We might call this getting a spiritual tan! The more time we spend with God, the better our tan will be. Others will notice this healthy spiritual glow in our lives.

Our view of God is expanded.

Worship opens our eyes to see and understand more of how wonderful and awesome our God is. ("Worship opens doors," Ps. 34:9b MESSAGE.) As I practice the discipline of God-oriented praise, I am able to worship with more elegant, majestic sentences, reflecting the greatness of God that is impressed upon me in worship. This is part of being transformed.

This deepening of my praise of God then spills over into my giving thanks. Instead of ending up looking at just myself ("Thank you Lord for saving *me*"), I end up looking at Him and giving Him glory in my thanksgiving ("Thank you, Lord, that in your greatness and deep agape love, you reached out to your rebellious creatures, providing salvation for them. Thank you for your working in my life to bring me to salvation so you have more glory to yourself").

---

27. W. E. Vine, *Expository Dictionary of New Testament Words,* 4 vols. (London: Oliphants, 1939-41; repr. in one volume, Nashville: Thomas Nelson, 2003).

Purposes of Worship

As this change in praying is going on in me, now when I pray before a meal, instead of saying only, "Thank you for this food," what comes to mind is, "O you who bring forth food from the earth and water it by your power, we thank you for what your hand has provided for us in love."

I'm not saying that simple prayers are wrong or deficient. Rather, as we spend time in private worship, the majesty of God gets more and more into our souls and flows out in our prayers. It is like growing spiritually in an upward spiral.

Our personal worship becomes the wellspring for public worship.

When we spend time in personal verbal worship, it will also raise the level of our public worship, a point we have noted earlier. Praise and thanksgiving will naturally flow out of us, elevating God and edifying those around us. Practice in private makes for power in public, an important point noted in chapter 12 in the quote by Ravi Zacharias: "Worship is a *personal thing* before it goes public. It is an *individual thing* before it is part of a community."

As our personal worship spills over into the public, others will tend to follow our lead. Instead of speaking off the top of our heads with superficial thoughts, the time we have spent with God, gazing on His character, thinking through who He is, will guide us in lifting Him up before others.

Personal worship opens up to us deep, powerful, and transforming thoughts, so when we are together with other believers, this overflows in our public worship. Of course, we want to avoid the trap of speaking grand sentences to impress others, or even to try to teach them. Our motive needs to be simply to glorify God in the best way we can. And in the process, to share with others the riches we have received in and through private worship.

As I am continually working through the Psalms in my private worship, the words and thoughts from my current psalm flow out in my worship like water from a spring: pure, refreshing, delightful to me, as well as to those around. In this way the growth and fruit I'm experiencing in my personal worship become a blessing and stimulation to others I am with.

Think of what would happen if everyone in a church or prayer meeting was practicing personal worship like this. Instead of being boring, prayer meetings would become richer and deeper, more powerful and transforming. The more Scripture we have living in us and the more we know about God, the more the Holy Spirit has to work with in our lives and worship.

The Holy Spirit has opportunity to point out sin.

When we give God glory for who He is without thinking of how that benefits us, this brings us into the presence of God. We step out of the darkness of this world into the light of His character. And there, light exposes sin.

When we praise God for His purity, the Holy Spirit can easily bring to mind our impurity. The contrast is stark: the holy light of His character shining on what is in my heart!

Peter's response to being in the presence of Christ after the miraculous catch of fish in Luke 5:8 illustrates how the presence of God makes us aware of our sinfulness: "When Simon Peter saw this, he fell at Jesus' knees and said, 'Go away from me, Lord; I am a sinful man!'"

When the light of worship in the presence of Christ reveals my sin and sinfulness, my first reaction, unlike Peter in this incident, is to draw back into the shadows, saying, "Oh, I'm not *that* bad!" And yet I must admit that in my flesh, I am worse that that. God, however, is not operating on the basis of what I am or can do but on the basis of what His love and grace have done, and thus He invites me into His presence and wants to cleanse me as I confess my sin.

This revelation of sin is important. If we don't readily confess what the Spirit points out and grasp how much we have been forgiven, we will resist the Spirit's conviction of further sin. Peter touches on this truth in 2 Peter 1:9, "But if anyone does not have them [the qualities in verses 5-7, which God wants in our life], he is nearsighted and blind, and has *forgotten that he has been cleansed from his past sins.*" We need to remember where we have come from, as well as what we are in Christ.

Many Christians have a hard time understanding their own depravity. We see ourselves as basically pretty good people. Many think that God chose them the way a man would buy a used car. He walks around it, kicks the tires, looks inside, checks the oil, starts the engine. He says to himself, "Looks pretty good; a couple of new tires, a tune up, and it will do just fine."

This perspective is totally wrong — we're not as good as a used car! In fact, there is nothing positive or useful at all about our flesh. As Paul wrote in Romans 7:18, "I know that nothing good lives in me, that is, in my sinful nature [*lit.* flesh]." We are more like a car that has been in an atomic blast: it is radioactive and filled with corpses of people who died of the Ebola virus, the bird flu, the plague, and other infectious diseases. In our natural, fleshly self, we are not only useless to God, we are dangerous to Him and His kingdom!

In Ephesians Paul wrote how we were "objects of wrath" (Eph. 2:3), meaning that we were worthy only of hell. But — a very big *but!* — God redeemed us in spite of what we were (see Eph. 2:4-5). His goal is now to transform us. This began when we were born again and adopted into His family. It continues throughout our lifetime, and it goes much faster when we cooperate with Him through worship! It's a case of keeping the tension between where we have come from and where we are going, staying in balance.

When we understand that we had no innate goodness to commend ourselves to God, that we were called, transformed, and accepted solely out of His love and because of what Christ did for us, then we can, in quiet submission, let the Holy Spirit point out the next sin He wants us to deal with. When we are standing in the light of His presence in worship through praise, it is easy for Him to do that. Then, confident in His love and care, we can freely agree with Him about the *next* sin He is pointing out and can accept His forgiveness. (Part 4 considers confession in much more depth.)

We nurture our first love for Christ.

It may seem odd to mention our love for Christ last, but it logically flows from the points above. We are convicted of sin as we enter the light of God's presence; we then receive forgiveness, which then leads to a greater love for the Savior.

There are two aspects of nurturing our love for God. First, we see the wonder of God's character, His greatness, awesomeness, power, and majesty. We can only love Him more and more because of who He is.

Second, the more we have our sin exposed and receive forgiveness, the more we will love Him, for we understand more and more the magnitude of His suffering and forgiveness in the face of our sin.

Remember the story about the visit that Jesus had at a Pharisee's house? He told a parable there of two debtors who were forgiven by a creditor (Luke 7:41-42) and then asked the Pharisee which one would love the creditor more. "The one who had the bigger debt canceled" was the Pharisee's correct answer (v. 43).

Apply that to us: the more we understand of our own depravity and how much we have been forgiven, the deeper will be our love for the Lord Jesus, for His sacrifice, for the heavenly Father's planning our salvation, for the Holy Spirit as He finishes the work of sanctification in us.

Worship opens our eyes to both sides of the picture: where we have come from, and what we are becoming; how much we have been forgiven, and how much we are loved. When we see this, we can only love our God and Savior more.

Let's finish here with a prayer, remembering this list of wonders the Lord is doing in us through praise worship.

Lord God, the Holy One whose glory is in His holiness, who hates sin and will punish it, but who loves sinners and has found a way to redeem them — to you belongs praise, all praise, for all time. We exalt you, Lord Jesus, as the Righteous One who at the same time is the Compassionate One. Lord, help us to grow in our ability to worship you and to apply the things we are learning. Amen.

Dave and Worship

When Dave rang the bell, Jack answered the door and greeted him warmly. "How did your week go?" he asked as they walked to the study.

"It was pretty busy with lots of homework, but I made sure to read the assigned chapter of the book early in the week so I could think about it and practice what I learned," replied Dave as he sat in his regular chair. "I really like it that the chapters are short so I don't get bogged down in them."

Jack nodded, "Yes, I like that too. So what struck you the most in this chapter on worship?"

Dave opened his book and paged through chapter 14. "First of all, I was surprised at all the purposes of worship. I thought it was just to give God glory."

Jack nodded, "God is very economical in all He does. That is, He usually accomplishes several things through our obedience to a command. Here you see God using worship to bring benefit to Himself, to us and to those around us.

" Yes," Dave said, "that's clear in the section 'Our personal worship becomes the wellspring for public worship.' I'd never thought about how my personal spiritual life affects those around me, but now I see how my personal worship will bless others. I'm beginning to get the idea that this is what church life is supposed to do!"

Dave continued, "This insight gives me another impetus to practice praising God, since it will help me to be a better part of the church. The growth God gives me through worship will spill over onto other people when we get a chance to praise God together!"

"Exactly right," replied Jack. "God has such wonderful ways of taking what we offer and multiplying it for the benefit of those around us. And as we worship, the Holy Spirit also is working deep within, exposing sin and leading on to confession. That, by the way, is what the next session is about — only from a little different perspective. So read chapter 15 for our next meeting."

Purposes of Worship

Study Guide questions for Chapter 14: "Purposes of Worship"

1. How does worship expand our view of God? (108-109)
2. How does personal worship influence public worship? (109)
3. How does the Holy Spirit use worship in our lives? (110-111)
4. What does worship have with our first love for Jesus? (111-112)
5. What do you do to nurture your first love for Jesus?

Part 4

Confession

Truth #5: Confession Brings Freedom

CHAPTER 15

Confessing in Layers

We have looked at worship as a discipline that is crucial for successful spiritual warfare. A second such discipline is confession.

Confession, unfortunately, is a lost art. It's not talked about much, and therefore it is not practiced much. We read in 1 John 1:9, "If we confess our sins, he is faithful and just and will forgive us our sins and purify us from all unrighteousness."

Here the word translated "confess" means "give assent to" or "acknowledge." Confession is essentially acknowledging our sin and agreeing with God's assessment of it. It's more than just stating our sin. Rather, it is a commitment to treat it as God would: when He says something is wrong, we commit to agree with Him and, as a consequence, to reject, renounce, avoid, and leave what is wrong.

On the other side, when He pronounces something good, we must give assent to His judgment and obey Him in doing that good.

When we spend time in personal worship, we are naturally led into confession. When the Holy Spirit has us in the light of God's presence, He can easily point out sin.

As I mentioned earlier, when I am in God's presence in worship, my natural reaction to revelation of my sin is to draw back into the shadows, saying to myself, "Oh, I'm not *that* bad!" My natural tendency is to minimize my sin — not really denying it, but not fully agreeing with God's estimation of it.

However, when we are convicted of a sin and come to God to confess it, it is essential that we be honest and transparent about it, both with Him and with ourselves. Confessing half-heartedly or in a way that protects us is *not* agreeing with God.

Peter Kingston, Wycliffe Bible translator, has pointed out that, after asking for and receiving God's forgiveness, we need to *renounce* that sin — rejecting it, turning violently away from it. Such a stance puts into action our agreement with Him that this sin is evil, destructive, and grievous to Him.

As an example, I could mention that one of my "weaknesses" is exaggerating. I don't do it purposely, but in the excitement of presenting something, my numbers often tend to get bigger or smaller than they really are, depending on what I want to emphasize.

My wise and gracious wife has helped me to be more honest by pointing out that exaggeration is not just a weakness, it is a sin! It is a polite kind of lying — a lie! That label is direct, even harsh, but it correctly reveals the essential nature of exaggeration, which I must affirm and renounce.

Layers of Confession

I long ago discovered a problem, however, in my experience with confession. I found that my confessing often did not bring the freedom from sin that 1 John 1:9 seemed to promise.

As a natural worrier, I can tell you that confessing my worry had little effect in my life. I would confess it but then within a few minutes would be worrying again.

As I prayed about this, asking God for help, an insight came in relation to lists in Scripture that I had memorized. For instance, the list of qualities of heavenly wisdom in James 3:17 are in a particular order "first of all . . . then. . . ." So is the list of qualities in 2 Peter 1:5-7: "Add to your faith goodness; and to goodness, knowledge; and to knowledge, self-control. . . ."

From this thought came the realization that worry is really only the first of a whole list of related sins. It is the visible transgression, but under it are a whole stack of other hidden sins. Worry is what we see, but the layers of sin under it are what give it power. Upon reflection, I found several layers underlying the surface sin of worry.

> *Worry*
>   ↑   comes from
> *fear* that something will or will not happen,
>   ↑   which comes from
> *failure to surrender* this thing to God.
>   ↑   I resist surrendering it because of my
> *refusal to trust God,* thinking He doesn't know best.
>   ↑   My refusal to trust stems from my
> *arrogance,* thinking that I know better than God how this should work out.
>   ↑   This pride flows from my
> *selfishness,* or valuing my comfort more than God Himself (that is, seeking security or significance from the wrong source).

Confessing in Layers

↑ This really is *idol worship.*

↑ My idol worship comes from my *unbelief,* rejecting what God's Word says about Him, about me, and my situation, and my demanding something to be happy.

↑ My unbelief is rooted in my *rebellion,* my innate refusal as a sinner to submit to God.

Looking at this list makes me shudder. The simple, "innocuous" sin of worry is a warning sign that there are deep, powerful, negative, destructive forces at work down inside my heart.

As you can see, the sin of worry starts at the bottom with rebellion and unbelief. These two serious, powerful, and destructive sins are not readily visible but are the source of all the surface sins we can see. It's like there's a gang of violent men seeking to control me, but they work through the most innocent-looking one to distract and deceive me!

Satan wants us to focus on the visible sin, on the superficial — "It isn't so bad; look at all the people who worry without visible negative consequences!" He does not want us to see the serious sources of superficial sin, for then he can keep us enslaved to them.

God, however, wants us to look below the surface. Proverbs 16:2 says, "All a man's ways seem innocent to him, but motives are weighed by the LORD." The deeper sins we are talking about here are the heart-motives that produce visible sin, especially wanting our own way instead of God's (which is rebellion) and wanting our ideas to prevail over God's values because we think we know better, because we believe our own ideas rather than God's Word (which is unbelief). When we look beyond the surface with the Holy Spirit's help, we can become aware of the "gang of sins" holding us captive and only then can confess fully.

God wants us to weigh our motives and be aware of them. He repeats this idea in James 4:3 when speaking about the source of visible conflicts: "When you ask, you do not receive, because you ask with wrong motives." In chapter 17 we discuss learning how to discern our motives so we can confess the wrong ones and affirm the good ones.

Sin is like a plant. Its unseen roots go deep down into rebellion and unbelief, nourishing it, making it strong, and bearing bitter fruit in our lives. (See fig. 15.1.)

Fig. 15.1. Confession in layers: worry

If we confess only the top sin, it's like mowing grass: the plant immediately begins to grow back. But if we pull it out by the roots, confessing all the way down to the bottom, then that plant is gone.

Unfortunately, the truth is that our hearts are loaded with the seeds of sin, so more worry will sprout. But this only gives us another opportunity to give God honor through further confession.

The principle is always the same: as we confess down to the root, agreeing with God that these sins are awful, hideous, grotesque, and destructive, then renouncing and turning from them, we are pulling out the plant by the roots and can be freed from those sins. And this whole process gives glory to God.[28]

---

28. We can go to the first instance of sin in the world and see how, right from the beginning, sin came in layers. In the fall, the focus is always on Adam and Eve's sin of eating the forbidden fruit, which is where they clearly disobeyed God. But I believe their sin was more complex than that — it was literally the fruit of several choices.

It really started when Satan struck up his conversation with Eve. Adam was with her ("she also gave some to her husband who was with her," Gen. 3:6). Why didn't he defend her? Why didn't he contradict the clear lie of Satan ("You will not surely die," 3:4)?

Here's the progression that I see, from the top down. Adam deliberately chose to disobey God's order and eat the fruit. Why? Because he was focusing on the attractiveness of the fruit and the promised positive consequences of eating it versus focusing on God. Where did that come from? He was following Eve's lead, not God's commands. Why did he follow Eve here? He had abdicated his responsibility to God as the head of his marriage. Why this abdication? Because he was rebelling against his duty to take care of the garden and see that its rule was followed (see Gen. 2:15-17). But why was he rebelling? The deepest root seems to be Adam's unbelief: he put more weight on Satan's lies than on God's Word. So the layers of Adam's sin look like this:

Confessing in Layers

Layers under the Sin of Impatience

Impatience is another one of my common sins. In discerning the layers of sin under it, God has freed me to take up and use His patience. Here's what fed impatience in me:

Impatience

↑ comes from

anger — I am upset because my wants (expectations, desires) have been thwarted.

↑ I am angry because I am

holding on to "rights." — I have made these wants the condition for being happy, raising them to the level of an idol.

↑ I demand my rights because of my

self-centeredness. I am thinking about *me* and *my* viewpoint, my fulfillment.

↑ This focus comes from my

arrogance, for I think that I know better than God.

↑ I am not believing God because I am

trying to secure my own significance or security, believing myself, not God.

↑ This attitude is essentially

unbelief, for I have refused to consider God's Word worth submitting to.

↑ I think this way because of my

rebellion; I have made myself the final authority in these things.

So the "plant of impatience" looks like figure 15.2.

As God has helped me deal with this sin and its root sources, two things have stood out to me. The first is that God considers patience very important. It is the first quality of love listed in 1 Corinthians 13:4 ("Love is patient, love is kind, . . .").

In thinking about why patience would be first in the list, the realization came that although an impatient person could embody all the other characteristics of

---

choosing to disobey and eat the fruit;
focusing on the fruit, not on God;
following his wife's lead, not God's commands;
abdicating his leadership responsibilities;
rebellion, not acting against what Satan was doing;
unbelief, accepting Satan's lies.

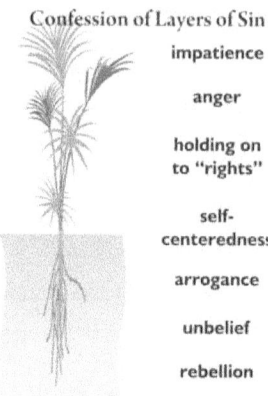

Fig. 15.2. Confession in layers: impatience

love, his impatience would nullify every one of them. I've seen this in practice. A friend of mine was a generous, kind, hardworking man — but he was extremely impatient. It was difficult to be around him, for his continual, rude impatience was always jerking my attention away from any positive thing he did or said.

The second point came from meditation on 2 Peter 1. Verse 3 says, "His divine power has given us *everything we need* for life and godliness through our knowledge of him who called us by his own glory and goodness."

What struck me as I thought on this verse is that nowhere in Scripture are we told to pray for patience. We are told to pray for other things like wisdom (James 1:5) or unity (Rom. 15:5), but not for patience. We are told to be patient, but not to pray for it.[29]

That is because God *has already given* us everything we need for life and godliness — including patience! So instead of praying for patience, when difficulties come and we feel our impatience rising, we need to pray something like, "Lord, help me to lay down my feeble, totally inadequate human patience and to take from your endless supply the mighty patience you have provided."

When I pray like that, there is a shift within me as my perspective is changed. I relax, and I can look at the situation differently, remembering that God is in control. It's His timing that is important, not mine, and I can rest in His goodness. This makes life easier for me and all those around me!

This, I think, is what James was talking about at the beginning of his book when he wrote, "My brethren, count it all joy when you fall into various trials, knowing that the testing of your faith produces patience" (1:2-3 NKJV). When we are "tested" and realize our patience is inadequate, we can turn to

---

29. In Col. 1:11 Paul does pray for the Colossians to be "strengthened with all power" so that they could have endurance and patience, but he does not pray directly for it.

Confessing in Layers

God and take up His patience instead, and this moves us on toward maturity.

Teaching Confession in Layers

When my boys were in their early teens, I taught them about many of the concepts we are discussing here. Here's what one of those conversations might have looked like.

> "OK, boys, let's sit up here at the table; I'd like us to have a look at the sin of lying. Remember last week when you got caught in a lie, I promised to help you learn how to overcome such temptations." Both boys nodded.
>
> "What do you see as possible sins under the visible one of lying?" I wrote LYING on the piece of paper on the table.
>
> Josh chewed on the end of his pen. "Well, asking myself why I would lie brings up selfishness; I want something for me — protection or respect or something material."
>
> "Yes, selfishness is a powerful manifestation of our depraved old nature," I replied as I wrote SELFISHNESS below LYING.
>
> Nat piped up, "Then there is a focus on the now — on non-eternal values. I'm thinking about what I'd like right now, getting out of trouble, not about the future."
>
> "Very good — I hadn't thought of that. This whole area could be called temporal or materialistic values. A clear example of this in the Bible is Esau selling his birthright for a bowl of soup." I wrote TEMPORAL VALUES. "Anything else?"
>
> Josh looked off in space, his wheels turning. "Obviously the bottom three are the others we've talked about before: rebellion leading to unbelief, leading to pride."
>
> True," I said and wrote these further down, leaving a space between them and the previous points. "There are some other possibilities to put here," I said, tapping the paper. Both boys looked blank.
>
> OK, how about these?" I asked as I wrote REJECTION OF GOD'S VALUES and below that FEAR, and then BELIEVING THE LIE OF SATAN. "One more thing that can often be near the bottom is the struggle for significance or security." I wrote these down too, completing the following list on the paper:
>
> LYING
> SELFISHNESS
> TEMPORAL VALUES
> REJECTION OF GOD'S VALUES
> FEAR
> BELIEVING SATAN'S LIE
> PRIDE
> DESIRE FOR SIGNIFICANCE OR SECURITY APART FROM GOD

CONFESSION

UNBELIEF
REBELLION

"What is Satan's lie?" asked Josh.

"Remember how in my class on spiritual warfare, I mention that Satan uses two main lies: 'God is not good all the time' — accusing God of sometimes withholding what is good for us or doing evil to us and therefore saying that God is not trustable — and 'Committing this sin will make me happier than obeying God.' Here both lies come into play. I tell a lie because I can't trust God and must protect myself, and lying will keep me out of trouble better than telling the truth, making me happier for the moment."

Both boys nodded.

"Remember what we've talked about before: knowing what underlies a sin helps us in two ways. It allows us to 'pull the sin of lying out by the root,' and it makes it possible for us to see how evil it is, even a white lie." I told them.

"So," said Josh, "When I am tempted to lie, I need to remember what's going on and confess the sins below lying."

"Right," I answered.

"Now all I have to do is want to be good!" said Nat the rebel with a laugh.

"OK, let's finish our time with prayer," I said, making a mental note to talk with Nat later about that last comment.

"Lord God, the Almighty One, who has defeated sin, who sets prisoners free, I praise you that we can come to you in confession and that you have promised forgiveness and cleansing. Help us to apply what we've learned today. Amen"

May you too, dear reader, be set free from the traps of sin by confessing in layers, pulling out the poisonous plants by the root. Take a sin that you have struggled with — perhaps gossip, maybe jealousy, pride, negative competition, or selfish ambition. Try to identify the underlying layers of the sin, writing them down. Ask God to give you wisdom and insight. Perhaps the first time you try it, you won't come up with much. Lay it aside, pray about it, and later come back and see whether you have any additional insight.

Take a look again at the examples given above. You can be sure that at the bottom of it are always unbelief and rebellion. Selfishness will also usually be in the mix, along with pride, and somewhere in there will be the desire either for significance or for security. Once you have a picture of what's there, then work at confessing all the way down to the root, renouncing each layer.

I encourage you to practice this regularly, taking a sin that plagues you and writing down the layers of sin that are under it. Confess them, renounce them — and see transformation in your life!

Confessing in Layers

Lily Pads: An Analogy with Dave And Jack

Dave pulled into the driveway and parked. He was looking forward to his lesson with Jack, but when he knocked on the door, there was no response. He went around to the back of the house, walked down toward the pond, and found Jack standing knee deep in the water, pulling up lily pads.

"Good morning!" Dave called, and Jack waved a muddy hand in response.

"I'll be up in a few minutes; just let me finish with this patch," he said. Dave watched Jack reach down deep into the water with both hands, feel around for a bit, then pull up a long dark root. With it came several lily pads and flowers, all tied together by the tuber. Jack threw them way up on the bank.

Pulling up the last bunch with its roots, Jack waded to the shore and dropped it on the bank. As Jack rinsed the mud off his hands at the edge of the pond, Dave asked, "Why don't you just pull off the pads and flowers instead of messing with those ugly, muddy roots?"

"Because lily pads are like sin," answered Jack. He paused, enjoying Dave's look of bewilderment. "Just like sin, lily pads are attractive to look at: beautiful, graceful white flowers floating among lovely green leaves. But they are destructive. If left unchecked, lily pads will fill the whole pond, choking out other plants and animals. And under those beautiful flowers and leaves hide ugly things: slime, bloodsuckers, worms, and snakes, to name a few!"

Jack leaned down and picked up one of the roots he'd thrown up on the bank. He held it up, a dark, gnarled, muddy tuber with long, white ugly stringers hanging from one side, and on the other the slime-covered stems ending in leaves and flowers. "Look at this. Like the root of sin, it's ugly. See what it's done to my hands?" Jack held up his free hand, stained a dark purple from the roots. "The last time I did this, one of my fingernails got infected from working with these. And smell this!" He held the root up toward Dave's nose. Dave pulled back as the odor of rotting mud and slime assailed his nostrils.

"Just like the stench of sin uncovered," said Jack, throwing the root back on the ground. "And like sin, unless you remove it far from where it was growing, it will reroot and grow again. That's why I've thrown these way up on the bank where there is no moisture to help them stay alive."

"Look at this." Jack held up a stem growing from the root; it was coiled up like a telephone cord. "This one was below the surface, waiting, slowly straightening out to bring its leaf to the surface. If I'd just picked off the leaves and flowers I could see, within a short time this young leaf would have been up on the surface to replace them, keeping the plant healthy and strong."

Dave stood thinking on what Jack had said. "It's like confessing in layers, isn't it?" he said. "If you only get rid of the pads and flowers, not the stem plus the shoots plus the root, it's going to grow right back!"

"Good application," said Jack as he turned and walked up to toward the shed, where he turned on the hose to wash the mud off his bare feet. "Confession in layers is the only effective way to root sin out of our lives. And as you read chapter 16, you'll see how to apply this to a very specific and significant area of your life."

Study Guide questions for Chapter 15: "Confessing in Layers"

1. What does "confess" mean? (117)
2. Describe what it means to confess in layers. (118-120)
3. Give some examples from your own life.
4. What are the benefits of confessing in layers? (118-122)
5. How will you apply this in your life?
6. How can you teach this to others? (123-124)

CHAPTER 16

Layers of Sin under Pornography

In this chapter we look at a specific application of confessing in layers: unmasking the layers of sin involved in pornography. Pornography can be defined as "input that stimulates relational/sexual desires that cannot be fulfilled legitimately." It is a huge factor in Western society, with so much sexual stimuli thrown at us every day. It comes in advertising, TV shows, movies, music, video clips, magazines, and newspapers. Its easy and secret availability on the internet makes it even more tempting. Exact statistics are hard to come by, but some surveys indicate that an amazingly high percentage of all pastors have viewed pornography on the Web during the past twelve months.

Satan knows that if he can get us ensnared in this sin, he will greatly weaken our spiritual life. Plus he can sow seeds of destruction in relationships and marriages, leading us to lives of hollow hypocrisy. Knowing how to fight and conquer the temptation to be involved in pornography in any form is critical.

Gender Differences

Pornography for us men is primarily visual — seeing something provocative or reading a description, and then replaying those images in our minds. Seeing or reading about an image can burn an impression into a man's mind that remains fresh and stimulating for a very long time. If I wanted to, I could recall a pornographic scene from a book I read in the sixth grade, over fifty years ago. I choose not to.

Pornography for females, I am told by women, is different: more relational, but still powerful. What women hear or experience is more important than what they see. Some women have told me that reading romance novels is a kind of pornography because it creates relational/sexual desires that cannot be legitimately fulfilled. The men in these novels understand women perfectly, always know the right thing to say, always meet their needs. The reason they can do this is that these men are created by woman authors! There are no such men!

Reading novels like this, however, stimulates the desire for such a man. If the reader is married, she will see what a lout her husband is in comparison to the man in the book. This can lead to dissatisfaction, which can then easily lead to a search for a better man. If the reader is single, she will be looking for someone who doesn't exist and will always be disappointed.

Layers under Pornography

So, what iniquities underlie the sin of lust fed by pornographic involvement? Here are the layers as I see them.

Pornography involvement
    ↑   comes out of
selfishness — I want to follow my lust for pleasure for myself, no matter how it affects those around me.
    ↑   This selfishness is fed by
reducing the woman to a means of pleasure, ignoring the fact that she is created in the image of God.
    ↑   This reduction arises from
having temporal values, thinking only of the present, devaluing the eternal.
    ↑   Having temporal values comes from
believing the lie that lustful dwelling on pornographic images will bring more happiness than obeying God and avoiding them.
    ↑   But also
believing the lie that the person I'm looking at wants me (that is, seeking significance from the person's approval/wanting me). In reality, she only wants money for posing; if I were there, she would tell me to get lost!
    ↑   This comes from
arrogance, believing I can judge better than God.
    ↑   To think this way reflects
unbelief, rejecting God's Word and principles.
    ↑   To reject God in this way is really
rebellion, choosing to do what I want, making myself the authority.

So this gives us the following layers of sin:

    pornography
    utter selfishness
    treating women as things
    having temporal values

believing Satan's lustful lies
arrogance
unbelief/rejecting God's Word
rebellion.

If we are serious about living for God and His glory, this list will give us goose bumps. These are terrible, destructive sins, grieving and quenching the Holy Spirit. They make us destructive tools in the hand of the devil rather than edifying ones in the hand of God.

As followers of Christ we should desire the opposite:

Walking in the freedom Christ brings:
    living a life worthy of the Lord,
    bearing fruit in all good works,
    growing in the knowledge of God,
    being strengthened by His mighty power
so that we can have great endurance and patience,
    joyfully giving thanks to the Father,
    who has qualified us to be partakers of the inheritance of
        the saints in the kingdom of light.
                            (see Col. 1:10-12)

Help in Application

I've read some good books helping men deal with sexual temptation and lustful thoughts and have gleaned some helpful things from them. In the book *Every Man's Battle,* the authors talk about "bouncing thoughts and eyes" away from stimulating sights, reminding me that I have no right to look lustfully at them. I have no right, both because I have a wife and because these women belong to someone else — they are someone's daughter or mother or wife.[30]

The authors also talk about focusing our thoughts on our wives, or, in the case of a single man, his potential future wife, or on Christ and His purity. The same would be true of a wife focusing on her husband, or a single woman on her future spouse or on Christ.

This advice has been helpful to me. As the authors say, it increases my affection and passion for my wife instead of sharing it mentally with a lot of other women. Every time I lust after another woman, I give her a bit of my heart and passion. If I do this regularly, there's not much left over for my wife.

Josh Harris's book *Not Even a Hint* — now retitled *Sex Is Not the Prob-*

---

30. Stephen Arterburn and Fred Stoker, with Mike Yorkey, *Every Man's Battle: Winning the War on Sexual Temptation, One Victory at a Time* (Colorado Springs, Colo.: WaterBrook Press, 2000).

lem (Lust Is) — is, in my opinion, the best book on the subject of sexual purity.[31] His serious acceptance of the biblical command that we should have "not even a hint of sexual immorality" (Eph. 5:3) in our lives points us to the very real possibility of living that way. He then goes on to give practical helps in living that standard.

Putting these insights together with the idea of confessing in layers, the Holy Spirit gave me the following prayer of confession to use when I have lustful thoughts or am tempted to think them. I pray this slowly, thinking about each point.

> Lord, you know what I just thought. I confess to you that this lustful thought is
> > utterly selfish,
> > totally destructive,
> > caustic to my soul,
> > pleasing to Satan, and
> > grievous to you, O God.
>
> Forgive me. I repent of and renounce these sins against you.

It gives me the chills when I confess through this list. To think that I'm pleasing Satan, and then that I am grieving God!

If I grieve God, I give Him pain, hurting the One who loves me so, the One whom I profess to love. Then I am not going to be a useful instrument in His hand. I'm going to limit what He can do through me for His kingdom. I certainly don't want that!

Since this confession goes to the roots of pornography, it strips off the mask of false pleasure and fulfillment that Satan puts over his temptations. It lets us see the ugliness and depravity that underlie them. It pulls back the curtain of lies that covers over the pit of ensnarement and the ensuing suffering and evil that await us when we accept and act on that lie. This should give us strong motivation to flee such temptation, to run into the arms of the Lord Jesus.

Breakthroughs with Confession

Using confession in layers can lead to great growth in our spiritual lives. After God began teaching me about confessing in layers, I was challenged by the pastor of my home church to pray for revival in my life.

As I prayed, the Spirit guided me in realizing that revival is not a warm, fuzzy, exciting happening where everyone feels good about following God. It starts with conviction of sin. It starts with exposing what we've been doing to

---

31. Joshua Harris, *Not Even a Hint* (Sisters, Ore.: Multnomah Publishers, 2003), reissued in 2005 as *Sex Is Not the Problem (Lust Is): Sexual Purity in a Lust-Saturated World.*

Layers of Sin Under Pornography

grieve God so we can repent. Then we can begin allowing the Holy Spirit to rule the whole of us and bring a new awakening of our first love. This conviction can be a painful thing, which is why most of us shrink from it.

Just at the time I began praying for revival, I got a bad case of the stomach flu and spent five days in bed. This was the Lord's way of calling me aside so He could have a word with me and answer my request for revival.

I was so weak that all I could do was pray, so I spent a lot of time talking with Him. God gave me some answers to my prayer for revival — in the form of pointing out a number of sins I needed to deal with. They were:

lustful thoughts
fear of man
drawing security from having money
lack of discipline in eating
pride
critical and negative thoughts and words
jealousy and competition
the desire to control others.

It was not that I was ignoring these sins; in fact I was quite successful in combating them. But what the Lord said to me was, "Your measure of victory in these areas is too low. I want you to adopt my higher standards and deal with them more severely." He was right, of course, and led me to a new surrender and a new commitment to obey Him in these areas.

After getting somewhat better physically, I was downtown at a store on a beautiful, warm September afternoon. When I got ready to go home, my car wouldn't start, so I called my mechanic; he said he'd be down shortly to help me. (There's one great advantage to living in the Middle East: mechanics make house calls!) I sat down on the wall by the entrance to the store and watched for the mechanic to come around the corner so I could flag him down.

As I sat there, a steady stream of people passed by, including many good-looking, tightly dressed girls. At that moment the Holy Spirit quietly said to me, "You are noticing too much!" He, of course, was right. Although I was trying to bounce my thoughts and eyes, still on an almost subconscious level, I was taking note of this and that nice feature.

I was definitely off base and immediately confessed to the Lord my wrong and sneaky indulgence in sinful thinking. I agreed that my thoughts were:

utterly selfish,
totally destructive,
caustic to my soul,

pleasing to Satan, and
grievous to God.

I repented and renounced this sin, agreeing not to take notice — although I still had to look down the street for the mechanic while all these girls were walking by. Within a few minutes, however, I was able to "look through" them instead of "look at" them, to look but not notice — a significant difference! That brought a new level of freedom and victory, more of what the Lord had in mind.

Watching What We Watch

The subject of looking and noticing points to an important precaution: watching our intake. We need to carefully stay away from material that stimulates us wrongly. In obedience to this principle, I've taken steps to protect myself.

In my Middle Eastern country most of the newspapers have semipornographic pictures in them daily — even the papers that call themselves a "family paper." So, when I walk by a newspaper stand, I intentionally look the other way or even cross over to the other side of the street to avoid seeing anything negative.

When it comes to reading, I'll have my wife read the newspaper first and warn me which pages I shouldn't look at, or I'll have her take them out of the paper. Or I'll ask her to read an article whose title indicates that it may contain too much explicit material, and then she tells me whether I should read it or not.

The point is, in everyday life we have enough stimulation that we can't avoid, so we should be taking precautions to avoid polluting ourselves unnecessarily with further impure input.

Application of this truth starts probably right now for all of us. Every time you watch TV or glance through a magazine or see a movie, there are enticing images. We can and should immediately turn away from these and state the truth in confession, protecting our souls from being burned with the acid of lust that Satan is constantly throwing at us.

A fellow worker, John Miller, shared a good goal and standard concerning watching films. He said, "I ask myself the question, 'Can I watch this to the glory of God?'"

John went on to point out that in resisting temptation, we should not just say No to it, but we should say Yes to God. We should flee to Him and replace the temptation with God Himself! And that is the real answer: turning from the temptation to God Himself. Our desire is to be such a worshipper that it becomes an automatic response to temptation by turning to God and viewing Him in all His glory.

Let's end this section with prayer.

Almighty Father, the One who is glorious in holiness, who hates sin, but loves the sinner, we praise you for your grace as you work in our lives. Help us to live in your power, to be different from the world in living a life pure in thought, word, and deed, and to be quick to confess and renounce when we fail. Help us to discern the layers of sin that underlie the obvious ones and to confess and renounce them. Amen.

Getting Open About Temptation

Dave settled into his regular chair, looking a bit uncomfortable. "This was a very convicting and difficult chapter," he commented.

Jack set his water glass down on the table before sitting in his chair. "You are right. The subject of our sexuality and our weaknesses there is a very personal, core issue. It goes so deep that most people are reticent to talk about it in any way other than joking. But our sexuality is a good thing, created by God and, if entered into properly, is a great force for creativity and bringing God glory."

Jack paused to let that thought sink in. "So, what did you get out of the chapter?"

Dave sighed. "Well, it was helpful that the author related it to confessing in layers. Lust is definitely something I struggle with a lot. I mean, there's temptation everywhere. The girls at my school are all flaunting themselves and many ads on the internet use sexy girls to get my attention. Which reminds me, I need to get an ad blocker for my computer. Even some of the reading assignments we get for literature class are lust-inducing!"

"So what are you going to do differently?" asked Jack.

"First of all, I went back to chapter 11 and reread the section 'Gaining My Freedom' — you know, the one about confession and reclaiming ground given to Satan?"

"Yes, I remember that well."

"I went through those steps and it helped, clearing out some past sin. Also using that prayer of confession near the end of chapter 16 was helpful, this one here under the title "Breakthroughs With Confession." I think I'm going to be using it a lot!"

"Good," said Jack. "That's entering into spiritual warfare with the armor on; it means advance for the kingdom of God as you persist.

"And there's another thing you can do to make it even more effective. After using that prayer of confession and receiving forgiveness, I found that it is important once again, in the authority of the Lord Jesus Christ, to withdraw any ground I gave to Satan in that sin I've just confessed. This is what I call my 'zero tolerance prayer,' tolerating no ground for Satan. It keeps him from getting even one square inch of my life for a foothold. I've found that the attacks were less effective after I began doing that."

"Makes sense," replied Dave. "I'll begin to do that, too."

Jack took his copy of the book and opened to the table of contents. "This week you'll be reading chapter 17. This will reinforce the things we've talked about today."

"OK," said Dave. "I can use all the help I can get!"

Study Guide questions for Chapter 16: "Layers of Sin Under Pornography"

1. Why have a chapter on this subject? (127-128)
2. How is pornography different for men and women? (127-128)
3. Trace through the layers of this sin, commenting on each layer. (128-129)
4. Why is the confession on page130 effective for those who love Jesus?
5. What is revival? Why does confession help bring revival? (130-131)
6. How can we guard against destructive in put? (132)
7. What changes will you make in your life after reading this chapter?

CHAPTER 17

Layers and Motives

We are now going to take this "confessing in layers" concept in a new direction and apply it to our motives. These are very important to God. According to Proverbs 16:2, "All a man's ways seem innocent to him, but *motives* are weighed by the LORD." Romans chapters 1–3 are all about how people's wrong motives lead them astray.

In Isaiah 29:13 God rejected the Israelites' (external) worship because their (internal) motives were wrong:

> These people come near to me with their mouth
>   and honor me with their lips,
>   but their hearts are far from me.

Similarly, evil in our hearts can sabotage our prayers: "When you ask, you do not receive, because you ask with wrong *motives*" (James 4:3). Earlier in James, the writer contrasts heavenly wisdom with earthly wisdom, pointing out the negative motives of the earthly thinking and what they lead to (highlighted in the brackets):

> But if you harbor [the motives of] bitter envy and selfish ambition in your hearts, do not boast about it or deny the truth. Such "wisdom" does not come down from heaven but is earthly, unspiritual, of the devil. For where you have [motives of] envy and selfish ambition, there you find [the fruit of] disorder and every evil practice [which are the results of wrong motives lived out]. (James 3:14-16)

Then in 3:17 James tells us, "The wisdom that comes from heaven is first of all pure; then peace-loving. . . ." Heavenly wisdom begins with purity, including purity of our motives; pure motives lead toward pure actions.

This is significant, for our attitudes, thoughts, and words and actions flow from our motives, as the following shows:

words and actions
↑
thoughts
↑
attitudes
↑
motives

How many of us in everyday life take the time to check out our motives? If we do, we usually look at only the superficial ones. For instance, we may help out on a work day at the church because we want to serve God and the community.

These discernable motives can look really good, but we are usually unaware of or ignore the negative ones hidden underneath. The real reason we join in to help on a work day may be simply that we don't want to look unspiritual or unhelpful — that is, we're motivated by a fear of what others may think of us. We then end up resenting the pressure we've given into and become angry at the others who didn't show up to help.

The Motives of Joseph and His Brothers

The story of Joseph in Genesis provides a clear example of how motives are lived out through attitudes, thoughts, words, and actions. When Joseph told his older brothers about his dream of them bowing down to him, they were very angry (Gen. 37:5-11).

Why was that? In their culture the older siblings, and especially the firstborn, were more important than the younger ones and got a bigger share of the inheritance, as well as the blessing of the father and the right to lead the clan — and Joseph was eleventh in line! Little brother Joseph's declaration that he would be honored over his older brother struck at their sense of importance and significance (loss of power), at their honor (loss of position), and at their security (loss of inheritance). Later, when Jacob sent Joseph to check up on his brothers, they acted out of their negative motives.

> So Joseph went after his brothers and found them near Dothan. But they saw him in the distance, and before he reached them, they plotted to kill him.
>
> "Here comes that dreamer!" they said to each other. "Come now, let's kill him and throw him into one of these cisterns and say that a ferocious animal devoured him. Then we'll see what comes of his dreams." . . . and they took him and threw him into the cistern. (Gen. 37:17-20, 24)

Layers and Motives

The older brothers' desire to protect their honor (significance), power (security), and inheritance was their motive, which expressed itself first in the area of attitude (anger, jealousy, and hatred), then in the realm of thoughts (revenge), leading to words (proposal) and action. Here's the progression from the top down:

action: seizing Joseph and throwing him into the cistern
words: "Let's kill him!"
thoughts: revenge, getting Joseph out of the way
attitudes: anger, jealousy, hatred
motives: desire to protect their honor, security (inheritance, position), and significance (leadership and power).

We are all like Joseph's brothers in that we all have negative motives. Personally, I find that my motives are always mixed, with some good, some neutral, and some bad, so I need to bring them before God and, as I like to say, "purify them in the light of His presence."

Even in writing this, I have mixed motives. Why do I want to share these truths with you? Certainly to help you grow and be more effective for God. In addition, I enjoy teaching. And then there is the desire to be admired and liked because I'm such a good teacher — at least that's what I'd like to think about myself!

I need to evaluate these motives before myself and God, reject those that are negative or neutral, and affirm the ones that are positive — then act out of these positive ones. The more we are aware of our motives, the better choices we can make.

In my case, the negative motive is obvious, wanting to make myself look good in your eyes. The one of teaching because I enjoy it is, I think, a neutral motive, not good, not bad. It is a weak reason, spiritually, for doing something. When there are good motives to be had, why use a weak one? Besides, one of the things underlying the motive of enjoying teaching is selfishness! So I reject the negative and neutral motives and affirm the positive one of wanting to help others grow as the reason for writing.

Why is this important? One of my colleagues is fond of saying, "Wisdom is doing the right thing, for the right motive, at the right time, and in the right way." Personally, I think that the most important aspect in this list is having the right motive; if our motives are right, we will be led away from wrong things, wrong timing, and wrong methods. But if our motives are wrong, even if the other things are right, they can be spoiled.

Consider a teenage boy who attends every meeting at his church, not just youth group, Sunday School, and church, but prayer meeting too. He is doing the right thing at the right time, but if his motive in going is to "hit on the girls," he spoils it not only for himself but for others!

The Fruit of Purifying My Motives

I don't examine my motives in every little decision I must make, but I certainly try to do so in the important ones. Taking time before God, I ask for wisdom in discerning my motives. Then I write as transparently as I can in my journal, listing all the motives I can discern in the situation.

As in confession, it takes courage to be honest with myself and really look down under the obvious ones to see what is there. After that, I bring each one before God, judging it in light of Scripture, rejecting the wrong and neutral motives as a reason to act, and affirming the positive, biblical motives, committing to act on them.

Here's a mundane example to show how this works. One weekend while my wife was away for a conference, I was sick. By the end of the weekend there was a stack of dirty dishes in the sink, but weak and sick as I was, I did not feel like washing them.

However, I knew that my wife does not like to come home to an untidy kitchen and dirty dishes, and I did not want to have to deal with her unhappiness. So I hauled myself out of bed and staggered toward the kitchen, grumpy to have to "suffer" in this way.

At that moment the Spirit convicted me of my wrong major motives. I was doing this out of fear of man and out of wanting to protect myself, not wanting to "get it in the neck" from an unhappy woman. This was self-centered defensiveness, not at all a good motive. It was also thinking evil of my wife, viewing her as an adversary. So I confessed all this to God, and He then helped me to see that I should clean up the dishes because I loved my wife and wanted her to have the joy of coming home to clean dishes and an orderly kitchen.

An interesting thing happened when I made that decision to act out of right motives: a sense of freedom came, followed by positive thoughts, and then leading to joy. Wrong motives trap us — think of how fear, anger, and jealousy bind and control us, leading us to unhappiness and relational problems — while right motives set us free from self and bring joy, which certainly helps in relationships. I even felt better physically. And when my wife came home, she felt loved and cared for as she saw how nice the kitchen was.[32]

---

32. When I shared this incident later, one woman told me that, no matter what the motive, I should do the dishes. She is right, for duty calls — but the right motives certainly make it better!

Layers and Motives
Dave Discovering the Layers of His Sin

"Well, Dave, how has God been working in your life since we met last?" asked Jack.

"This week I had an interesting opportunity to apply what you've been teaching me," Dave said. "I say interesting because it involved both confession and discerning of my motives. A friend was supposed to meet with me on Wednesday and help me with some homework in preparation for a test. He didn't show, and I couldn't get him on his cell phone.

"I was fuming — I'd basically arranged my day around this appointment — plus it was important to me, I needed the help for the big test the next day. I was really angry at my friend.

"Then I thought of the layers of confession and got out my journal to sketch out what was happening. Here's what I wrote:

Anger
Self-centeredness
Selfishness
Pride
Unbelief
Rebellion

"I realized," Dave said, "that my anger came from not getting my way. I was being self-centered, thinking only of me, and this came from selfishness."

"That's accurate, I think," said his mentor. "When people say, 'You made me angry,' they are hiding from that actual fact: 'You just revealed my ugly self-centeredness!'"

Dave nodded and continued, "Then there's pride: thinking my plans are more important than my friend's, that I know better than God how things should work out.

"Then unbelief in not trusting God to work through this situation — I was not thinking biblically at all."

"What should have been your thoughts?" asked his mentor.

"Well, as you have mentioned, Psalm 23:1 speaks to this, 'The LORD is my shepherd, I shall not want.' Certainly I can trust God in this situation to give me what I really need, not just what I want."

"Excellent," said Jack.

"And rebellion, of course, is at the root as I rebelled against what God allowed."

"Good. An important question here is: do you see anger as a sin?"

Dave hesitated, "Well, my anger was not very righteous!"

The mentor nodded, "We certainly all have experienced that. But there is another side to anger. As an emotion, anger can be neutral, kind of like a warning light blinking on the dashboard of life. How we respond to it makes it positive or negative."

"Well, I guess that's where examining my motives came in, clarifying what I was really thinking. My anger alerted me to the need to do that," said Dave. "See, further down the page there, below the list of sins, is a list of my motives."

I want MY agenda to be fulfilled.
I want my friend to help ME so I can do well on the test.
I don't want interruptions in MY planned schedule.
I want to do well on the test so I'll feel good.
I want to do well on the test to glorify God.
I want to have this prep out of the way so I can watch a
      basketball game tonight.

"So, after discerning these motives, what did you do with them?" asked Jack.

"First, I did as you suggested, rejecting the negative and neutral ones, and affirming the positive ones. That means I ended up with only one: 'I want to do well on the test to glorify God.'

"After confessing down through the layers and purifying my motives, there came a sense of peace and freedom, freedom from fear and anxiety and anger. Then this thought came, 'God will help me, if not through this friend, in another way!' That freed me even more. So I spent a little time praying about the test before going back to my room, and you'll never guess what happened!"

"What?" asked Jack.

"As I was walking across campus, I met the prof who would be giving the test the next day. In our conversation he asked if I had any questions about the material to be covered in the test. He then answered all the questions I had — and I'm sure did a better job then my friend could have done!"

"Wonderful!" exclaimed the mentor, "What a great example of how confession, purifying our motives, and prayer open the way for God to work in our lives in a powerful way. Remember we talked about Psalm 50:23? It says, 'He who sacrifices thank offerings honors me, and he prepares the way so that I may show him the salvation of God.'

"You chose to give thanks when you didn't feel like it, and that opened the way for God to give you the help you needed."

Dave nodded.

"What you experienced there, Dave, is a victory in the spiritual battle. Your fight was not against your friend but against the world system of selfishness, the self-centered flesh, and the destructive devil. That's a taste of what God has for you as you apply these truths!"

"If this is what life will be like using these tools you're teaching me, it's

Layers and Motives

going to be a great adventure," said Dave.

"That's true," replied his mentor, "But it's unlike strictly human adventures, where the focus is on being entertained with the thrill and challenge. Rather than being a whitewater rafting adventure, it is more like a being-on-a-sinking-ship-in-the-ocean-without-help-in-sight kind of adventure!

"For us the adventure is the challenge of cooperating with God when it's difficult and thereby seeing Him glorified. It's a road on which we will be weary at times because things don't
always work out as quickly and neatly as this situation; we will have to go through many unglamorous happenings, but He will carry us through."

"And speaking of carrying through, your assignment is to read chapter 18 this week."

Study Guide questions for Chapter 17: "Layers and Motives"

1. Why is it important to know our motives? (135-137)
2. Give an example (from your own life, if possible) of how motives influence attitudes, which then influence thoughts, which in turn influence words and actions. (136-137)
3. What does it mean to "purify my motives?" (138)
4. How will you apply this concept in your life of discerning and purifying motives?

CHAPTER 18

Confessing ahead of Time

Let's start this chapter with a prayer:

We lift you up, Lord Jesus, as the final Authority in all, the Most High. You are the Most High in wisdom, in knowledge, in power, in goodness. We praise and exalt you for who you are. We thank you for this opportunity to learn more of what you have given to help us in temptation, learning how to confess ahead. Help us to glean what we should today and apply it. Amen.

The key idea of this chapter — confessing ahead — came while praying through and putting on the armor of God. Confessing ahead is a powerful way to prepare ourselves for dealing with temptation. As I mentioned in the previous chapter, when God began answering my prayer for revival, He did it by pointing out sins I needed to deal with more seriously. The initial eight grew to a list of over thirty! Each of these is a weakness, a tendency to sin where Satan could effectively attack me if I am not prepared.

Confessing ahead helps me be prepared. It is the concept of confessing to God my tendency to sin in the areas of my weakness before I do so. I've begun doing this three or four mornings a week.

It has proven helpful in four ways. First, it reminds me of my weakness in each of these areas, preparing me for when I will be tempted there. Second, it is a chance for fresh surrender and strengthening of my resolve to stand against these temptations with the armor of God — a kind of focusing again on truth. Third, it is a chance to ask God for His help in standing against the wiles of Satan. And fourth, it opens the way for further conviction, for God to point out new sins or another aspect of a sin.

To give you an idea of the kind of things God wants us to deal with, here's the list of my sins, pretty much in the order that God revealed them to me.

- lustful thoughts
- fear of man
- thinking/speaking critical and negative thoughts and words
- money: stinginess and drawing security from having money rather than from God

Confessing Ahead of Time

- eating too much, too fast, too often
- pride: taking credit and thereby stealing God's glory
- being touchy and insecure
- jealousy and competition
- the desire to control others rather than empowering them
- self-pity rather than praise
- trying to get from people what only God can give
- trying to protect my dignity and significance, not believing they are safe in God
- not having/nurturing my first love for God
- materialism: too much thinking, dwelling, dreaming about projects and things
- greed: wanting more and more success, activity, excitement, fulfillment
- impatience: wanting to resolve things right now, not waiting for God's timing
- trusting myself: not praying while talking with others, just saying what I think
- speeding: driving fast because it makes me feel good, in charge, masculine
- legalism: doing things because they make me feel spiritual, better, superior
- graceless, harsh speaking
- swearing in my thoughts
- laziness
- complaining
- worry
- anger
- fear
- failure to focus: letting myself be distracted from the task at hand
- lack of follow-through
- gossip
- being pushy in my own strength
- being contrary and unkind

The "How to" of Confessing Ahead

In asking God to help me be strong in Him and the power of His might, I use the list of sins to pray something like the following:

> Lord, I confess to you my tendency to entertain lustful thoughts. Lord, help me to flee from them, remembering how destructive they are. Help me to "not notice," to bounce my eyes and thoughts away from sexual stimulation.

CONFESSION

> I confess my tendency to allow myself to be controlled by fear of man. Lord, I tend to let others' thoughts influence me more than your thoughts. Forgive me and help me to reject fear of man and to fear you instead, giving value to your opinion, not other people's.
>
> I confess my tendency to think and speak critical and negative thoughts. Help me to reject them while they are in the forming stage, to neither think them nor speak them.
>
> I confess my tendency to get my security from having money, from not spending it, from seeking a high in getting a good deal. Help me to wisely use the resources you've given me, while not being controlled by them.

That should give you an idea. I think of this "confessing ahead" as a kind of rehearsal for the battle to come, thinking/speaking truth and committing myself to applying it before the actual attack comes. In confessing ahead, I am practicing the proper and powerful response so it will be more natural to me when the temptation comes.

As a practical point, I often confess through about a third of this list each time, so it isn't an overwhelming amount and I can pray through it with more thought.

The Fruit of Confessing Ahead

Confessing ahead has resulted in some significant growth in my life. Here's what I wrote about it in two prayer letters:

> As part of the revival God began in my life last fall, He clearly convicted me of a number of sins, including fear of man and not keeping the speed limit.
>
> Fear of man is basically putting some person's evaluation above what God thinks. I can grasp that pretty well.
>
> That speeding one, though, is a tough one for me. Our house in Connecticut is located on a back road where the speed limit is 30 mph. However, most people drive 50 or 60. It just gripes me to have to drive so slowly — and certainly no one else drives that speed! When I'm driving fast, I feel more in control, more powerful, more manly. Slow driving feels like someone else is in control!
>
> In spite of my natural desires, however, in obedience to God, I decided to drive 35, giving myself the 5 mph margin that police give drivers in a radar trap — that is, the enforced speed limit. Each day I confessed ahead my tendency to drive too fast and asked God for help to drive the proper speed.
>
> So I'm driving along sloooowly, and up behind me zooms somebody in his shiny new SUV. I can see the driver in my rearview mirror, fretting at

getting stuck behind this slow guy (me!) — and there's nowhere to pass on this road, so both of us have to suffer with this until we reach the highway three miles away.

On top of this, I can hear my father's voice from the past commenting on my driving: "Well, there's grandpa, out on the road, going nowhere. Why doesn't he just get off the road and let those who have somewhere to go get by?!!!!"

I'm shrinking down inside, embarrassed and frustrated. And what is this embarrassment? It is fear of man. If God says to obey the law, should I let some kid who's in a hurry to hang out at the mall push me to disobey the Creator of the universe?

So here is God, dealing with two sins in my life with one swat: fear of man and speeding. As I've continued to confess ahead and stick to the speed limit with God's help, denying self, driving slowly, and ignoring those eager beavers behind me, two things have happened. First, it doesn't bother me so much anymore to drive the speed limit. And second, the thought of what those behind me think has lost a lot of its power. By my refusing to give in to what others are thinking, my fear of man is fading.

There is a lot of freedom in fearing God rather than man. As it says in Proverbs 29:25, "The fear of man brings a snare, but he who trusts in the Lord is safe."

Psalm 62:5 sums up both lessons: "Find rest, O my soul, in God alone; my hope comes from him"!

From a second letter, which tells of the ongoing work on my fear of man:

There are certain questions I don't like to be asked, such as, "Why didn't you do it this way?" This is more of an accusation than a question. It is followed by a silent but definite comment on my intelligence: "You dummy!"

What gets to me even more are unjust accusations like: "You never do anything right!" Or "This is all wrong!" when it's really just a matter of opinion. I am immediately goaded to defend myself, which usually brings on a negative reaction from the other person and leaves a mess to clean up in our relationship.

In last month's prayer letter I mentioned how driving the speed limit led to being freed more from fear of man, and confessing ahead has continued the process of freeing me. In a continuation of this new freedom, the Lord used meditation on the armor of God to bring another breakthrough in my strong tendency to defend myself vigorously, even when the other person hardly knows they've accused me.

As I've mentioned before, every morning for the past 37 years I've meditated/prayed through Ephesians 6:10-18, putting on the armor, and this past week the Lord gave me a new insight from it, which shows the depth and richness of Scripture! As one author has said, "There is a cumulative value to investing small amounts of time in certain activities over a long period."[33]

Verse 12 says, "For we do not fight against flesh and blood but against principalities and powers." When praying that God would help me live this truth, something clicked in my head — actually it clicked on both an intellectual and emotional level at the same time, a genuine "aha!" experience — and I realized that when I am bothered by accusations, whether implied or direct, this also is fear of man. I'm caring too much what the other person thinks; I have the belief that it is very important that others see things from my point of view, to approve of what I think is right. When they don't agree, I'm intimidated, fearing what they think. I'd never made the connection before, obvious as it is!

If an accusation isn't true, why do I let it bother me so much? Because I want to be justified in the eyes of the accuser — but that isn't necessary, for God and I know the truth, and that's enough. If it isn't true, deny it and let it pass. If it is true, I need to admit it, ask forgiveness if necessary, learn from it, forgive myself, and move on.

There is a lot of freedom in fearing God rather than man, as I mentioned before. Proverbs 29:25 says, "The fear of man brings a snare, but he who trusts in the Lord is safe." Now as I continue to confess ahead my weakness in this area, God will strengthen me toward obedience to Him.

You can see the cascade of positive events that comes from rejection of temptation and a commitment to obedience. To listen to the conviction of the Spirit, to confess and reject sin brings a flood of growth in that area and those surrounding it. Confessing ahead facilitates this process.

Confessing ahead is another example of God's kingdom being "right side up" from the world. Confessing before you sin is certainly different from natural thinking.

This is a developing concept for me. Recently it took a new twist, inspired, I believe, by the Spirit. Instead of confessing each item, I began praising God for what He is doing in each of these areas — praising Him for the discernable change in each one as I cooperate with the Spirit in dealing with each temptation that arises. And also praising Him for the progress He's going to bring in areas where I'm not doing well.

As with any discipline, there is the danger of making it a legalistic "this must be done every morning" type of rule. To avoid this, I will follow the same principle as in my meditation on the Psalms: listening to the Spirit. This activity is not just a discipline, it is one facet of the gem of my love relationship with Jesus Christ. The purpose is to love Him, to glorify Him, so I need to discipline myself to follow His leading.

---

33. Andy Stanley, *The Best Question Ever: A Revolutionary Approach to Decision Making* (Sisters, Ore.: Multnomah Publishers, 2004), p. 68.

Confessing Ahead of Time

Following God's leading, sometimes I'll use a psalm just one day, sometimes I'll spend two or three weeks meditating on one. There is a sense when it's time to move on to the next one. I expect that the Holy Spirit will guide me the same way in confessing ahead. He will show me other sins, weaknesses, and temptations to confess ahead, and some of these others will drop by the wayside for a time.

I also expect that there will be a cycle in this, as there is in many aspects of spiritual life. God is taking us on an upward spiral in which He brings us again and again through the same scriptural truths and the same problems, but each time He's giving us a higher understanding and application of truth.

Satan will seek to discourage us in this, saying, "Look, you're still stuck in the same sins! There's no progress in your life; you might as well give up and give in to these temptations because they will never go away!"

The truth, however, is that the temptation isn't the sin, and as we apply the same answer we did last time, we again will have victory. And even if we fall and confess, this is occurring on a different, higher level than before. Plus, as we confess ahead, we will be more prepared to deal with these personal temptations when they arise.

As you practice confession, giving the Spirit time in your personal worship to point out sin you need to confess and looking for the layers below the obvious sins, you can make a list to use in confessing ahead, like mine above. And as time goes on, the Holy Spirit will show you other sins that you can add, equipping you more completely.

Discerning Ahead

Another aspect of looking into the future is the concept of discerning ahead. This is thinking through what would happen if we sinned in a certain area. What are the layers of people, events, and situations that would be influenced for the negative if I sinned in certain way?

I first thought about this concerning the sin of adultery, writing in my journal how my relationships would be affected if I were to be unfaithful to my wife. Many believers think that they would never do such a thing, but as the Bible (not to mention good old common sense) warns, "If you think you are standing firm, be careful that you don't fall!" (1 Cor 10:12). We all have the flesh, and given the right situation, we all can and do make wrong decisions. I don't want to underestimate my flesh or the desire of Satan or the power of temptation.

It all starts on a very innocent level, like just finding the company of a person of the opposite sex exciting, and instead of cutting off that emotional attraction, enjoying it. This can lead to an emotional attachment, to spending too much time together, then to touching, and eventually to adultery. We are all capable of sinning in this way. As someone said, we don't just fall into adultery; we first have to wade out into it in small steps.

If we think through the results ahead of time, however, visualizing what that sin will bring, it helps us to clarify the evil early on in the temptation process and to strengthen our conviction to avoid it.

Here's what I wrote in my journal:

If I commit adultery, it will damage my relationship:

with God (He will be grieved, I will be shamed, and my usefulness will be curtailed),

with myself (How could I forgive myself!!!???),

with my wife (she will feel betrayed),

with my sons (How could they trust me again? What would my example do to them?),

with my teammates (I would shock and hurt them, be a terrible example),

with my disciples (I would destroy their trust in me, give them an excuse to sin),

with my family at home (discouraging believers, ruining testimony to unbelievers),

with all those I've shared Christ with (negating what I've said),

with my supporting churches (discouraging them, losing support),

with my mission agency (I would be a terrible example and would have to resign),

with my pastor friends (giving discouragement and a bad example).

The list goes on, but this is enough to make me want to stay as far away as possible from anything that will lead me into adultery! Just the results in the first four relationships (with God, myself, my wife, and my sons) are enough to put up a high wall against the desire for using some other woman for my personal enjoyment. It is chilling to think that the pursuit of personal pleasure could negatively affect so many relationships!

I have had opportunity to use this perspective. Most every semester that I taught in the university in our Middle Eastern country, there has been at least one woman — student or teacher — who would begin pursuing me. It was quite thrilling to have a good-looking woman after me (although I'm sure they were more after my passport than me!).

However, remembering where this sin could lead and the terrible possible outcomes, the first thing I would do was to tell my wife about it. That brought everything out in the open. Secret thoughts and desires are powerful when kept under cover, but properly confessed thoughts and desires lose a lot of their hold over you. Then I would bring my wife to class with me. My pursuer usually quickly got the point that she didn't stand a chance against my wife and pulled back.

As an aside, I must add here that not every wife would have the strength to deal with such a situation. For some husbands, confiding in a male friend may be the best thing to do rather than telling your wife.

Discerning ahead is a preparation you can do with any sin, and we should implement it, especially with those sins to which we are more naturally prone. We'll talk more about this point in chapter 23, on standing against the wiles of the devil.

May God give you wisdom as you stand in the battle!

Dave's New Insights

"This chapter sure gave me some new understanding!" exclaimed Dave. "I had never thought about confessing ahead."

"You are right," replied Jack, "this was a new concept to me, too. Have you tried it out?"

"Yes," said Dave. "The list of my sins I'd made in my journal for chapter 18 on confessing in layers gave me a good start on this." He flipped open his journal, "Here they are: anger, self-centeredness, selfishness, pride, unbelief, and rebellion. I used this to 'confess ahead' a couple of times this week, and it was helpful."

"In what way?" asked Jack.

"Well, it prepared me for a difficult encounter I had on Wednesday. One of my classmates wanted help from me with a class, but I wasn't able to meet him at the time he wanted, so he became angry and said some hurtful things. I felt my own anger rising, but the Spirit reminded me of what I'd confessed ahead in the morning, and I was able to back down from defending myself and my pride. And remembering how self-centered I am helped me to view my friend differently, not as my adversary, but as a needy person."

"So," said Jack, "you think that confessing ahead made you more aware of what was happening?"

"Definitely," replied Dave. "And as the book says, the Lord answered my prayer and made me more sensitive to what the Spirit had to say so I could avoid falling into my own weaknesses."

CONFESSION

"I'm glad to hear that you are willing to put these truths into practice right away," said Jack. "One of the worst things we can do is to take information like this and store it in our 'nice and interesting' file, but never use it."

Dave nodded and asked, "How much should I read for next time?"

"I think chapters 19 and 20 will be enough to read and practice," replied Jack.

Study Guide questions for Chapter 18: "Confessing Ahead of Time"

1. What is confessing ahead? (142)
2. What are the four ways it can help you? (142)
3. How can you practice confessing ahead? (143-144)
4. What kind of fruit does confessing ahead bring? (144-146)
5. What is discerning ahead? (147)
6. How do you do this? (147-149)
7. How will you use confessing ahead and discerning ahead in your life?

Part 5

Lifting Our Souls

Truth #6: Lifting Our Souls to God Brings Insight, Direction and Joy

CHAPTER 19

Using Meditation and Journaling

Some days don't go well. We end up frustrated, grumpy, and unpleasant. Our attitudes, words, and actions are anything but glorifying to the Lord. We know this is wrong, but somehow we seem stuck in our emotions. How do we handle such situations in a godly way?

Psalm 143 provides us with guidance in the form of two measures, both in verse 8. These give us direction in preparing for and handling our sinful tendencies. The first measure is, "Let the morning bring me word of your unfailing love, *for* I have put my trust in you." Note the "for," which shows the connection between the two. Trusting God opens the way for hearing/thinking/perceiving by faith God's unfailing love.

The question is, Do I wake up thinking of God's unfailing love? Or do I wake up worried and unhappy or just "blah"? Or am I just thinking about what I'm going to do today without giving a thought to God's love for me?

If I am not thinking about God's love, it could indicate that I am not putting my trust in God. So my unsettledness, worry, or focus on the present are all signs that I need to come back to God, surrender all to Him, and trust Him.

Practically, this means I need to spend time worshipping God so I can remember how trustworthy He is! In fact, we could say that such unsettledness, worry, and temporal focus are all symptoms of "worship deprivation"!

The second measure in verse 8 is the core of what we want to look at: "Show me the way I should go, *for* to you I lift up my soul." Note again the connector "for," which makes it clear that David expects the Lord to respond to his uplifted soul. Here the question is, Are we getting guidance when we need it? If we have not lived up to the first measure, we probably will not do well on the second one either! If I am not trusting God, it is unlikely that I would come and be totally open with Him; I won't be trusting Him to guide me into what is best.

The action that David here sees as opening the way for God to give guidance is *lifting his soul to God.* Nice phrase — but what does it mean? How do you do it? It took some meditation and research for me to get some understanding of it.

What It Looks Like

Our soul consists of our mind, our will, and our emotions. Therefore, lifting my soul to God means, I believe, telling Him what I am thinking, wanting, and feeling. Once my thoughts, wants, and feelings are out in the open, I can examine them in the light of God's Word and surrender to His truth. That is, lifting our soul to God is:

> honestly telling Him what's
> > on my mind — what I'm thinking,
> > in my will — what I'm wanting, and
> > in my emotions — what I'm feeling;
> then processing all this,
> leading to surrender.

This lifting up calls for genuine transparency before God, something we should be developing as we practice worship and confession. Lifting our souls to God is an extension of these two privileges.

Psalm 86:4-5 gives us encouragement in this. "Bring joy to your servant, for to you, O Lord, I lift up my soul. You are *forgiving and good,* O Lord, *abounding in love to all who call to you.*"

I like the New King James rendition even better: "Rejoice the soul of Your servant, for to You, O Lord, I lift up my soul. For You, Lord, are *good,* and *ready to forgive,* and *abundant in mercy* to all those who call upon You."

God's warm, loving character woos us to transparency: "For You, Lord, are good, and ready to forgive." I don't have to fear His condemnation when I am honest with Him. He knows it all anyway, and He is going to be merciful with me. He is ready and eager to forgive as I am open and honest before Him.

I'm sure you can see how this ties in with worship: as we worship God and see His character more fully, then we are going to trust Him more and be more open with Him! Note also that God encourages us to lift our souls to Him by promising that He will bring joy to us: "Rejoice the soul of Your servant, for to You, O Lord, I lift my soul."

King David did a lot of "lifting of His soul" to God in the Psalms. Let's look at another example, Psalm 43, by an unnamed psalmist, possibly David.

> [1]Vindicate me, O God,
> > and plead my cause against an ungodly nation;
> > rescue me from deceitful and wicked men.

Use Meditation and Journaling

Here we have the psalmist describing a desperate situation, telling God what he wants: vindication, defense, and rescuing. This is lifting his will to God.

²You are God my stronghold.
   Why have you rejected me?

Here the psalmist expresses his viewpoint: it looks to him like God has left him. This is lifting to God his thoughts.

Why must I go about mourning,
   oppressed by the enemy?

Here the writer is pouring out his heart, telling God how he feels. Has God rejected him? Where is God's help? Why must he mourn and feel oppressed? This is lifting his emotions to God. The psalmist, however, does not stop with telling how he feels.

³Send forth your light and your truth,
   let them guide me;
let them bring me to your holy mountain,
   to the place where you dwell.

In this verse the author is beginning to process his feelings, thoughts, and wants. He asks for God's input, His light and truth, to bring him back to a proper focus, leading to proper action:

⁴Then will I go to the altar of God,
   to God, my joy and my delight.
I will praise you with the harp,
   O God, my God.

The writer has begun to focus on God rather than his problems, remembering that his joy comes from God, not his circumstances. His perspective is changing, and it leads him to worship.

Note the warmth of the last line, "O God, *my* God." Then the last verse brings our author to a new level.

⁵Why are you downcast, O my soul?
   Why so disturbed within me?
Put your hope in God,
   for I will yet praise him,
   my Savior and my God.

The author is still in trouble, but he has been encouraged, he's gotten new perspective, he is able to see beyond the moment to what God, His Savior, will do. He has been given joy and guidance.

Psalm 43 has been a great help to me, leading me in lifting my soul to God. In one situation, after being arrested several times, being put on trial for sharing my faith, and finally acquitted, the police came again to my door to tell me that I was being put on trial for sending Christian propaganda into a city in the northern part of the country. Not true, for I'd had nothing to do with the gospel letters sent to the residents there.

The trial was going to take place in a little town way in the north of the country, where the people were conservative and prejudiced against Christians. Two other workers had recently been put on trial in the area and, instead of being released until the next hearing, had spent three months in prison waiting for the second trial date.

I asked several others to make the trip with me, but no one, other than my wife, wanted to risk getting put into prison with me! I thanked my wife for her courage but told her that someone had to be around to take care of the kids. So I went alone.

Just a week earlier I'd memorized Psalm 43 and was very glad to be able to meditate on it during the all-night bus trip up to this little town. I certainly was feeling abandoned and needed God to plead my cause! Although I felt adrift, I was encouraged to "put my hope in God," remembering that I would be able, in the end, praise Him who is "my Savior and my God."

The beginning of the court hearing was not too promising, as it took the officials half an hour to get my name and passport information straight! Then they asked me about the letters they had received complaints about. I told them firmly that they were not from me, that I had nothing to do with them, that the address given on the letters was not mine.

After listening to me, the judge said, "Well, that doesn't matter. We are going to try you on the basis of whether it is illegal to send such letters into the country or not. If it is illegal, you will go to prison!"

Then something happened that showed me God was delivering me from deceitful and wicked men. The judge said, "We will send this case to a specialist in the capital. Whatever he says will decide the case." Then he named the specialist — a law professor who just happened to be a friend of mine! That was a little gift from God, reminding me to trust Him.

My friend did not defend me. He simply stated what the law said about this, that such mailings were perfectly legal. And I was acquitted!

It was a pretty stressful way to learn about lifting my soul to God. And it was followed immediately by another chance to trust God, for the day after I returned to the capital from this trial, the police came at midnight and arrested me again on other false charges, keeping me in jail for a week.

The encouragement from meditating on Psalm 43 and lifting my soul continued through this time too, which is a whole other story. The point is that lifting my soul to God, along with the psalmist in Psalm 43, turned these experiences into victories for God and chances to grow for me.

Christ's Example

The most powerful biblical demonstration of lifting one's soul to God is Christ's prayer in the garden.

> "Father, if you are willing, take this cup from me; yet not my will, but yours be done." ... And being in anguish, he prayed more earnestly, and his sweat was like drops of blood falling to the ground. (Luke 22:42, 44)

Jesus was totally honest with His Father, telling Him that He really didn't want to go through what was before Him, but then He surrendered. And Jesus' desires to avoid the coming suffering were so strong that He had to work through them three times!

None of us will ever go through anything as intense as Jesus did. His example, though, shows us that whatever our circumstances are, we can lift our souls to God, come to surrender, and be given the grace needed to walk in obedience through any situation.

Lifting My Soul through Journaling

One effective way of lifting my soul to God is through journaling. My journal is not a diary that I write in every day but a book to record thoughts, ideas, prayers, worship, and poems, a place to tell God what I'm thinking, feeling, and wanting.

I often find that my thoughts and emotions get jumbled up inside my head. I can't see the whole picture in order to make a good decision. It feels like the TV screen in my mind is too small to show me the whole scene. But when I get it all out on paper (or on my computer screen), writing before God and myself what I'm thinking, feeling, and wanting, then I can see more clearly what's going on.

It also helps to get things out that otherwise would be buried in my subconscious, making it possible to evaluate everything in the light of Scripture. This brings guidance and joy.

It's almost like magic the way "lifting my soul to God" brings peace and resolution to my turmoil, minor or major. Answers come, insights are given, understanding wells up. It is not magic, of course — it's the Holy Spirit rejoicing in working hand in hand with us to give the guidance and joy He has promised.

It also is amazing how little things can trip me up. They are just below the surface of my life, things I'd kind of pushed down and ignored, but they have power to hurt me. Journaling has helped to bring them out, to clarify things so I can process them. That really helps to settle my mind and emotions.

For instance, one night I woke up at 3:00 A.M. really angry. "What do I have to be angry about?" I wondered. Not having an answer, I got up, found my journal, and began to write. I told the Lord how I was feeling, and in the process, out came the names of nine people I was angry with.

The first was my doctor, whom I had visited the day before. I had asked him an informed, intelligent question; his response was a put-down. I shrugged it off as his problem with insecurity and went on through my day. I evidently internalized the put-down, however, and it later popped out in my sleep. I forgave him and the other people who came up — and then slept like a baby!

If I hadn't lifted my soul to God, I think I would have lain awake the rest of the night and would have been tired and grumpy the next day, which is just what Satan would have liked!

I should add that I use my journal for this only as often as is necessary. Sometimes I will go for a week without writing anything. Sometimes I write every day or several times a day. It depends on whether I am struggling with something or working on learning or responding to inspiration. Often I write worship prayers, record thoughts and insights, or enter quotes that strike me.

Another important function the journal plays is helping me to consolidate things God is teaching me. I often take time during or after my quiet time to write insights from studying the Word, or from events that have happened recently.

Sharing the Fruit

There is a saying that "impression without expression causes depression." If we don't take the time to express our impressions from an event or a series of happenings, then our emotions and thoughts can be weighed down by all the images and emotions.

It has been my practice for the last thirty years to write a prayer letter each month for friends who intercede for us. The first section is always a summary of what God has been doing in my life.

In the beginning I did not realize how important writing this prayer letter was for me, but I now understand that it has been a kind of therapy, a way of giving expression to my impressions. This practice has helped me to "tie up" these events by verbalizing the insights God has given me through them. Then I could put these lessons on the shelf, so to speak, and have them ready to use again myself or share them with others. And of course the prayer letters then passed these insights along to those who read them.

A Demonstration

Let me give you an example from my journal

> Lord, I am disturbed by my impatience, my immaturity, my pride and anger. I have, on one hand, sought from my wife the security, significance, consistency, and affirmation that only you can give. Yet, I am not taking up your grace, it seems. I am not getting up the shield of faith. I am walking in my own strength. I am struggling for significance, unwilling to let go and rest in you, it seems.
>
> Lord, help me to let you rule, reign, right things.
>
> I am also disturbed by my lack of passion for you. Things are ho-hum. I think more about doing than being with you. Lord help me back to my first love. Help me to walk with you in love, in surrender, in right balance. I am weak, self-centered, lazy, undisciplined, Lord. Forgive me.

The next day I wrote,

> Thank you, Lord, that in your wisdom and grace you work to open us and help us grow. Thank you for helping me face my pride and stubbornness and deal with them. . . . I praise you for the joy of knowing you.

Here you can see the outcome of lifting my soul to God: a sense of God's guidance and thankfulness leading to joy.

Another Example of Journaling

Distressed by what was a wrong decision on my part, journaling brought perspective, peace, and healing.

> Last night I should have gone to the Bible study, but I was lazy, wanted to get to bed early, wanted to rest. But even though I went to bed early, still I did not rest. Forgive me, Lord, for not following through; it is possible I

could have given Rudy some good input at the study, but that's only a "what if" statement; I must not dwell on it.

Also there is the fact that I did not open my heart to you much yesterday, going from one task to the next, not "checking in" with you. Thank you for your patience and forgiveness in that. Help me today, Lord, to be open at each step, listening to your leading.

Praise you, Lord, that in the midst of my conflicting thoughts and swirling emotions, you stand firm, sure, right, good, willing and able to forgive, to transform, to move us on to the next thing. I praise you for this opportunity to look to you in my weakness, uncertainty, and failure; to trust you and your love; to let go of my self-accusation, failure, and laziness. Thank you that I can hold on to your forgiveness, love, and faithfulness and rise above my wrong decision so I can live for and with you today.

Thank you that I don't have to earn back the right to walk with you, nor do I need to punish myself or be on probation. Praise you, Lord Jesus, that your death and resurrection are far more than enough to cleanse and transform me. I praise you for the opportunity to believe, to give thanks, to praise in the midst of weakness, failure, and uncertainty, for you are powerful, righteous, and omniscient! Glory be to you!

As the Great Forgiver, certainly you are "the Mighty One of Jacob" exalted in Psalm 132:2, 5. What a gracious and forgiving God you are, to call yourself by the name of a deceiver, a cheat, and a rebel! Jacob rejected your faithfulness, shamelessly bargained with you, manipulated others, lied and deceived, favored one wife over another, loved some of his children, tolerated others, was a terrible father, shrank from responsibility, spoiled some sons, deeply wounded others, was unrepentantly self-absorbed, and passed on a legacy of poor parenting to his children. And you are willing to call yourself the God of Jacob!

That means you are also pleased to be my God—for like Jacob, in my natural self there dwells no good thing; I am no better than him. You are pleased to call me by name; to forgive, accept, and transform; to work with me to the end, as you did with Jacob. And since you are the "Mighty One," your resources of patience, wisdom, strength, creativity, knowledge, and love are infinite, boundless, ever-flowing. I praise you that in you there is forgiveness, from you flows forgiveness, and in your forgiveness I can forgive myself.

Here you can see how journaling led to looking at the Word (Psalm 132), looking at God, and coming to a release of my self-accusation and discouragement.

Use Meditation and Journaling

Getting Rid of "Junk Stress"

In lifting my soul to God, one thing He showed me was that I was constantly creating "junk stress" for myself. Stress is an inner response to outward stimuli. Two people in exactly the same situation can have exactly opposite responses. Two men run to cross the street, but the light turns red before they reach the curb. As one waits, he looks at his watch, taps his foot, and figits with his briefcase, obviously stressed out. The other man looks around, comments to himself on an interesting car or on progress at a construction site, and looks relaxed. The difference is the inner response.

I used to be more like the first man, stressing about making it through a traffic light, about getting everything done, about accomplishing one more thing before going home, about being late to meetings, and so forth. But in lifting my soul to the light of God's presence, it became clear how this stress not only was unnecessary but stemmed from wrong values, greed to do more and more, doubt about God's ability to order things, and fear of man. I was squandering energy, time, and brainpower.

Confessing these wrong, sinful attitudes and actions led to the ability to think more clearly. I could then practice "letting go" of what is temporal, "holding on" to what is eternal, and "rising above" the stress I'd so competently manufactured for myself.

Lifting our souls is like letting God shine the flashlight of His wisdom down inside to show us what needs to be cleaned out. This is sometimes painful, but it's always good!

Study Guide questions for Chapter 19: "Using Meditation and Journaling"

1. What is "lifting my soul to God?" (155)
2. What are the three aspects of my soul that I should lift to God? (155)
3. How did Jesus lift His soul to the Father? (158)
4. Why is it good to lift our souls through journaling and how do we do it? (158-159)
5. How does lifting our souls in journaling equip us to help others? (159-160)
6. What is "junk stress" and how can I get rid of it? (160-161)
7. What difference will this chapter make in my life?

CHAPTER 20

Transparency

For many of us, it is difficult to be transparently honest about our thoughts, feelings, and wants. We daily practice the art of hiding them from those around us and, often, from ourselves. So how do we develop the habit of being truthful and open with God and ourselves, and then others?

Simply put, transparency flows out of worship. As we discussed earlier, if we are spending time in the light of God's presence, we will be seeing our sins and confessing them. Then, as we learn to be transparent with God and ourselves, it is easier to be transparent with others. We can learn to reject the motive of making ourselves look good (even to ourselves!) or of protecting our reputation. Instead, we can replace this negative motive with that of wanting to please God and help those around us grow.

The Example of the Psalms

Such transparency is definitely biblical. Take a look at Psalm 73 and notice the transparency of Asaph, the author. He begins by complaining to God about how he's trying to live a righteous life and is getting nowhere, while the evil get rich and live a life of comfort.

> For I envied the arrogant
>   when I saw the prosperity of the wicked.
> They have no struggles;
>   their bodies are healthy and strong.
> They are free from the burdens common to man;
>   they are not plagued by human ills.
> Therefore pride is their necklace;
>   they clothe themselves with violence.
>   (vv. 3-6)

And Asaph continues to complain through the next six verses. Then in verses 13 and 14 he says,

> Surely in vain have I kept my heart pure;
>   in vain have I washed my hands in innocence.

Transparency

> All day long I have been plagued;
>   I have been punished every morning.

Asaph is being very transparent here, likely not knowing that he will provide a model for countless others in being honest before God. In verses 16 and 17 he continues.

> When I tried to understand all this,
>   it was oppressive to me . . .

Humanly speaking, it is hard to make sense out of the injustice and seeming randomness of life. It is oppressive, discouraging, depressing. Fortunately, Asaph doesn't stop here but goes on:

> . . . *till* I entered the sanctuary of God;
>   then I understood their final destiny.

The little word "till" signals the switch in Asaph's thinking. When he entered God's presence in the temple (like us coming into God's presence in worship), then the Lord seems to have given His view of the matter, which is a long-range perspective. Asaph had been thinking only about the short-term outcomes, not about where these evil people would be spending eternity.

In verse 22 we come to even more transparency.

> When my heart was grieved
>   and my spirit embittered,
> I was senseless and ignorant;
>   I was a brute beast before you.

Asaph is being pretty blunt about himself here: "senseless and ignorant," and "a brute beast" — and he is correct!

Then in verses 23-25 we see the result of Asaph transparently lifting his soul to God: new insight into God's faithfulness and love; new higher, godly desires; and new commitment to follow the Lord.

> Yet I am always with you;
>   you hold me by my right hand.
> You guide me with your counsel,
>   and afterward you will take me into glory.
> Whom have I in heaven but you?
>   And earth has nothing I desire besides you.

Asaph shows us both how lifting one's soul is done and the rich outcome he receives: a renewed first love for God, a deepened eternal perspective, and freedom from the snares of this life.

This psalm has been of great comfort to me over the years, and certainly to many, many people over the centuries. If Asaph had held back and hidden his struggles, think about how much he would have lost and how much we would have missed!

Caution

Let me end with a word of caution. We do need to be wise in what we share in our transparency and with whom we share it. Our journal needs no editing — we should be absolutely open before God. But beyond that, we need to be careful. What I may share in a men's accountability group will be different from what I share in a mixed crowd or with children.

It is important for you to know that we will get some flak if we share openly. People have different ideas of how transparent one should be, and some will be threatened by our openness. One time I wrote a prayer letter circulated to a limited number of people telling of how I was being pursued by a good-looking woman teaching at the university where I was working. I asked for strength, wisdom, and protection.

I got a letter back from another missionary telling me that I shouldn't write such things in my prayer letter! His view of discretion, however, would result in less prayer, but I needed help. Furthermore, being open like that helped to hold me accountable!

Here again, we must follow God rather than men, for He is the One who knows all and guides in all.

A Benefit of Lifting Our Souls: Greater Obedience

When lifting our souls to God, we may not get immediate answers or relief, but in His time He will give the answers we need — and the answer may come as a new challenge to apply what we already know to be true.

Here's an example from an entry in my journal:

> Praise be to you, O Lord, for how you are working in my life, pointing out my negative and critical thoughts (although I don't enjoy it when you use my wife to point them out, especially in public, but must thank you for it anyway). Praise you that you are more interested in our sanctification than in our comfort.

Transparency

  Thank you for the thought that no one can actually snatch away my significance or dignity or joy. I may give them to others, surrender them, but don't need to because they are dependent on you, not on my human feelings.
  Lord, guide me today in living for you, in joining you in what you're doing.

Now, let's see how God answers my prayer for guidance by giving me an opportunity to practice thinking truth.

  Later the same day. Lord I am angry with my friend because of the double standard I perceive: he feels free to point out my sins and mistakes, but if I point out his, he often comes back with "You're competing!" Maybe I am, but the right response, a more godly response, would be, "You may be competing, but you are right!" That's what I'd like to hear but am not getting. But, Lord, as you have forgiven me, so I forgive him. Help me to have your perspective on this. I praise you for it all.

As you can see, my ongoing struggle for significance and security, along with my failure to find it in the world around me, drives me more and more into the truth of God's Word and into the freedom He has for us.

Here's another example, this time from a prayer letter, showing how God used the lifting of my soul and meditation on His Word to consolidate the lessons He'd been teaching me and to bring me out of a difficult situation.

  Dear Friends
  Superficially everything seems to be going well, but underneath, things have been in secret turmoil. The major hint is that I've been waking up at 2:00 A.M. and can't get back to sleep for 2 or 3 hours. Although this is a great time to pray and do other things (I'm writing this at 3:00 A.M.), a few nights of this makes one really tired.
  The cause of this insomnia seems to be having a lot of irons in the fire while the fire is going out! On a number of fronts things are not going as I'd like: the Light Church is experiencing only mediocre progress; some of our leaders are being tested in dangerous ways (tempted to marry unbelievers); plans for our multi-church Easter celebration are stymied by lack of a venue and vacillation in the commitment of our closest partner; the coffee business is not expanding, held up by delays in production of our coffee-cup-top filter; advertisements for our tours have brought in zero results; cash flow is a problem; the nationwide men's conference, for which I am primarily responsible, is looking like it may bomb out with low attendance; there are a number of projects which aren't getting sufficient attention from me because of time crunches. And the list goes on.

In all this, the Lord has reminded me of the need to constantly lift my soul to Him, journaling regularly.... Tonight as I was meditating on Scripture trying to get back to sleep, Ps. 37:4 came up: "Delight yourself also in the LORD and he will give you the desires of your heart." With that, the light came on! The deeper cause of my sleeplessness jumped out at me: my focus has been on these events and desires, not on God.

I was subtly trying to draw my delight from things going well, not from God Himself. This is virtually putting the cart before the horse, actually preventing things from going well! So now I am in the process of unhitching the horse and reharnessing it in front of the cart: deliberately finding my delight in God, in His character, in His revealed Word while giving up my desire to see each of these things go my way. May He work what is best in each one, bringing glory to Himself, whether that be through what I consider failure or through it going well. That releases me from a whole unnecessary load and will make me easier to live with!

"May all those who seek you rejoice and be glad in *you*" Ps. 40:16.

The struggles in our souls can be deceptive and confusing at time. The root causes can be hidden so that only God in His grace can reveal them to us as we cooperate with Him in lifting our souls and meditating. Here's an example of how He does this, as written in another prayer letter.

Dear Friends,

From all outward appearances it had been a good day: a couple of positive discipleship lessons, business goals accomplished, and a warm and productive team meeting. However, inside I was in turmoil: dissatisfaction, anger, jealousy, and negativeness swirled around in my heart.

As soon as we got home from the team meeting, I got out my journal and began to write about what I was feeling, lifting my soul to God. A string of emotions poured out on the page where I could look at them more objectively and begin to examine them in the light of Scripture.

The last few weeks Psalm 27 has been my springboard for worship: "The LORD is my light and my salvation — whom shall I fear?" God is the One who brings light into our darkness, He illuminates our way, showing us what is causing us to stumble; He shows us the next step. Then, as we let Him, He moves to save us from what is threatening us.

In this case what was threatening me was my old self. After letting God shine the light of His Spirit down into my soul, what emerged as the root of all the turmoil was, surprise (!), my desire to be significant; after our recent return to the field, I was having trouble fitting into things again.

This uncertainty was manifested by my craving to have control over the events and people around me, to be important because I was in charge. This desire is ungodly and destructive. Having control of everything is, of course, an impossible goal, so I ended up frustrated and angry.

Transparency

Having shown me the source, God then led me to confess my unbelief and rebellion against the truth, to reject this desire to be important through power, and to surrender to the Word. He has already given me all the significance anyone could ever desire: created in the image of God, chosen before the foundation of the world, redeemed by the blood of the Lamb, adopted into the family of God. I needed to start thinking and acting like who I am in Him!

Another factor in this is that we were still in jet lag and had not recovered from a very intense one-month trip. Low emotional and physical resources can lead to a skewed view of things. So after dealing with the root cause, I took the evening off and did some relaxing and profitable reading before going to bed early.

Life is so complex from our viewpoint, while it can be quite simple when we look at it from God's perspective. He gives light from His Word and Spirit. We need to take the time to look, listen, and obey.

Let's finish in prayer.

> *Lord God, Creator and Sustainer of all, you know the most secret thoughts and desires of our hearts. You know our thoughts before they are formed. There is nothing hidden from you, and for this we praise you. We thank you, heavenly Father, that you delight in our coming to you in transparency, telling you what we really are thinking, wanting, and feeling, for then you can guide us in working these through, bringing us to a new and deeper surrender to you. Help us, Father, to frequently admit our need of your help by lifting our souls to you. Amen.*

Practice with Jack and Dave in Journaling

"How is it going with lifting your soul to God through journaling?" asked Jack.

Dave pulled his journal out of his backpack and flipped it open to his last entry. "Here, take a look," he said.

Jack took the notebook and read, "Lord, I am unhappy with the way things went this morning. I was tired, the toaster didn't work, I'd forgotten to iron my shirt, and because I was tired and got up late, I was behind schedule. I felt frustrated, impatient, angry. In fact, I was angry at you for allowing these things into my life. I was angry at myself for forgetting to iron my shirt and for not being more disciplined in getting to bed earlier the night before. I wanted things to go smoothly, and these little bumps in the road really upset me — or better put, revealed more of my self-centeredness."

Jack continued reading: "Forgive me, Lord, for being angry with you. It shows that I'm not trusting you, not thinking about your goodness, but

LIFTING OUR SOULS

about my comfort. Forgive me for not praising you for these irritations. Really, how important are these things anyway, especially compared to what people living in China suffer for their faith, or in Somalia or countless other places in the world? I have it really good, and here I am complaining! Forgive me for my unthankfulness."

As Jack handed the journal back to him, Dave commented, "It was really freeing to write those things out. It was like putting down a load I was carrying. It really brought some joy back to me!"

"You've certainly got the idea, Dave," said Jack. "God wants freedom for us from the burdens we carry unnecessarily. The statement that we 'carry baggage from the past' is really correct. And with the help of journaling, we can lay aside those unnecessary hindrances one at a time."

"That makes me excited about how God is going to use this in my life!" said Dave.

Jack smiled. "Remember that, Dave, the next time you don't feel like taking the trouble to lift your soul to God."

Study Guide questions for Chapter 20: "Transparency"

1. How do we learn to be transparent? (162)
2. How does "lifting our souls to God" help in transparency? (162-164)
3. How should we be careful in our transparency? (164)
4. How does lifting our souls transparently help us grow in obedience? (164-166)
5. What will now change in your life?

Part 6

Filling with the Holy Spirit

Truth #7: The Filling of the Spirit Brings Humility and Power

CHAPTER 21

How to Be Filled

A fourth basic spiritual discipline, beside worship, confession, and lifting our souls, is being filled with the Spirit. If we neglect this discipline, we will have times when we feel totally without help, just like in figure 21.1.

Fig. 21.1. Out of gas!

I admit that I sometimes feel this way in life: out of gas, out of strength, pushing everything uphill. This is also what it's like trying to live for Christ without the filling of the Spirit. We have been give a beautiful, powerful car (our new life in Christ, including a new nature, gifts, meaning in life, direction), but if we try to get somewhere by pushing it (to live and serve Him in our own strength, without the filling of the Spirit), we aren't going to get very far.

Trying to push our life, our family, our ministry, and our work ahead in our own very small strength will bring little lasting results — and lots of frustration and exhaustion. We all would say "Of course!" to that. But how often I find myself doing things in my own strength!

Jesus talked about the need for us to have His power when He said, "I am the vine; you are the branches. If a man remains in me and I in him, he will bear much fruit; *apart from me you can do nothing*" (John 15:5).

Jesus' words here should ring in our ears everyday: "apart from me you can do nothing." In order to do anything of lasting significance, we need His power, which comes through abiding in Him. Part of abiding is being filled with the Holy Spirit.

Let the Spirit Guide

I've heard it said that being filled with the Spirit is not like filling a bottle with a liquid but more like letting the Spirit sit in the driver's seat of your life. Upon reflection, however, I would say that this picture is not quite right either.

The Holy Spirit wants to be our Navigator, telling us when and where to turn, how fast or how slow to go. God still lets us sit behind the steering wheel of our life, making the actual decisions of which way to turn and when to step on the brake and the gas — He intends, though, that we make these decisions at the direction of the Spirit.

He wants us to work in cooperation with the Spirit. He wants us to obey out of love for Him. Since the Spirit is the Navigator, not the driver of our life, it is possible for us to make willful, wrong decisions that bring pain, problems, and probation. Or we can listen to and obey the Spirit as He applies the Word or prompts us.

This Navigator/driver arrangement shows the great heart of God. He does not force us to obey, and when we disobey, He goes with us in the mess we are about to make. He never abandons us but is willing to suffer the pain that our self-created accidents bring Him as He sees us needlessly sidetracked and hurting. He is faithful to His promises, No matter what we may do, while He lets us suffer the consequences of our refusal to obey the Navigator, He does so that we might come to ourselves and submit again.

What hinders us from having a Spirit-filled, Spirit-guided life? Scripture mentions two things that prevent us from being filled with the Spirit. First, according to Ephesians 4:30 we should not *grieve the Spirit*. We grieve Him by consciously choosing to sin.

Second, in 1 Thessalonians 5:19 we are commanded not to *put out the Spirit's fire.* In the words of the King James Version, "Quench not the Spirit!" To quench the Spirit means to resist His leading. When the Spirit prompts us to do something, like obey a portion of Scripture, witness to someone, say a kind word, or help others and then we don't obey, we have quenched Him.

So grieving the Spirit means we disobey what we know, while quenching means we don't follow His prompting. When we continually refuse to obey Him, He withdraws and waits for us to "come to ourselves."

The Spirit will allow the natural consequences of bad decisions to bring difficulty and pressure to bear on us. And then if we still don't respond, He will send someone to confront us.

Make Your Choice

God leaves the decision to us of whether we will be filled with the Spirit. Ephesians 5:18 says, "Do not get drunk on wine, which leads to debauchery. Instead, be filled with the Spirit."

There are two important points in this verse. *First,* getting drunk is a choice, as is being filled with the Spirit — neither happens automatically.

An important distinction here is that being filled is different from having the Holy Spirit come to dwell in us. Every believer receives the Holy Spirit when he or she is born again. Romans 8:9 tells us, "If anyone does not have the Spirit of Christ, he does not belong to Christ."

In contrast to our one-time experience of being baptized by the Spirit into Christ at conversion, being filled with the Spirit requires ongoing cooperation on our part and occurs over and over again. The word translated "be filled" in Ephesians 5:18 contains the idea of continual fillings. This need for ongoing cooperation on our part is true of so much of the spiritual life: God provides, but He gives us a critical part in the process. We must chose to obey both these commands: "Do not get drunk" and "be filled with the Spirit."

The *second* point is that being filled with the Spirit will lead away from what is wrong (debauchery) and will result in a changed life. Perhaps better put, it leads to a continually changing life, going from good to better as the Spirit works in us and we cooperate. This can be clearly seen in the series of commands that follow Ephesians 5:18, all of them having to do with how to have godly relationships.

To use a simple illustration: being filled with the Holy Spirit is like being a sunflower that is nurtured, fertilized, and watered properly, and that gets enough sunlight. The outcome is a plant with strength, lushness, productivity, and beauty. Failure to be filled with the Spirit is like being a sunflower in poor soil, without any fertilizer, not having sufficient water or enough sun. The outcome is a weaker, smaller, and far less fruitful flower. Both are sunflowers (that is, both are believers), but only one is taking the power provided — and the difference shows.

The "How to" of Being Filled

To be filled is not complex. It requires just two things from a believer: confession/renunciation of known sin and then asking God for the filling of His Spirit.

Each morning in my quiet time, following worship, I pray through putting on the armor. As part of "being strong in him" (Eph. 6:10), I spend time in confession. After that I ask for the filling of the Spirit.

In fact, I don't just ask that the Spirit will fill me, but that He will overflow from me into the lives of others around me, so that when they meet me, they will meet Him too. I ask Him to be the Navigator and Captain of my life. Then I go on to surrender my day to Him, praying through all that I know will happen, asking Him to go before me, to guide and direct. This is submitting to the Spirit's lead, surrendering to Him the right to navigate the "car" that is my life.

I well know that after my quiet time I am going to sin, hopefully unintentionally. When I become aware of my sin, I need to confess and again ask for the filling of the Spirit, surrendering to Him again the right to navigate my life. Then He can go on to empower and lead, for the glory of Christ.

Here we see again how these different disciplines we are looking at one at a time are actually all intertwined. Worship leads to confession, which leads to surrender, which leads to being filled with the Spirit and transformation.

Power from the Spirit

How is the power of the Spirit manifested in us when we are filled? In Ephesians 3:14-19 Paul prays for the believers in Ephesus, asking for power for three specific outcomes.

First, "I pray that out of his glorious riches he [God] may strengthen you with *power* through his Spirit in your inner being, *so that Christ may dwell in your hearts through faith*" (vv. 16-17a).

This power Paul is asking for is as great as God's glorious riches, which are immeasurable. And the purpose of the power is to change us from within, to make us grow in faith so Christ can dwell more widely, deeply, and powerfully in our hearts. This is something I pray for myself and others each day.

Nothing outwardly spectacular or even noticeable may happen when we receive this power, but over time what the Spirit accomplishes in us will be stunning. As we become people of greater and greater faith, it will result in more and more praise, trust, and obedience, with more glory going to God.

Second, the passage goes on to say, "And I pray that you, being rooted and established in love, may have *power,* together with all the saints, *to grasp* how wide and long and high and deep is the love of Christ, and *to know* this love that surpasses knowledge" (vv. 17b-19a).

Look at figure 21.2, which is an attempt to display the greatness of God's love.

How to Be Filled

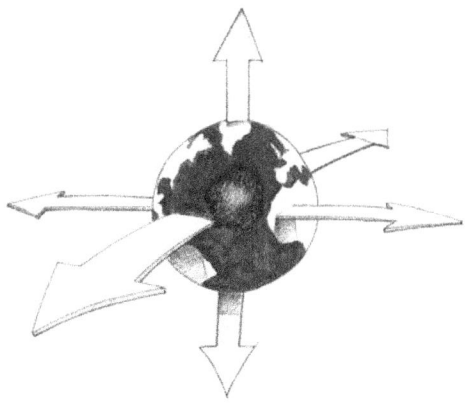

Fig. 21.2. The greatness of God's love

God's love is:

>immensely *long* — it goes from eternity to eternity;
>incredibly *wide* — as wide as the universe and beyond;
>incomprehensibly *high* — as high as the heavens; and
>immeasurably *deep* — as deep as the depth of the universe.

The whole earth is swathed in His love; we move in it, breath it, sleep in it. We can never be separated from it. There is nowhere we can go in this universe that will bring us outside of the love of Christ.

Now these are nice words, but the reality of them is way beyond what our intellect can comprehend ("to know this love that *surpasses knowledge*"). An intellectual grasp is not enough, we need to know it spiritually, volitionally, emotionally, experientially, and any other way possible; to do this we need the Spirit's power to grasp, to understand that we are immersed in Christ's love all the time! This can only come from being filled with the Spirit and asking for this power.

Now comes the *third* and most exciting part of this passage. Verse 19b adds the outcome: ". . . and to know this love that surpasses knowledge — *that you may be filled to the measure of all the fullness of God.*"

Think of that! God wants us to be filled to an incomprehensible degree — the measure of all His fullness!

I don't pretend to know all this filling to God's own fullness entails, but it is definitely desirable. It certainly has to do with the filling of the Spirit and all that He brings to us in gifts, wisdom, power, direction, and godliness. This is a fullness that will overflow on all those around us. What is the only requirement for this fullness? It is simply to know, to grasp, *how much Christ loves us!*

Listen to the next verse: "Now to him who is able to do immeasurably more than all we ask or imagine, according to His power that is at work within us" (v. 20). Here again are some of the dimensions of God's greatness — that He is able to do *immeasurably more* than all we could possibly imagine, *far more* than all we could ask for. And then the clear statement that this power *is already* at work in us.

This truth of God's provision and our cooperation is echoed in 2 Peter 1:3, which teaches us that "His divine *power* has given us *everything we need* for life and godliness through our knowledge of him who called us by his own glory and goodness." This "everything" is available, ready to be taken up; we just need to learn to use it! And it begins with being filled with the Spirit.

We may not see or feel it, but by faith, believing God's Word, we can know it is there. And with time, as we cooperate, as we give God more and more space to work in and through our lives, we will see the outcome of this.

Cooperating through Prayer

This passage of Ephesians 3:14-19 that we have looked at is a great one for cooperating with God in prayer. I pray through it almost every day as I intercede for all those on my prayer list, as well as for myself. It's already structured as a prayer, so it is easy to use.

> I pray that out of his glorious riches he may strengthen you with power through his Spirit in your inner being, so that Christ may dwell in your hearts through faith.
>
> And I pray that you, being rooted and established in love, may have power, together with all the saints, to grasp how wide and long and high and deep is the love of Christ, and to know this love that surpasses knowledge
> — that you may be filled to the measure of all the fullness of God.

Regularly praying this passage does three things in me. First, it helps me to remember that I cannot live without the power of the Spirit. Second, it reminds me to ask daily, and throughout each day, for the filling of the Spirit and results in my having more power for more faith. Third, it results in my knowing more and more of how great the love of Christ is. This helps me exercise faith in praising Him in and for all things. As we know more and more that He is good, powerful, and loving and that He sends or allows all things in our lives for His glory and our good — this leads us to trust Him more and more.

Culture Clash

The final verse in the "be filled with the Spirit" (Eph. 5:16) passage is very countercultural: "Submit to one another out of reverence for Christ" (v. 21). Normally when we think about being powerful, we would expect others to submit to us. Here the filling of the Spirit will produce just the opposite!

This is another example of God's kingdom being "right side up" from the "upside down" world. When we are weak, then we are strong; when we give, then we get; when we are powerful, we submit!

Think what it would mean if all believers properly submitted to each other? If we were all filled with the Spirit at all times? No pride, no fighting, no competition. Instead, there would be a constant overflowing of love, grace, and goodness. Unfortunately, because we act so much out of our flesh rather than our new nature, it is more often the opposite.

However, we have hope: if we are daily in worship and being filled with the Spirit, He will be transforming us, moving in us to make these verses in Ephesians 5 true in our lives.

It is interesting that in these passages on power, no gift of the Spirit is mentioned. Nothing outwardly spectacular happens, but something inwardly begins to occur that will end up being spectacular: transformation so we can live everyday life on a higher plane. This is living a life worthy of God!

Dave Finding Filling of the Spirit

"Good morning, Dave!" Jack said, on meeting him at the door. "How are things going? Any new insights from your application of what we've been studying?"

"Yes, there are!" replied Dave as he took his usual seat, arranged his backpack, and took out his journal. "I've been using both the 'confession in layers' and the 'discerning of motives' aspects. Both of these are flowing out of journaling or, better said, of lifting my soul to God." Dave's voice was filled with excitement.

"Here's how it happened. We are planning to have a Bible study on campus, and several of us believers are inviting our friends. In the planning sessions, however, we've had some sharp differences of opinion about how we should proceed. I found it
really frustrating that some want to focus on social activities without any biblical input; I think we should plunge right into the Bible — after all, that's what we've invited our friends to do! At least I have.

"Anyway, I began to journal about my frustrations, telling God what I was thinking, feeling, and wanting, and then, as you say, processing this information. It was really helpful to get everything out and see it more objec-

FILLING WITH THE HOLY SPIRIT

tively. In the process, out came a number of sins, including my desire to control the situation, to make everyone do what I think is best (why can't they get with it?!). But I was not leaving room for the Holy Spirit to work. Here, let me read the layers of sin that came out. The visible sin was:

frustration (anger), underneath it
the desire to control everything,
then selfishness,
pride,
not trusting God,
failure to surrender this situation to Him,
lack of prayer, and at the bottom
unbelief and rebellion.

"That's a thorough list!" commented Jack.

"Yes, and along with it, out came my motives. I wanted to see my friends come to Christ, which of course is a good one. Then I want to be successful in this venture, which is probably a neutral one. On the other side, I wanted to look good, competent, and wise in the eyes of my unbelieving friends, and if we just have social stuff, they won't have an opportunity to see what a good teacher I am! Also, I like being in control because it makes me feel secure and significant."

"So, what was the outcome?" Jack asked.

"First I had to confess my sins, laying aside my negative and neutral motives and affirming the positive ones. Then I asked for the filling of the Spirit, surrendering my desires to God and asking Him to work in the situation.

"When we had another planning meeting yesterday, we came to a good conclusion: a social event to start with, then beginning the weekly Bible study the following week, and having a social time once a month. It came out pretty easily once I stopped being an obstructionist!"

"Excellent!" said Jack, "That's because all that confession and repentance gave the Holy Spirit room to work both in you and through you. This comes from the filling of the Spirit! And the next chapter, 22, will help you more in this area."

Study Guide questions for Chapter 21: "How to be Filled"

1. Why do we need the filling of the Spirit? (171)
2. How does the navigator/driver agreement illustrate what it means to be filled? (172)
3. What hinders us from being filled with the Spirit? (172-173)
4. What do we need to do to be filled with the Spirit? (173-174)
5. How is the Spirit's power seen in us when we are filled? (174-176)
6. What are the benefits of praying through Eph 3:14-19? (176)
7. What "culture clash" is waiting us as we are filled? (177)
8. How will you apply the truths of this chapter?

CHAPTER 22

Results of Being Filled

As we daily practice the discipline of being filled with the Spirit, there will be major positive changes in our lives. They will come slowly as God works from within, but they will be powerful. In this chapter we consider four of these important results.

One Result of Being Filled with the Spirit: Revival

One thing He is going to do is work at bringing an ongoing revival within us. I'm not talking about some warm, fuzzy, exciting happening — although that could be part of a revival that begins to spread. No, I'm talking about an increasing insight into God's greatness, a growing grasp of His love, a gracious revealing of our weaknesses, a deepening surrender, a widening wisdom, a broadening effectiveness in obedience. And this is going to come about as we let the Holy Spirit point out sin in our lives.

As some have suggested, we can think of our heart like a house, where the Holy Spirit comes to live when we become believers. Once inside our "heart home," the Spirit begins to knock on locked doors, areas of our life that we want to hide from Him. He wants to open access to everything, especially the secret, hidden cupboards and closets where we keep our favorite sins, so He can clean them out.

As we give Him permission to do this, acknowledging, confessing, and renouncing those sins, we are going to have an ongoing revival in our lives. This begins with listening to His conviction and being willing to confess and leave sins. As we do this, He will be bringing up the next sin on His agenda of growth for us. As we confess and deal with it, then He will bring up the sin after that to be dealt with. Our cooperation will move this process forward.

We should ask, "Why is there so little revival among us?" Part of the answer is that we in the West do not like discomfort; our highest value is to be comfortable. Satan knows this and has been very successful in using this desire for comfort to get conviction and confession off the agenda of the church and the individual believer.

Our sins, though, should not be our focus, for that leads to unhealthy introspection and morbidity. We must recognize and confess them, but our focus should be on our holy and forgiving God, agreeing with Him as He points out sin, rejoicing in His forgiveness and the power He gives us to obey.

A Second Result: A Growing Freedom "from" and Freedom "to"

God is in the process of freeing us from bondage to fears, wrong ideas and attitudes, impure motives and desires, and the memory of difficult past experiences. Galatians 5 speaks to this. Verse 1 says, "It is for freedom that Christ has set us free. Stand firm, then, and do not let yourselves be burdened again by a yoke of slavery." Paul here is referring to the Galatians being enslaved again to the law, but the concept can secondarily be applied to anything that binds us.

In verse 13 Paul gives the other part of freedom, "You, my brothers, were called to be free. But do not use your freedom to indulge the sinful nature; rather, serve one another in love."

Freedom *from* sin, freedom *to do* what is right. The Spirit's aim is to free us to walk in freedom so that we can worship better, serve Him more, have true joy, live in truth, and bring Him glory.

Real life: freedom from the fear factor. When my wife and I were in our forties, she went to a women's conference, and our two boys went on a weeklong trip with their school. I was home alone, and as I lay in bed one night, a strong fear came over me: "What if they are involved in accidents and are killed?"

This was not an idle thought because in our Middle Eastern country the rate of traffic fatalities was very high. The thought of losing them was almost too much to bear. I wrestled with this, but finally turned to God and began to pray. "Lord, you have given my wife and boys to me. I acknowledge that they are not mine but gifts on loan from you. If you choose to take them to yourself, I choose to let them go. We have had wonderful times together, but if you decide it is time for them to come to you, I can know that this is the best, and that you will sustain me when they are gone."

With this surrender to God of the most precious things in my life, my fear left and a great peace came to my heart. I was able to sleep well. From that time on, there was a new freedom in my life. And this freedom has carried over into other areas, for as I began to "let go" of other people and things, the Holy Spirit has had increased freedom to work more powerfully in my life.

I saw this expanding freedom as God continued to teach more about

Results of Being Filled

surrender and giving up ahead of time when my mother developed Alzheimer's and was deteriorating. We watched her going downhill for several years and did our mourning during that time, letting go of her and our relationship with her.

When she, as a believer, died at age eighty-five, we were of course sad and experienced a short grief cycle, but there was also much joy to know that she was released from her suffering and was dancing in the streets of heaven.

But then another death occurred for which I was not prepared. We had a beautiful dog in the States, half Husky, half German Shepherd. She had one brown eye and one blue eye, and she embodied the joy of life. Just to watch her bounding through the fields made us happy. She was a delightful creature. Our son was taking care of her while we were overseas.

One morning we got the news that she had been hit by a car and killed. It was like a blow to the stomach for both my wife and myself. I shocked my friends by saying that it would have been easier for me if one of my boys had died!

Then it struck me — of course! I'd given up my boys to the Lord, but I had not given this dog to Him; I'd just assumed we'd have her for the next ten or fifteen years, so when God took her, it was like having something torn out of my hand. That prompted me to go through my life again and resurrender everything to God.

Such surrender has a powerful, positive side benefit: it prepares us for possible martyrdom. When all belongs to God and we are only stewards, it's much easier to go when the call to the other world comes. We never know what the future may hold. It is good to be ready.

Freedom from celebration aversion. In my fiftieth year the Lord brought a new area of freedom to me. All my life I'd struggled with participating in celebrations — I didn't like them. Christmas, Easter, and Fourth of July were all interruptions to life rather than joyous events.

As time went on, the Lord showed me that part of this attitude stemmed from my not being able to work on those days. I drew security and worth from work and was deprived of these on holidays. God gradually dealt with those wrong sources of worth and security and gave some freedom there. But the more foundational cause was directly revealed to me one day in my quiet time.

While praying about something totally unrelated, it suddenly came to me that my father's viewpoint was the source of my problem. He had communicated to me by his attitude and actions that celebrating was not manly; it was only for women and children. He never actually said this, but his example had been a powerful teacher of these values. As a result, all these years I'd fought subconsciously against celebrations, feeling it was not masculine to participate.

Immediately a question came to my mind, "What does God think about celebrations?" The answer was just as immediate, "Why, celebrating is God's idea. Look at all the celebrations He gave to the Jews in the Old Testament. Look at how Jesus attended celebrations. Think of His parables of the lost sheep, the lost coin, and the lost son (Luke 15), each of which ended in a party! Celebrating is a very male thing to do, as well as female!"

This revelation was a new step in the progression of freedom God was bringing into my life. Such is the freedom God has for each of us, if we are willing to let the Spirit work in us.

Light from above. This process of moving into freedom is described very poetically in Proverbs 4:18: "The path of the righteous is like the first gleam of dawn, shining ever brighter till the full light of day." As we walk forward with Him, more and more comes to light: burdens we can drop, sins we can forsake, obstacles and temptations we can skirt. It is the work of the Holy Spirit to teach and enlighten us about these, to break the bonds of darkness. It is our part then to avoid them once we can see them.

Without the Spirit's work and enlightenment, we will trip over the same things again and again. With the Spirit's work, we can learn what's wrong and avoid the stumbling blocks the world, the flesh, and the devil put out for us.

To have His light, we must be filled with the Spirit. As James puts it in 1:22-25, "Do not merely listen to the word, and so deceive yourselves. Do what it says. . . . The man who *looks intently* into the perfect law that gives freedom, and *continues* to do this, *not forgetting* what he has heard, but *doing it* — he will be blessed in what he does."

Yes, "he will be blessed in all he does." What a tremendous promise, for those who with the Spirit's power apply what they know from the Word!

A Third Result: Power in Ministry

As we are on our second journey through Ephesians 6:10-18, we are still focusing on being "strong in the Lord and in his mighty power" (v. 10). We've talked about how worship is our great privilege that transforms us, and about confession, including confessing in layers, checking our motives, and preparing for temptations. Now we are looking at being filled with the Holy Spirit and the results of being filled. Thus far we've looked at two results: revival, and a growing freedom "from" and freedom "to."

A third result of being filled with the Spirit is power in ministry. When we

Results of Being Filled

are filled with the Spirit and have continuing revival in our lives, which is His work *in* us, the Holy Spirit begins to work *through* us. Often we are unaware of this happening.

We need to cooperate with Him by cultivating a growing determination to not grieve or quench the Holy Spirit — obeying what we know, following His guidance. And we need to desire to be a useful and effective instrument in His hand. Then He gives us increased power in ministry.

I can share a personal example of a time when the Spirit asked me to deny myself. In 2001 we were asked to start up a new ministry focused on outreach, hoping to find spiritually interested people and pass them on to church startups. We called this ministry "The Net" because it was to be like throwing out a wide net to draw in as many as possible.

After setting up a business that gave us a legal platform for ministry, our second step was to open a bookstore. The two younger couples working with us had ideas quite different from mine about how this should be done. They were Gen X people, from reasonably affluent situations, with a goal of excellence in everything and seemingly no compunction about spending money.

In contrast, I am from the early baby boomers, who like things basic; plus I am of Scottish background and get great satisfaction and a feeling of significance from doing things cheaply and quickly.

Our differences came out strongly when talking about how to fix up the place we rented for the bookstore. I wanted to just paint it and be done with it, but the others wanted to strip off the old wallpaper, replaster, and put down new carpeting. This would cost about $1,500 — to me, a totally unnecessary expenditure! Also, the money they wanted to spend was in *my* work fund!

In addition, we had been given a good number of elegant bookshelves: black metal with glass shelving, very adequate for our needs. However, the others didn't like the color; they wanted white ones. Painting the black ones was not a option in their minds. And new white shelves would cost another $1,500! Again, from *my* work fund.

We had a pretty stormy team meeting talking about these issues. I was really hot, literally: red in the face, talking loudly and rapidly, punctuating my comments with the jab of a finger.

When we got home from that meeting, I spent some time talking with the Lord about these teammates who didn't know the meaning of money and were so slow in getting things done!

The next morning, after writing in my journal about this, I was praying for God to help these folks change, when it was as if the Lord asked me, "Are you being sweetly reasonable in this?"

I knew right away what He was referring to, for the word usually translated "gentleness" in the New Testament can also be translated "sweetly reasonable." Isn't that a beautiful phrase? Wouldn't you like everyone to be sweetly reasonable with you?

I had to admit that I was not being one bit sweetly reasonable but was being stubborn and selfish. Then a sudden impression came to me: "Let them have what they want!"

"But Lord. . . ." I was interrupted by the same thought: "Let them have what they want!"

What could I do but surrender? At the next team meeting I voted for redoing the place and buying the new bookshelves. After the meeting, one of our teammates rode home with me. On the way he commented, "Well, that went smoothly!"

"Didn't you notice that I changed my position on every point?!" I asked.

"Oh . . . ah . . . well, I guess you did," was all he could reply.

A superficial evaluation of what happened might be that they won and I lost. But the reality was very different. I may have lost on these two issues, but I found later that my influence on those younger couples had increased greatly — there was more power in my ministry to them — because the Lord got me to give up what was of little worth (getting my way, saving money, and being fulfilled) and to value what is truly important (relationships, cooperating with the Spirit's work in me). The Lord prevented me from quenching His Spirit — and the credit goes to Him, not to me! The result was His power in ministry.

What we're talking about here is the long-range perspective. You've heard the saying "Nice guys finish last"? This is often true, but only in the short run. It's like watching a five-mile race on a track. The guy who sprints through the first few laps rarely wins the race in the end. The selfish, dishonest, rebellious guy may "win" in the beginning, but those who trust and obey God, not quenching or grieving the Spirit, are those who "win" in the end. As it says in Psalm 37:9-13,

> evil men *will* be cut off,
>   but those who hope in the LORD *will* inherit the land.
> A little while, and the wicked *will be no more;*
>   though you look for them, they *will not be found.*
> But the meek *will* inherit the land
>   and enjoy great peace.
> The wicked plot against the righteous
>   and gnash their teeth at them;

Results of Being Filled

but the Lord laughs at the wicked,
    for he knows their day is coming.

God is going to give you opportunities to apply this perspective. This whole thing we are talking about flows from the filling of the Spirit (giving up, surrender, willing to lose in the short run) and results in having God's power in the long run.

These truths have to do with the concept of brokenness. This involves being brought to a new level of surrender and openness to God because of a new perspective on our smallness, the value of relationships, the daily gift of life, and the greatness of God. The power of the world's hold on us is broken to a greater degree.

Brokenness often comes through difficult circumstances like an illness, an accident, a death, a traumatic event, or a deep disappointment. When we respond to these happenings with faith, trusting God and praising Him, we are "broken in the right place," as one book put it,[34] and are reshaped into a more useful instrument for the Master's hand. Then as we are filled with the Spirit, He will do powerful things through us.

If we resist this breaking process, reacting with anger, self-defense, resistance, or rebellion, then we will be broken in the wrong places. We will become bitter, negative, and destructive to ourselves and those around us.

Personally, I define this brokenness as "learning not to trust myself, but trusting God instead." In the "right-side-up kingdom of God" we often have to trust by faith, going against our instincts, responding positively because we know His character, not because we understand.

As we spend time in worship and get to know His character, we find that our trust deepens — that worship influences all else that happens. Worship is the wellspring of much transformation in our lives. As we give God glory and honor, He is at work in deep levels in and through our lives.

A Fourth Result: Renewal of Our First Love

The fourth result of being filled with the Spirit is a rekindling of our heart's love for God. Notice Christ's words to the Ephesians in Revelation 2:4-5: "Yet I hold this against you: *You have forsaken your first love.* Remember the height from which you have fallen! Repent and do the things you did at first. If you do not repent, I will come to you and remove your lampstand from its place."

---

34. See Allen Nelson, *Broken in the Right Place: How God Tames the Soul* (Nashville: Thomas Nelson, 1994).

In God's sight, losing our first love is a very serious offense. We can see the truth of this reflected in a marriage. When spouses get over the "in love," infatuation stage (which rarely lasts longer than two years), it is easy to drift into a superficial relationship focused on the practicalities of life, forgetting the excitement, intimacy, and joy of when they met. It often results in two people living parallel, but not unified, lives.

This is not what God intends for a marriage or for our relationship with Him. Love should actually move from the initial infatuation stage to a continually deepening love, a growing passion for each other. It takes intentionality and work to nurture that kind of love.

A secret of happiness. As a help in nurturing our first love, I want to mention here something I've found to be a secret of happiness: compare down rather than up; that is, look at those who are worse off than us, not those who are better off.[35] Everyone naturally tends to compare up — to compare what they have with those who have more: more talent, more good looks, more education, or more wealth. Such comparisons always bring unhappiness and dissatisfaction. For example, my wife can always find men who are better looking, more educated, or richer than I am. But when we make these comparisons, we are committing two huge errors.

First, we are unthankful for what we have. We are jealous of what others have, greedy for more than God has given us. Instead of comparing up, we should compare down, looking at those who have less than we do. If we have only a bicycle, we should compare ourselves with the fellow who has to walk; we should praise God for our bicycle, not compare ourselves to the fellow who has a car, for then we will not be thankful but complain. If we have a car, we should compare ourselves to the fellow with a bicycle, not with the man with a Mercedes.

In applying this principle to our relationship with our spouse, we should focus on his or her good qualities, not their lacks. My wife may not work as quickly as I do or think like me, but she is a fine believer, diligent, orderly, thoughtful, careful with money, a great help, and wise in many things: a beautiful person — that's what I should be thinking about!

One man I knew tried to use this in reverse, but it did not work well. When his wife complained of his dangerous motorcycle racing (he raced motocross until he was sixty-three and had many accidents), he would say, "Look, I don't drink, smoke, or gamble; be thankful I'm that good!" He was unwilling, however, to address the areas where he *did* need to change!

---

35. According to a lesson plan I developed for my English classes, the seven secrets are to (1) count your blessings, (2) compare down, (3) distinguish what are needs and what are only wants, (4) do what you should, (5) speak the truth in love, (6) forgive, and (7) know God.

Results of Being Filled

The *second* mistake we make in comparing up is thinking we know better than God. He gave me this woman as my wife, and she is all I need. He did not give me someone with other qualities, because I don't need them. I can praise God for just how He made my wife and how He has matched us.

In marriage, it is important to spend time mediating on the many fine qualities of our spouse — especially when he or she has done something to irritate us. I need to work at remembering what initially drew me to my wife, the things that made me fall in love with her. This renewed focus on her and her positives intensifies my love and appreciation for her.

It is the same in our love relationship with Christ. When we remember His divine character, the stunning beauty of His being, and the powerful outworking of His plan in history, it will strengthen our first love for Him.

Remember the first days. Another discipline to help nurture our first love for God, and for our spouse, is to think about the early days of our relationship. I think about my wife and the walks we took in the fields under an August moon, the shine in her almond-shaped eyes, the gracefulness of her walk, the music of her laugh, the excitement of touching her hand. These memories refocus my perspective, fanning the flames of love and romance.

The same is true of our relationship with God. I need to remember the initial glow of coming to know Him, the excitement of my early walk with Him, the nuggets of truth I found in the Word, the victory over sin, the joy of sharing the Word.

We need to spend time with Him, to think about Him, to delight in Him. When we are filled with the Spirit, He will draw us into delighting in Jesus, for this is one of the Spirit's roles ("He [the Spirit] will bring glory to me by taking from what is mine and making it known to you," John 16:14). Following Psalm 37:4 is a great discipline: "Delight yourself in the LORD and he will give you the desires of your heart."

My spiritual father, Dave Shinen, Wycliffe Bible translator to the Yupik Eskimos, used to say that if you delight in something or someone, then when your mind is free it goes automatically to that object of delight. In our courtship days, no one had to remind me to think about the woman who became my wife! In fact, it was hard *not* to think of that special person when I was supposed to be working or studying.

Worship is a way we can delight in Christ and nurture our first love for Him: thinking about who He is, about how great, glorious, merciful, and gracious He is. We need the help of the Holy Spirit to keep our love a "first love." Notice Paul's prayer: "I keep asking that the God of our Lord Jesus Christ, the glorious Father, may give you the Spirit of wisdom and revelation, so that you may know him better" (Eph. 1:17).

Jesus agreed that we need the Spirit's help in this. The powerful discourse of Jesus in John 16 emphasizes that one major purpose the Holy Spirit has is to glorify Christ (see especially vv. 13-14).

The Holy Spirit is to teach us more and more about Christ. All Scripture is God centered and, in the New Testament especially, is Christ centered. So we should be eager for the Spirit to teach us how to be Christ centered in our thoughts and our love.

Being well watered. The filling of the Spirit allows us to drink from the wellsprings of God. Worship is the first wellspring of life and growth. The Word is the second. They are of course intertwined, but also distinct. We'll be talking about how to draw from the well of the Word in chapter 29.

If you cultivate your first love for Christ, God will use you greatly. Your life will be fruitful, and you will have joy that the world cannot take away.

> *Lord God, Creator of heaven and earth, the sea, and all that is in it — the Almighty One, who knows when each sparrow falls, who holds the stars in place. You are the Holy One who hates sin and will punish it but who loves the sinner and provided a way of salvation. To you we lift our hearts in worship. To you we give honor and glory and praise. It is you we love, for your love is overwhelming; it is rich, deep, and pure. Lord Jesus, continually renew our first love for you. Amen.*

Dave and the Holy Spirit

"This chapter was really helpful to me," Dave said as he got out his notebook. "It kind of put things together."

"Tell me about it," replied Jack.

"Well, the four items covered in the chapter have been touched on before: revival, freedom, power in ministry, and renewal of our first love for Christ. However, this chapter put them into this new context of the filling of the Spirit."

"What difference did knowing this bring into your life?" asked Jack.

"It brought into focus for me how being filled with the Spirit is the wellspring from which all these good things come. It reminded me of how very important it is to deal with sin, to be open to conviction, to daily ask for the filling of the Spirit. As you know, I tend to try to do things in my own strength, even though I know I need God's help. This chapter brought home in a new way my weakness and the power of the Spirit."

Jack leaned back smiling. "Wonderful! You are internalizing the big picture, seeing the importance of 'being' before doing. What stood out to you the most?"

Dave opened to the end of the chapter, "The last and most important point, that the filling of the Holy Spirit nurtures our first love for Christ. It's like a sandwich: the filling of the Spirit on one side, renewed love for Christ on the other, and me in the middle! Practicing the discipline of confessing and asking daily for the filling is going to keep me right in the middle of what God has for me!"

Jack laughed. "Well put. This insight will help you with the next part, 'Deeper Thoughts on Putting On the Armor.' Your assignment is to read chapter 23."

Study Guide questions for Chapter 22: "Results of Being Filled"

1. What is revival and how does the Holy Spirit want to bring it to us? (179-180)
2. How does the Spirit give us "freedom from" and "freedom to?" (180-182)
3. Give an example from you life of having "freedom from" and "freedom to."
4. How can we cooperate with the Spirit in having more power in our lives? (182-184.)
5. What is "brokenness" and how can we cooperate with the Spirit in this? (185)
6. How can we cooperate with the Spirit in nurturing our first love? (185-188)
7. How will the contents of this chapter influence the way you live?

Part 7

Deeper Thoughts on Putting on the Armor

More On Truth #2: We Can Win By Putting On and Using the Armor of God

CHAPTER 23

Background

We have looked at different disciplines that help us be "strong in the Lord and the power of his might," the major ones being worship, confession, lifting our souls, and being filled with the Spirit. As part of these primary disciplines, we also considered discerning motives, discerning ahead, praying through our day, and journaling.

In this chapter we consider some background perspectives regarding the spiritual armor. We then devote the rest of this seventh part to a more in-depth look at actually putting on the whole armor of God. There will be some good, useful repetition of truths, as Peter does in 2 Peter 1:12-15.

The Wiles of the Devil

Ephesians 6:11 says, "Put on the whole armor of God, that ye may be able to stand against the wiles of the devil" (KJV), that is, against his deep and deadly deceptions. Here are four brief reminders about this verse.

First, putting on the armor is a command, not a suggestion. God tells us straightforwardly to obey Him in this. It's not like my choosing to wear a tie or not. If I don't put on the armor, there can be dire consequences for me and many around me.

Second, we should put on *all* the armor, not just part of it.

Third, if we put it all on, we *will* be able to stand against the devil's wiles. That's often not what I feel when in the midst of a strong temptation, but it is the truth, as 1 Corinthians 10:13 affirms: "No temptation has seized you except what is common to man. And God is faithful; he will not let you be tempted beyond what you can bear. But when you are tempted, *he will also provide a way out* so that you can stand up under it." A large part of the "way out" is putting on the armor of God so we can stand against the wiles of the devil.

Fourth, Satan knows each person's weakness and sets traps for him or her in those areas. The disciplines we've discussed (worship, confession in layers, and lifting our souls) all provide insight into what our areas of weakness are, so we can be prepared for attacks there. The Lord knows what is coming in our day and wants us to be ready for it. Often during my worship time, when the Holy Spirit convicts me of a sin, He is actually warning me, preparing me for where the devil may attack. I am alerted to be looking for this temptation with my armor in place.

When I pray through Ephesians 6 each morning, I ask the Lord to help me recognize the wiles of the devil before I fall into them. Over the years, the Lord has answered this prayer on increasingly deeper levels.

As I mentioned in chapter 22, this is the outworking of one of my favorite verses, Proverbs 4:18: "The path of the righteous is like the first gleam of dawn, shining ever brighter until the full light of day." As we walk with God, we can see more and more clearly the traps set for us along the way and can learn to avoid them.

In contrast, "The way of the wicked is like deep darkness; they do not know what makes them stumble" (Prov. 4:19). Without the light of God to guide us, we would keep stumbling over the same things again and again, repeatedly falling into Satan's traps.

The schemes of the devil in my marriage. My wife and I have been married over thirty-five years. Overall, it has been a very good marriage, rich, strong, and growing. Still, there is a lot of room for further progress.

Since Barbara was born and grew up in Germany, our marriage is a cross-cultural one, giving us more than the average relational factors to deal with. Besides the natural male and female differences, we have two cultures, two mother tongues, and two very different family backgrounds. In my family, when you were sick, you were treated like a king. In Barbara's family, the attitude was, "Hurry and get well; you're being a burden!" That gives you an idea of how far apart our backgrounds were!

Barbara's German nature makes her, on one hand, very private and, on the other hand, tough. For my part, I am both quite insecure and very transparent. These differences guarantee clashes!

At times when I have sought to be more open with her about my inner thoughts and feelings, her response sometimes has communicated, "Don't whine, be a man!" She doesn't say that, but that's exactly how I feel it!

Such exchanges have prompted some pretty strong discussions, with me being the aggressor, speaking out of hurt — that is, out of self-pity. Such an attitude on my part has not contributed to harmonious teamwork in our marriage and ministry! Obviously the devil was very much at work, using my weaknesses to stir things up.

Now, thinking in terms of layers, what were the problems here? I wanted affirmation, support, and compliments from my wife; I wanted to be able to tell her my inner desires and then to receive emotional support. These are not wrong desires, but they had become idols — that is, I was demanding them in order to be happy.

So in the top layer of my "stack of sins" was discontent. Under that was wrong expectations (my wife must act this way if she loves me), then self-pity, and then idol worship (without her reacting in my desired way, I can't be happy). Next was my seeking from her what really comes only from God (significance, security, dignity), then pride, followed by unbelief and rebellion. Here's how they stacked up:

discontent
wrong expectations
self-pity
idol worship
looking to wrong source
pride
unbelief/rebellion.

That's a pretty ugly list. Each one of these sins was a trap, a "wile" or "scheme," the devil was using against me. But in this case the Lord had plans to use this primarily to expose and deal with my sin of self-pity.

Many people wouldn't even consider self-pity a sin — but it is, for it is a statement of unbelief. Is God lovingly in control or not? Giving in to self-pity actually says, "No. I have to watch out for myself, grabbing what encouragement I can from the words and actions of people around me. If I get this, life is fine, but if those around me fail to give me what I want, then my life is terrible." This is human thinking: unbelieving and destructive.

God calls us to a higher level of living. When negative, accusatory words are spoken by people around me, support not given, or no comfort offered, I am slowly learning to respond with prayers like this:

Thank you, Lord God, for this opportunity to live by faith, remembering that your love and acceptance are sufficient. To know you is enough for joy, period! Thank you for this challenge to rise above and live in the unseen, to rise on the wings of faith above the fiery darts of Satan and soar into the security of your love. Help me to learn from the grain of truth in this accusation and to give you glory in my response!

The Holy Spirit often brings Psalm 62:5 to mind, which always brings things into focus for me: "Find rest, O my soul, in God alone; my hope comes from him." This verse makes me face the question, Where am I trying to find rest? or From where do I expect help to come? I must *not* seek these from people or possessions or success, for they are fickle, feeble sources. God "*alone* is my rock and my salvation; he is my fortress." If I seek shelter in Him, "I will never be shaken" (Ps. 62:2). Standing on these verses helps me be aware of the traps the devil has for me, so I can avoid them.[36]

Standing with the armor on. Once we've begun to understand the wiles Satan uses against us, we have to learn to use the armor of God to stand against them. Application is a learning process. In my case mentioned above, I struggled for a good while to consistently rise above self-pity. In the end, as I willfully chose to praise God for the opportunity to rely only on Him, not on people, God changed my emotional attitude. So now, instead of feeling sorry for myself when I do not receive encouragement or compliments, I am able to view it as a challenge, an adventure in applying grace and truth.

In learning to stand against this wile of Satan, I end up giving God glory, as well as blessing those around me with more positive responses. It takes time and practice — with the Spirit's help, I am still learning to apply this — but it is worth every effort, for it is an investment for eternity!

So, in summary, if I keep on the whole armor, I *can* stand against the wiles of the devil. The wiles the devil uses against me utilize my weaknesses. In journaling (lifting my soul to God) about my struggles, God will help me see these weaknesses so I can better spot them before falling into them at a later time. By confessing in layers, I can learn other weaknesses that underlie the obvious ones. Then in confessing ahead, I can be prepared for encounters with these wiles.

Fighting the Right Enemy

The doorbell rang at midnight. I rolled out of bed and stumbled to the door. When I opened it, three policemen pushed their way in and told me I was

---

36. Here's another example of discerning traps and avoiding them. In the early years of my marriage I was pretty hot tempered—"explosively touchy" is a better term!—easily hurt and angered by those who unknowingly snatched away my dignity or sense of significance. However, the "messes" I had to clean up in relationships each time I gave vent to my feelings prompted me to find better ways to deal with my anger!

Lifting my soul to God through journaling and confessing in layers led me to an understanding of the underlying causes: insecurity, self-pity, looking to others for the significance and security only God can supply, as well as failure to forgive others and myself. These were the wiles the devil was using effectively against me.

As God worked, making me more aware of my weaknesses and teaching me to think truth instead, real progress was made in my life. He is teaching me to live the truth of Proverbs 12:16, "A fool shows his annoyance at once, but a prudent man overlooks an insult." Also helpful is Proverbs 29:11, "A fool gives full vent to his anger, but a wise man keeps himself under control." When Satan sought to catch me in these sinful tendencies, God reminded me to use the weapons he'd supplied to stay clear of these traps.

Background

under arrest! I knew I had nothing wrong, but I also knew that this made no difference in the country where we lived.

When we are treated unjustly, when our rights are trampled on, how should we view those who have done this? My first and natural response is anger toward those who treat me unjustly. However, for many of us, the most important reaction is not our first (which often pops out naturally), but our second, which should spring from Scripture. Ephesians 6:12 says, "For our struggle is not against flesh and blood, but against the rulers, against the authorities, against *the powers of this dark world* and against *the spiritual forces of evil in the heavenly realms.*"

We are ultimately not fighting people but Satan and his agents. Our true enemy is thus not some person who is doing us wrong but Satan and his forces, who are using this person. Satan is a powerful foe, and it seems his kingdom is well organized. In sharp contrast before him and his forces, we in ourselves are weak.

However, when we put on and use the armor of God, Satan has a hard time defeating us. But if we forget who the real enemy is and struggle against people instead, we will certainly lose.

Satan and his forces cunningly use people for their evil, destructive purposes and want us to view those people as the enemy. However, according to Ephesians 6:12, it is clear that those people are not our real enemy, even though they are acting like one.

Jesus' words of forgiveness from the cross reflect this truth, when He said, "Father, forgive them, for *they do not know what they are doing*" (Luke 23:34). People who mistreat us usually do not know they are fighting for Satan against God. Our attitude toward them must be one of forgiveness in our hearts and graciousness in our actions.

Supernatural Response

When people have been cruel, destructive, and evil, a response of forgiveness seems so wrong. It is unnatural to not view these evil men as the enemy — this is a supernatural viewpoint. Since our real enemies are supernatural ones, so both our response and our weapons need to be supernatural. Psalm 37:1-2 gives good perspective on this:

> Do not fret because of evil men
>   or be envious of those who do wrong;
> for like the grass they will soon wither,
>   like green plants they will soon die away.

This gives us the eternal perspective. God will deal justly on the human level in His time; it was not my business to extract revenge from these policemen who were taking me away, even if they acted like my enemy. Verses 3 and 4 say:

> Trust in the LORD and do good;
> > dwell in the land and enjoy safe pasture.
> Delight yourself in the LORD
> > and he will give you the desires of your heart.

We are called to look away to the Lord, to rejoice in His goodness — in short, to worship in the midst of difficulty. Our trust of Him will lead us to doing what is right and good. Our delighting in Him (rather than in worrying about making our circumstances delightful) opens the way for Him to give our hearts both the right desires and the fulfillment of those desires.

But for me, the key item comes in verses 5 and 6:

> Commit your way to the LORD;
> > trust in him and he will do this:
> He will make your righteousness shine like the dawn,
> > the justice of your cause like the noonday sun.

We have to lay down our natural desires for immediate justice and commit all this to God, to trust Him to work it out. And that is what He does, in His time.

In the instance where I was unjustly arrested, several of us were put on trial for sharing our faith. The lawyer who opened the case against us wanted to put us away for seven years! In the end, however, the prosecuting attorney actually defended us, defining clearly everyone's freedom to choose a religion, to learn about his or her religion, to form a congregation, to worship together, and to share his or her faith with others. What Satan meant for evil, God turned around for good, strengthening the legal situation of the Christians in the country.

Satan tried to use the police for evil, but they were not the real enemy. God guided us in trusting Him and responding well — forgiving these men in our hearts — opening the way for God to display "the justice of [our] cause like the noonday sun," to bring good out of evil!

Thinking in these terms is like seeing beyond the physical world into the spiritual one, as when Elisha and his servant were in a city surrounded by the enemy army (2 Kings 6:15-17). The servant only saw the human army. Then Elisha prayed that his servant's eyes would be opened to see the much greater

Background

army of God surrounding the enemy — and God granted it!

So it is with us. May we, by faith, be able to recognize the true enemy manipulating humans, as well as see our true Defender and obey Him.

Violence and Forgiveness

Another, much more serious incident occurred in our country that illustrates how living in God's perspective defeats the real enemy. Five young men brutally murdered three believers; two were nationals, and the third was a foreign worker. The reason given for killing them was that they were establishing a church in a conservative Muslim city.

Two of the martyrs had been married. Their wives, one a national and the other a foreigner, were soon interviewed by the local press. Both of them independently said the same thing: "I am proud of my husband for being willing to die for Jesus. I know he's in heaven now. And as Jesus said on the cross, I forgive those who killed Him, for they did not know what they were doing." This was within hours of hearing how their husbands had been brutally tortured and killed!

One columnist writing in a national newspaper said, "That one sentence of the widow [on forgiveness] has done more than 1,000 missionaries could do in 1,000 years!" Because the widows realized their real enemy was Satan, not the young men who killed their husbands, they could respond biblically with forgiveness.

Most of us would say, "I could never respond like that!" Humanly speaking, that is true. But consider a saying in the country where I worked: "A lake is made drop by drop." This is true spiritually as well as physically: small things repeated often build up, for good or bad.

These widows obviously had had a close walk with God, meeting with Him every day, reading His Word and praying. I would venture to guess that they also were applying this truth of knowing who the real enemy is on a daily basis, forgiving those who gypped them in the market, those who circulated lies about those "dirty Christians," and the local children who mistreated their sons and daughters because they were Christians. As they lived by the truth that they were not fighting against flesh and blood in everyday happenings but against spiritual forces of evil, then when the big event came, they were ready; their spiritual lake was full, so to speak.

In addition, we can count on the truth that God gives us grace when we need it. Looking at a situation theoretically, we can recognize that in our own strength we probably could not make a biblical response. But when we are actually in that situation, God gives us the strength, the insight, and the wisdom to move through it properly.

The one caveat is that we need to be ready to appropriate His grace: we must be practicing walking daily with the Lord Jesus, thinking His truth, and regularly taking up the grace that He gives us each moment. A traumatic happening, then, requires only that we continue doing the same thing, just on a bigger scale.

In your life. Maybe you have someone who is treating you like an enemy — perhaps a fellow student, someone at work, a neighbor, or even your spouse. The first step of dealing with such a person is right there in Ephesians 6:12. Every time you think of or see this person, recite that verse we just read: "For our struggle is not against flesh and blood, but against the rulers, against the authorities, against the powers of this dark world and against the spiritual forces of evil in the heavenly realms."

Acting then on this truth, we first can forgive him or her, just as Jesus forgave his killers. This sets us free emotionally. Second, we can affirm our forgiveness every time we think of or see that person. (See chap. 26 for further discussion of forgiveness.) Third, we can pray for this person. God has brought this one into your life for at least two important reasons: God will use this person both in you and through you, as you cooperate with God.

Here's one progression that God wants to be working in you through difficult relationships:

> We also rejoice in our sufferings,
>   because we know that suffering produces perseverance;
>   perseverance, character;
>   and character, hope.
> And hope does not disappoint us,
>   because God has poured out his love
>   into our hearts by the Holy Spirit."
>   (Rom. 5:3-5)

Perseverance, good character, and hope are the rewards of finding our joy in Jesus, not in having things go our way. It is so easy to forget such spiritual truth when in a difficult relationship, for it is so contrary to our natural thinking. That's why memorizing such portions and using them aggressively is so significant.

Great opportunities. Each difficult person in our lives is a tailor-made lesson for us, designed by God for our good. As one person said, great difficulties are God's compliment to us: He's saying that we are now mature enough to take

Background

up and use His grace in this larger difficulty. The question is, Are we going to cooperate with God in accepting His grace and learning the new lesson He has for us?

Our cooperating with God begins with thanking Him for this person and for what He is going to do *in our lives* through him or her. Then it continues with our asking God to help us cooperate in what He is going to do *through us* in this situation. He has brought or allowed this difficult relationship to give us a stage upon which to demonstrate God's grace to those around us. As we interact with the difficult person, either in grace or in anger, we are saying something about our faith to everyone around us.

Beyond that, God wants us to love this person into the kingdom. This means praying for that one, asking God to bless him or her, to open eyes to truth, to give us opportunities to do good to that person. God is using him or her to bless us with the opportunity to grow, and now we need to bless this difficult person in our thoughts and prayers. Then see how God answers those prayers.

Lord God, you are the Most High, the final authority, the Almighty One, who will never be defeated. Thank you that you have given us your Word to guide us, to give us your perspective. Help us to think and live the truth that no man is our enemy. Help us to know how to apply this truth, and to love the difficult people in our lives. Thank you for what you are going to do. Amen.

Knowing Our Future

Ephesians 6:13 says, "Therefore put on the full armor of God, so that when the day of evil comes, you may be able to stand your ground, and after you have done everything, to stand."

Note that this starts with "therefore," pointing us back to verse 12 on how our fight is against spiritual rulers and authorities, not against flesh and blood. The consequence is that we cannot fight with human means, so we need the armor of God.

Then the command is repeated, "Put on the full armor of God." Repetition means this is important! God is very interested in us getting and practicing this truth: if we put on the full armor, we *can* win the fight!

In this verse Paul makes one prediction and two explanations. He says "when the day of evil comes . . . ," an implied prediction that an evil day will come. Such days will come to us all. Satan will attack through many means: sickness, accidents, loss of loved ones, relational problems, economic problems, war, and violence. But whatever comes, this verse tells us to keep the armor on, "so that . . . you *may* be able to stand your ground." So if we keep on the armor, we'll be ready for the evil day and be able to stand our ground, not giving into Satan's attacks. And that should take us back to remembering what wiles he uses against us.

Doing God's "everything." Paul makes this little addition: ". . . and after you have done everything, to stand." The "everything" mentioned here is according to His measure, not ours.

As time has gone on in my life, I've come to see that much of the activity that passes for spiritual work is not necessarily what God would have us to do. Projects, programs, and "progress," to name some, often make us feel like we are doing well. But is that the "everything" of God?

He is much more interested in the development of the character of Christ in us. And this is seen in obedience to Him in everyday relations. God often has much lower standards than we do for busyness, but much higher standards for holiness and godliness. Part of putting on the armor is spending the time with Him so we can be transformed in character and then work hand in hand with Him, not in our busyness, but in His business.

When the evil day comes, we often are forced to cut back on activity and focus on the essentials. A man with cancer can't do all the things he used to — because of lower energy levels he must spend much time resting — which gives him more time to spend with God. Spending regular time in the Word should help us to see what God's "everything" is.

Asking God daily to reveal to us what His "all" is for us today is a good practice. Then when the evil day comes, we will be ready.

An arresting illustration. Now, in conclusion to this chapter, let me tell you a bit of how having on the whole armor of God helped me to stand in my evil day. In the arrests I mentioned at the beginning of this chapter, where the police acted like our enemies, we knew that the arrests were coming. In fact, I was encouraged by some people back home to flee. But the response that came from the Spirit was, "How can I tell the local Christians to stand under persecution if I flee when faced with it?"

I ended up in jail with a number of the local believers, and after spending a week together in a cell, our relationships were considerably deepened.

During one interrogation, I was being questioned in a roomful of police. Suddenly all of them jumped to attention as a man in white shirt and tie came striding up to where I was sitting. He looked me over and spoke sternly, "Why don't you go back to your own country and work on the problems there?

Background

America has plenty of problems, you know!"

"Well," I answered, "America certainly has many problems, but there are plenty of people working on them. I want to stay here and be of help where I can."

The man, who was the chief of the National Police headquarters in our city, turned away in frustration. He later told a mutual friend that I was a "bad person" because I wouldn't give up and leave the country!

From my perspective, I see this whole arrest and the pressures of interrogation and threats as an evil day. I was able to stand in that evil day only because of having the armor on and therefore being able to endure, to move through the experience with God's power.

With all the pressures of those days — frequent arrests, the police getting me fired from the university, teammates staying away, our landlord trying to evict us, being expelled from our meeting place — there was indeed plenty of reason to give up and go home. However, thinking truth, keeping on the armor, recognizing the spiritual battle against Satan, and being willing to cut back to the essentials made us able to stand.

God knows what evil days will come; fortunately, we don't. Our part is to daily put on the armor and to practice using it so we will be ready.

Dave and His Specific Confession

Jack was looking for a book in his library when Barbara showed Dave in. "Hello, Dave," Jack said, coming over to give him a warm handshake. "How was your week?"

"Have I got news to tell you!" Dave said enthusiastically.

"I'm all ears," said Jack. "Let's get settled and pray, then you can give me the news."

Dave sat in his usual spot, and Jack, after sitting in his, prayed. "Lord, creator of this day, provider of this time to share, guide us, open our eyes to what you would have us to learn, to understand, to apply. May your Spirit be our teacher. Amen."

Dave jumped right in. "Two sessions ago you talked about discerning what wiles Satan uses against me. And last lesson was about fighting the right enemy, not viewing people as the enemy. Well, I began to journal about the difficult guy on my floor, Jared, and a whole bunch of things came out. Some of them I kind of already knew, like how I was viewing him as the enemy and acting accordingly. I saw him as an irritation in life, an annoying motion in my peripheral vision. Out of this God showed me several sins and made me aware that these were traps that Satan could use against me."

"And what were those sins?" asked Jack.

Dave opened his journal and looked at his notes. "One was selfishness — I was thinking only about myself and how Jared made my life miserable when he was around. I was not thinking at all about Jared's need to know God.

"Second was a desire to put comfort above obedience. I wanted nothing to do with Jared because he made me uncomfortable.

"A third was pride; I looked down on Jared, thinking that I was better — that is, that I'm a reasonable guy, but he's a jerk.

"A fourth was tied to my pride, a reluctance to forgive Jared — I kind of felt like he deserved to be shunned. But as you have said, God doesn't make forgiveness optional.

"So I confessed these sins of mine, then went on to specifically forgive Jared for his selfish, unkind, hurtful, and crude speech and behavior."

"That's very good, Dave," commented Jack. "You were specific, not forgiving some general idea, like his being obnoxious."

"Yes, you emphasized that in the lesson on confession: name the sin clearly so it can be dealt with — in this case, forgiven. Then I thanked God for bringing him into my life and asked Him to help me love Jared and help me learn from him what God had to teach me."

"So what happened — and I'm sure that something happened!" laughed Jack.

"It sure did," said Dave, putting his journal down. "The crazy thought came to visit Jared. That sure wasn't from me! So later when I went by his room and saw the door open, I knocked and went in.

"We actually had a decent conversation — he said he was glad that I stopped by. He really seems to be a kind of lonely guy. I suggested we go out for a pizza some night, and we'll do that tonight!"

"So, you have started on a new adventure!" said Jack. "As you use these tools we're talking about, you will have lots of adventures like this, seeing God turn irritations into growth, deepening, and new life for those around you!"

Dave nodded, "I am praying now for Jared's salvation. Before, the thought never entered my head, and if it had, I would have dismissed it as impossible. Now, with the perspective you've given me, I can see how God could use me to help Jared become a child of God! At the same time, I want to be cautious, knowing that this may be a long road."

"Good point, Dave, " replied Jack." You may be only the sower of good seed in Jared's life and not see him actually come to Christ. Someone else may have that privilege, but your part is just as important. Follow the direction of the Spirit and see what He does, both in you and in Jared. For next week's discussion, read chapter 24."

Background

Study Guide questions for Chapter 23: "Background"

1. What are the wiles the devil will use against you? (193-195)
2. How can "confessing in layers" help you be ready for the devil's wiles? (195)
3. Who is the right enemy? Why is it so difficult to remember this? (196-197)
4. What will help you to remember to fight the right enemy? (197)
5. What prepared the wives for the martyrdom of their husbands? (199)
6. How is each difficult person in our lives a blessing?
7. How will this change your perspective on people? (200-201)
8. How can we cooperate with God in embracing this blessing in faith? (198)
9. What three things can you know for sure about your future? (201-202)
10. What is the difference between God's "everything" and mine? (202)
11. How have you, or will you apply the truths of this chapter?

CHAPTER 24

The Belt of Truth

As you will remember, the first three parts of the armor all have to do with relationships. The belt speaks of our relationship with God, the breastplate of our relationship with ourselves, and the shoes of our relationship with others. In this part we will take a more in-depth look at each of these, sharing further insights. Again, there will be some repetition, for repetition of significant truth is important; spiritually, we are all slow to grasp and implement it!

Ephesians 6:14a says, "Stand firm then, with the belt of truth buckled around your waist." (See fig. 7.1.) The belt of truth is the foundational part of our armor. For the Roman soldier, it held his uniform together: his breastplate, his skirt, and his scabbard were all fastened to it. Without it, his effectiveness would have been greatly diminished.

Spiritually, I believe the belt of truth refers to the basic truths of the Bible, the whole gospel. To state them briefly: on one hand, because of the fall, we human beings are born sinners, separated from God, deserving only hell. On the other hand, God in His great and, humanly speaking, irrational love, has made a way of salvation and calls all humanity to repentance and eternal life. The belt includes these two sets of truth.

Putting on the belt has to do with establishing a balance of the two sides of truth in our lives as followers of Jesus Christ, a balance like we see in scales. Here we are going to explore this concept a bit further. One side of the scale represents negatives, the other side stands for positives. The balance can be seen in King David's words in Psalm 86:1-2.

> Hear, O LORD, and answer me,
>   for I am poor and needy.
>   [the negative side of the scale: "in my natural self dwells no good thing"]
> Guard my life, for I am devoted to you.
>   [the positive side of the scale: God makes us holy in Christ]

The Negative Story

On the negative side of truth, we could list the following:

> In our old nature, without Christ:
> we deserve only hell
> we deserve punishment
> we deserve eternal separation
> we deserve condemnation
> we deserve nothing good.

To expand a bit on these:

> We all are sinners and have sinned. (Rom. 3:23)
> We all deserve eternal death, which is separation from God. (Rom. 6:23)
> We are God's enemies, dangerous and destructive to His kingdom. (Rom. 5:10)
> We are hostile to God, unwilling and unable to obey Him. (Rom. 8:7)
> We follow the ruler of this world, not God. (Eph. 2:2)
> We gratify the sinful cravings of our flesh. (Eph. 2:3)
> We are by nature objects of wrath. (Eph. 2:3)
> Nothing good lives in our flesh, that is, our innate, incorrigible self-centeredness. (Rom. 7:18)

You can see how grim our situation is without Christ. In fact, it is more than grim — it is totally hopeless. In our natural selves we deserve nothing good, only pain, suffering, and eternal death! Such a stark revelation certainly flies in the face of our culture, which tells us that we deserve the best, what is good and comfortable.

This attitude comes out in the question often asked, "Why does God allow good people to suffer?" God tells us that there is no one good (Rom. 3:10) and that we actually deserve far worse than what we are getting now. Our culture is wrong, God is right! The additional truth is that suffering is an important part of our growth, and a part of many unbelievers' coming to Christ. Much suffering also comes from Satan and from our own and others' wrong decisions — but God uses it for good.

We don't usually think about the negative side of truth — that is, what we actually deserve. We don't *want* to think about it, it's too painful! In enjoying our walk with God, it is easy to forget where we have come from and what our old nature still is. It is important to remember these unpleasant truths, however, for this helps us in two ways.

First, it *moves us toward true humility.* One definition of humility is to see ourselves as God sees us, both in our natural depravity and in our being in Christ. We have to keep both sides in focus. Humility is very important because it is the doorway through which grace flows into our lives (James 4:6).

Second, remembering these negative truths *keeps us healthily dependent on God,* rather than trusting our natural selves.

In his second letter Peter speaks of the importance of remembering what we were. After listing out in 1:5-7 the qualities we are to have in our lives as believers, he says, "But if anyone does not have them, he is nearsighted and blind, and *has forgotten that he has been cleansed from his past sins*" (v. 9). Peter then goes on in verses 12-15 to speak three more times about how important it is to remember this:

> So I will *always remind you* of these things, even though you know them. (v. 12)
> I think it is right to *refresh your memory* as long as I live in the tent of this body. (v. 13)
> And I will make every effort to see that after my departure you will *always be able to remember* these things. (v. 15)

Obviously remembering where we have come from is important to God, as well as to Peter — mentioning it three times in four consecutive verses! We might say that Peter was used to getting threefold warnings and directions, so it's not surprising he did the same for his disciples!

The Rest of the Story

Now let's balance the negatives with the positive side.

We deserve only hell	— but He has given us heaven.
We deserve punishment	— but He has given us pardon.
We deserve eternal separation	— but He has made us His sons and daughters.
We deserve condemnation	— but He has given us a commission to serve.
We deserve nothing good	— but He has given us all spiritual blessings.

The balanced picture is a lot better! Think again of the scale. If we have too much emphasis on the negative side, it becomes unbalanced in this direction, and we can become depressed. If we have too much emphasis on the positive side, we have a different imbalance. We can become proud, self-dependent, and spiritually lazy, thinking we have arrived.

The Belt of Truth

What we want is a balanced grasp of these two aspects of truth, like the scales in figure 24.1. Note that it is the tension on the arms of the scales that keep them balanced. There will always be a tension between these two sides. The natural tendency is to remove the tension by giving in to one side or the other, but it is a good tension, a creative tension, necessary for true balance.

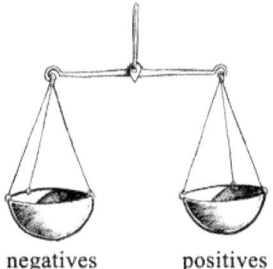

negatives   positives

Fig. 24.1. Proper negative-positive tension

Here's more truth from each side to help keep us balanced.

Our natural state	*God's provision*
We all have sinned. (Rom. 3:23)	He has made atonement for all sin. (1 John 2:2)
We all deserved eternal death, separation from God. (Rom. 6:23)	He has provided eternal life for all; all believers have it. (John 1:12)
We were God's enemies, dangerous and destructive to his kingdom. (Rom. 5:10)	He has adopted us and prepared good works for us to do. (Eph. 2:10)
We were hostile to God, unwilling and unable to obey Him. (Rom. 8:7)	He has brought us into His Kingdom and given us His Spirit of obedience. (1 Pet. 1:2; Col. 1:12-13)
We followed the ruler of this world, not God. (Eph. 2:2)	He has freed us to follow His Spirit and obey the Word. (Rom. 8:9)
We naturally gratify the sinful cravings of our flesh. (Eph. 2:3)	He gives us power and desire to do what is right. (Phil. 2:13)
We are by nature objects of wrath. (Eph. 2:3)	He has made us His dearly loved children. (Col. 3:12)
Nothing good lives in our flesh. (Rom. 7:18)	We are made righteous in Christ. (1 Cor. 1:30).

For me, it is powerful to see these contrasts, to see what God has provided in spite of what I deserve. I am humbled by what He has done, despite what I naturally am. And that is exactly what our response should be: humility leading to surrender, praise, and worship in every area of life. These truths lift our eyes above the mundane and help us live right now in the spiritual realities of eternity.

Putting on the Belt

The obvious question that comes up now is: "How exactly do we put on the belt of truth?"

Here's how I do it. After my worship time in the morning, and after I've prayed to be "strong in the Lord," I continue with something like the following.

"Lord, help me to put on the belt of truth today by remembering that by nature I am a child of wrath, that in my old nature dwells no good thing, that I deserve nothing good, that I deserve only punishment, separation, suffering, failure, and defeat. And remembering, as it says in Ephesians 1, in spite of what I am naturally, you, the Holy God, have blessed me in the heavenly realms with every spiritual blessing in Christ. You chose me in Him before the creation of the world to be holy and blameless in your sight. I praise you that this is what I am in you.

"In love you predestined me to be adopted as your son through Jesus Christ, in accordance with your good pleasure and will — I thank you that you desired me as your child — to the praise of your glorious grace, wherein you have made me accepted in the beloved, and which you have freely given me in the One you love.

"In Christ I have redemption through His blood, the forgiveness of sins, in accordance with the riches of your grace, O God.

"Thank you, Lord, that in Christ I stand before you chosen, made holy, and dearly loved. Amen"[37]

---

37. This prayer is, of course, only one example of how we can put on the belt of truth. We are certainly not tied to any particular form, for the content is the important thing. Overall, the belt reminds us of the two sides of truth. It is also a declaration of God's wonderful love to the unseen audience of angels and demons around us. And it an exaltation of God's goodness, justice, and grace.

In putting on the belt of truth each day, I remind myself of where I came from and to where God brought me. In doing this, I use variations of the two lists. "Lord, I put on the belt of truth today, remembering that although I deserve rejection, punishment, and death, in Christ I am chosen, called, cleansed, created anew, claimed, commissioned, and completely loved." This is from Colossians 3:12 and is really a summary of what we are in Christ. I don't just reel this off unthinkingly but tend to pause on each point to think a bit about it in something like the following:

In Christ, I am:
    chosen   — This is His work, not based on my worth but on His agape love.
    called   — He has actively, diligently worked in my life to bring me to Himself.

The Belt of Truth

What I am doing in this prayer is reviewing the full good news, reminding myself of God's great provision, His great love, His great forgiveness, and His great acceptance of me. When we keep all this in sight, then we will live out of His grace for His glory with His great power.

Speaking the two sides of truth in this way is actually "preaching the gospel to myself," as Jerry Bridges calls it in his excellent book *Respectable Sins*. He points out that it is natural to think that the gospel is only for unbelievers, but the reality is, it is for sinners, which we as believers also are. Reviewing the gospel like this frees me up to face my sin as I see how wonderfully accepted, forgiven, and loved I am by God. It also motivates me to deal with my sin: if God loves me so much in spite of what I am in the flesh, I certainly want to love Him back by obedience. This grasp of the gospel gives me also a strong sense of gratitude, leading to praise and thanksgiving.[38]

The gospel causes us to face the shame there is in our lives. Shame can come from abuse heaped on us by others, fear of man, our own mistakes and foolishness that embarrass us, or, more profoundly, from the inner knowledge that I am flawed in my basic makeup by original sin. It also enables us to embrace the truth of our shame, to bring it into the light of our forgiveness and acceptance in Christ, and to be freed from it.[39] Putting on the belt daily is a powerful means of gaining this freedom, remembering that we are deeply and unreservedly loved by God.

The gospel also speaks clearly of our being adopted into the family of God. J. I. Packer says that the concept of our adoption by God "is the nucleus and focal point of the whole New Testament teaching on the Christian life."[40] As Packer goes on to point out, there are two measures of God's love in the New Testament: the cross and the gift of sonship. First John 3:1 says, "How great is the love the Father has lavished on us, that we should be called children of God! And that is what we are!" A statement of amazed wonder and joy.

As I speak the gospel to myself daily in putting on the belt of truth, the amazing truth of God's rich, unreasonable, outrageous love begins to sink in.

---

cleansed	— He has atoned for my sin, declared me legally innocent.
created anew	— He transformed me from a dangerous enemy into a new creation.
claimed	— He has made me His child.
commissioned	— He has prepared good works for me and equipped me to do them.
completely loved	— I cannot decrease or increase His love by what I do.

All these are things He's done for us, and we can rest secure in them. They are the foundation of our relationship with Him, the belt of truth, on which all the other parts of the armor depend.

38. Bridges, *Respectable Sins,* pp. 33-35.

39. This concept is partially developed in *The Shame Exchange,* by the Breedloves and the Ennises.

40. Packer, *Knowing God,* p. 194.

DEEPER THOUGHTS ON PUTTING ON THE ARMOR

Here's an entry from my journal on this theme, flowing from meditating on Ephesians 1 and 2.

> Praise be to you, Father in heaven, for your perfect love, your perfect interaction, your perfect grace in our lives. You chose us before the foundation of the world, meaning you wanted us to be your children. You bought us with the blood of the Lamb, paying a huge price to own us. You predestinated us unto the adoption of children through Jesus Christ — according to the good pleasure of your will.
>
> You were not the least bit reticent about this but were whole-hearted, eager to have us in your family. Making sure that we became your children gave you pleasure; adopting us was an act in which you were glad, happy, pleased, and experienced joy! And this adoption was "to the praise of the glory of your grace, in which you have made us accepted in the beloved," as the KJV says so poetically.
>
> And the most astounding thing about your love is that when you planned our adoption, we were your enemies: bitter, rebellious, negative, destructive, hurtful foes. Rightfully you could have immediately condemned us to hell, separated us from your presence for eternity. "But because of your great love for us, you, God, who are rich in mercy, made us alive with Christ even when we were dead in transgressions — it is by your grace that we have been saved" (Eph. 2:3-4).
>
> We exalt in this, we praise you, we give thanks from full hearts for the warm and wonderful love that you pour out on us every day, including your gracious rebukes and correction — after all, you are the perfect Father with every aspect of fatherhood manifest in your relationship with us. And our response is to love you back by obedience to your Word.
>
> According to Ephesians 1, your attitude toward us, your interaction with us, your words about us are filled with enthusiastic, positive, loving thoughts; it is a delight and pleasure to you when we come to you in prayer; you are pleased with time spent with us.
>
> It is not like when we knock on some people's door and when they open it they say in a disappointed voice, "Oh, it's you." No, when we come into your presence in prayer or worship or thanksgiving or thought, you say, "Oh!! It's *you*!! I'm so glad You came. I am delighted to see you!! I was just thinking about you, how much I love you, how you are one of my favorite sons — of course, all my children are my favorites, but that doesn't diminish my love for you. I am so glad you are my child; I have no regrets about choosing, calling, and adopting you; in fact every time I think of you, I am pleased; I delight in you; you are fully accepted in my heart. It is such a pleasure to have you in our family, to know you, to spend time with you.
>
> "Come to me more often; I enjoy your prayers, your intercession, your praise time, your thoughts of me throughout the day.
>
> "I look forward to eternity when we can spend unbroken time together

The Belt of Truth

always in heaven, where you will be continually in my presence spiritually, mentally, emotionally, physically. Live in my love. Live in obedience that we both may have more pleasure and joy."

We praise you, Lord, our heavenly Father, for this your love toward us. Help us to honor and glorify you by reveling in your love, rejoicing in your acceptance, responding to your desire to spend time with us by coming to you each day, loving you back with obedience. Help us to live in the warm, light-filled, graceful beauty of your rich, deep, powerful, ever-flowing, enthusiastic love for and acceptance of us. Glory be to you in our lives every minute of today!

Dave on Negative and Positive Truth

Jack answered the door, greeted Dave, and led him into the den.

After they'd settled in their seats, Jack leaned forward, "Anything to report about putting on the belt of truth?" he asked.

"Yes," said Dave, "I found it somewhat painful to remind myself of what I am and deserve naturally — it really is an ugly picture if you look it full in the face. But it is a relief to list out the positives God has done for us, how much He loves us — it really is inspiring and comforting — uplifting. As you said, that phrase in Colossians 3:12, that we are "chosen people, holy and dearly loved" is a powerful one, and I spent time meditating on it."

Jack nodded, "The greatest desire of the human heart is to be loved unreservedly, wholeheartedly, constantly, deeply — and this is what God does with His agape love. We just have to believe it! In spite of what we were and what our flesh still is, we *are* chosen, holy, and dearly loved!"

Dave continued, "I had a sense of the negative and positive in my life before, but using the lists you gave me really lays it out. It is powerful to see these contrasts, to see what God has provided. I feel humbled!"

"That," replied Jack, "is exactly what our response should be: humility leading to surrender, praise, and worship in every area of life. These truths lift our eyes above the mundane and help us live right now in the spiritual realities of eternity."

They both sat quietly for a few moments.

"Repeating this truth every day to God for His glory, and then to ourselves for true comfort and perspective, helps us to grasp it a bit more deeply each time. The end result is transformation, something we'll talk about in another lesson."

Dave leaned back in his chair, "Two things stand out to me as I've tried to practice putting on the belt of truth. In beginning to accept the negative truths about my old nature, I find it easier to admit to God my mistakes and sin. I don't feel so strongly the need to hide my failures from God or myself."

Jack nodded. "Yes, that is a great side benefit of putting on the belt: we grow in our transparency to God and to ourselves. And this will lead to greater transparency with others."

Dave continued, "Another thing I noticed is that, in thinking through the two sides of truth, I am not so quick to trust my own ideas and perspectives. There's too much of a chance that my flesh is active there. I want to come to God to check them out first. This whole truth has given me a much bigger grasp of reality."

"That will keep you from falling into Abraham's error of trusting in his wife rather than God, which led to his having Ishmael!" commented Jack. "Keep putting on the belt every day, Dave, and you'll see more and more benefits. And read chapter 25 for our next session."

Study Guide questions for Chapter 24: "The Belt of Truth"

1. What relationship does the belt refer to? (206)
2. What are the two sides of truth the belt presents? (206-210,)
3. In what two ways does remembering the negative side help us? (207-208)
4. How do we put on the belt of truth? (210-211)
5. What does this do to help us keep the balance of the two sides of truth? (210-211)
6. What does this have to do with "preaching the gospel to ourselves?" (211)
7. How will you go about using this new information in your life?

CHAPTER 25

The Breastplate of Righteousness

The breastplate was a critical part of the Roman soldier's armor. It covered his vital organs. Its usefulness was tied to the belt, because if it wasn't fastened properly, it could swing out and hamper the soldier's ability to fight. When it was correctly attached, it protected him well from the weapons of the day. (See fig. 7.1.)

There is an exact parallel here with the spiritual application. We first have to have the belt of truth in place, understanding who we were, how much we have been forgiven, and who we are now in Christ. Then our relationship with God is in place: we know we are forgiven, accepted, and submitted; we have no known unconfessed sin.

After that, we can put on and use the breastplate of righteousness: "Stand firm then, with the belt of truth buckled around your waist, with the breastplate of righteousness in place" (Eph. 6:14). God entrusts us with this breastplate of His righteousness, imputing to us the righteousness of Christ. He allows us to carry it into the day, even though He knows we are going to fail and bring Him disgrace. This is confirmation of His love, acceptance, and forgiveness in our lives.

Just as He has forgiven and accepted us, so we can and must forgive and accept ourselves. This second piece of armor addresses our relationship with ourselves.

Forgiving ourselves is not just telling ourselves that we're OK so we can feel better. Rather, it is (1) understanding and accepting the forgiveness that Christ has bought for us at great cost and (2) applying this forgiveness to each situation.

To be a Christian we have to believe that Christ's death and resurrection paid the penalty for our sin and that God has forgiven us — believing that in His eyes we are holy and accepted. (Eph. 1:4-5).

Lots of us Christians, however, don't take the next step of granting, or applying, that forgiveness to ourselves. We don't want to forgive ourselves, or we don't feel we can forgive ourselves. Many therefore walk around without the breastplate on, angry and disgusted with themselves. This exposes them to attack by the enemy, especially on an emotional level.

Causing an Accident

When I do something foolish, I very quickly can start berating myself. I remember once that I forgot to look to the right before pulling out of a side street, and I drove right into an oncoming car. Immediately I started berating myself, "You idiot, you can't ever do anything right! When are you ever going to learn?!" This in spite of the fact that I'd never done this before!

Such words also trigger the fear of man: "What are others going to think when they hear about my stupidity? What a fool I am!"

However, in rejecting this human thinking, we can take up and put on the breastplate, which involves forgiving ourselves as Christ forgave us. We can plunge into God's thoughts, namely, that the sacrifice and resurrection of Jesus truly paid for our sins, that just as God has forgiven and accepted us, so we can forgive and accept ourselves. To affirm such truths is to apply His finished work to the event of the moment.

In my accident, that would mean first confessing to God my impatience, lack of attentiveness, and driving error. Then asking for and accepting His forgiveness and the assurance that His love is not dependent on my being exemplary all the time. I take responsibility for what I have done and pay the consequences on the human level. Then I must forgive myself on the basis of Christ's sacrifice, as stated in Colossians 3:13: "Bear with each other [including yourself] and forgive whatever grievances you may have against one another [including yourself]. Forgive as the Lord forgave you." This also helps to free me from the fear of what others think of me.

But suppose I am really angry at myself for what I've done. Can I just ignore the anger and say that I forgive myself? No, we need to process our emotions. It may mean going through the cycle of grief in a brief way:

> anger and unbelief
> bargaining/depression
> acceptance of the event and my responsibility
> coming to a new balance.

I have to process my anger at myself for failing, looking at it biblically (accepting the fact that, no matter how hard I try, I will still sin and make mistakes unintentionally; I am a sinner, I am human, I cannot be perfect).

I need to remind myself of the other side of truth: God loves me unreservedly; my mistakes and sin cannot change that. In Christ I am chosen, holy, and dearly loved — not because I am good, but because He is good.

The Breastplate of Righteousness

Then I need to release my anger, to let go of my disappointment in myself, and to reject my perfectionistic standards for myself. Lifting my soul to God through journaling helps me in this.

I must look at myself as both fallen and redeemed, a person who can and will make mistakes — but who has also been forgiven by the perfect sacrifice of Jesus Christ, not by my perfect behavior.

I must acknowledge and reject my tendency to draw my sense of significance from being competent rather than from God's love for me. I must be willing to live the painful truth of 2 Corinthians 12:9 that God's power is made perfect, *not in my strengths, but in my weaknesses.*

Not Everyone's Problem

I realize that some people do not struggle at all with forgiving themselves. They may wisely fully accept God's forgiveness. Or their makeup is such that they are easygoing about their errors and sins, letting go of these quickly, and moving on. Or they aren't really aware of their faults and sins, so are untroubled by them. Or they habitually blame others for their own mistakes — a sinful practice that needs to be corrected.

However, for people like me who are somewhat perfectionistic, this practice of consciously forgiving myself is really important. I tend to have too high standards for myself. I have found out the hard way where this perfectionism leads: to self-centeredness, depression, self-punishment, oppression of others, difficulty in believing God, and reliance on self rather than God.[41]

If we think in terms of layers of sin, we can see that punishing ourselves, or holding onto anger at ourselves, flows from unbelief and rebellion. We really don't believe that Christ's sacrifice is enough. We think we have to add something to it. We are really stealing honor and glory from God because we don't believe He did enough! Here's how it may look in layers:

> odd, unhealthy behavior
> depression/self-centeredness
> punishing myself
> anger toward myself
> not forgiving myself
> saying Christ's sacrifice was not enough
> pride
> unbelief/rebellion.

---

41. See chapter 30 for another personal story of my need to forgive myself.

The "How to" of Forgiving Myself

When I do something foolish, like causing that accident, initially I am disgusted with myself and may call myself names, like, "You are such a idiot!" or "Dumbo strikes again!" But cleaning up the physical mess takes precedence, distracting me from my negative thinking. Later, that sense of failure, of self-accusation, will again rise up inside. Then I will take time to write out my thoughts.

Here is an entry from my journal after I was faced with another of my sins.

> Lord, I have failed again, impulsively saying things that miscommunicate. When will I ever learn to *not* make such sweeping generalizations that are so easily disproved? I'm always seeking to win debates, to triumph over the other, instead of sticking to giving them something new to think about. I am such a slow learner, slow in depending on you, not praying while in such discussions, slow in discerning and rejecting my natural tendencies to win, and slow to recognize when I've said enough.
>
> Lord, you know this far better than I do, the selfishness, the desire for attention, for winning, for gaining significance and honor in the eyes of others. This is unbelief; I am rebelling against your Word and insight. Forgive me.

Note that this is confessing in layers, from selfishness right down to unbelief and rebellion. I actually did not intentionally think of confessing in layers, it just came out as a result of having learned to think in terms of layers of sin.

My journaling continued:

> Forgive me for these sins, Lord, for my failure to think truth and to turn to you. Forgive me for trusting myself rather than you. And I thank you, Lord God, that the sacrifice of the Lord Jesus was sufficient to buy forgiveness for my sin.
>
> I acknowledge the further sin of wanting to berate and punish myself for these failures. I confess my lack of belief, my thought that I could add to your work of forgiveness. As you have forgiven me, so in your finished work, I forgive myself.
>
> Lord, help me to walk in the light of your forgiveness, rejoicing in the freedom it brings. Help me to lay aside my wrong, perfectionistic standards that lead me to depend on myself rather than you. Thank you for how you are going to help me. Amen.

This is effective because it is set in the framework of thinking scripturally, lifting my soul, and confessing in layers.

Every morning as I put on the armor of God, after putting on the belt of

The Breastplate of Righteousness

truth, I take up the breastplate of righteousness, praying, "Lord as you have forgiven and accepted me, so I forgive and accept myself. As you love me, so I choose to love and accept myself."

Very often in praying this I sense a release as I have been struggling, often subconsciously, with some failure to meet my perfectionistic standard. There are almost always ripples of discontent in me because I have been throwing stones at my own reflection in my soul.

In summary, putting on the breastplate is really taking God at His Word on the one side and spotting and rejecting our human thinking on the other. Knowing truth without rejecting the opposing lie does us little good. Having the breastplate without putting it on makes it useless.

Jack's Chance to Forgive Himself

Jack cradled his bandaged right hand in his lap, his face still drawn with pain as he smiled at Dave's arrival. "Have a seat, Dave. Pardon me for not getting up to greet you."

"No, no problem," said Dave, his shock betraying itself in his voice. "What happened?"

"Well, I'm embarrassed to say that I did something foolish and am paying for it. While I was sharpening a chisel this morning, the old electric motor driving my grindstone stopped. When I pulled on the belt to get it going again, the motor started suddenly, pulling two of my fingers into the pulley, crushing and cutting them."

Dave winced just thinking about it. "Wow, that must have really hurt!" he said.

"At the moment, I hardly felt a thing," Jack said, "but when the shock wore off, it certainly did smart! And that pain came because I wasn't very smart!"

"So what did you do?" asked Dave.

"After stopping the flow of blood, I found I could wiggle my fingers, so nothing seemed to be broken. Barbara cleaned the wound and bandaged it, and I've taken a couple of Ibuprofen tablets. The pain should lessen shortly."

"Aren't you going to the emergency room?" asked Dave.

"No, I don't see a need for that at present. The cut is disinfected, and there doesn't seem to be any damage to my bones, so I will wait to see how things develop. Besides, I didn't want to miss our mentoring time this morning."

"Are you sure you want to have our lesson?" asked Dave.

"Definitely," said Jack. "Barbara is going to bring us some tea and cookies to fortify us. While we're waiting, let's pray."

Dave bowed his head as Jack began, "Lord God, Creator of heaven and earth, sustainer of all you have made, we worship you this morning for your greatness, your wisdom, your power. We give you honor for your holiness, your purity, your goodness. We submit ourselves to you this morning. I praise you for allowing this incident with my hand, for you will use it for good in my life. Guide us this morning as we look into your Word. Open our hearts, teach us what we need to learn. Amen."

Jack leaned back in his chair. "Actually, Dave, this accident of mine is a perfect illustration of what we've talked about in being able to forgive ourselves.

"Think about my accident: it was fully my sin and error that brought it on: impatience and laziness leading me to not turn off the switch before pulling on the belt. Humanly speaking, I could berate myself for that, 'You idiot, can't you ever do anything right? When are you ever going to learn?!' This also brings in fear of man: What are others going to think when they hear about my stupidity? 'What a fool he was!'

"However, in rejecting this human thinking, I can take up and put on the breastplate, forgiving myself as God has forgiven me. In the place of human thinking I can embrace God's thoughts, especially that the sacrifice and resurrection of Jesus truly paid for our sins. As God has forgiven and accepted us, so we can forgive and accept ourselves. This is applying His finished work to the moment.

"In my accident, that would mean first confessing my impatience and foolishness to God, asking for and accepting His forgiveness and assurance that His love is not dependent on my being smart all the time. Then I have to forgive myself on the basis of Christ's sacrifice as stated in Colossians 3:13: 'Bear with each other [including myself] and forgive whatever grievances you may have against one another [including myself]. Forgive as the Lord forgave you.' This also helps to free me from fear of what others think of me."

Dave was scribbling notes as fast as he could. "I won't forget this illustration soon!" he said. "Maybe this is one reason why God allowed this accident to happen!"

"I'm sure it's one reason, Dave," smiled Jack, then wincing as a twinge of pain shot through his hand.

Thoughts on Perfectionism

Perfectionism, I believe, is definitely a sin, for it arises from the attempt to earn my own worth/significance/security by my performance plus other people's good opinion of me. It is something that can never be fully achieved.

Under this goal is the old desire, first manifested in Satan, to have what God has, to be perfect like God for my own profit. God is definitely the only One who is perfect. With Eve the desire to be like God had to do with the power to know good and evil; with me it is wanting to be without sin or error in my own strength.

Under that is selfishness. And under that is unbelief and rebellion. Each layer is pleasing to Satan but grievous to God:

perfectionism
desire to earn my own significance and salvation
attempt to be like God — perfect
selfishness
unbelief
rebellion.

When I look at these layers of sin, it is a good incentive to forgive myself as Christ has forgiven me! It also frees me to be realistic about what I can accomplish.

This brings up a side issue. We have a lot of talk about excellence, especially in Christian circles. I agree that we should do things well, but often people confuse excellence with perfectionism.

We need to evaluate what needs very high standards (like brain surgery) and what doesn't (like putting your pajamas under your pillow). Doing something well, with true excellence, may require a 90 percent effort. Moving it toward perfectionism — that is, getting another 9 percent done — often requires another 90 percent effort. It is *mostly* not worth it.

I have read that this need for another 90 percent helps explain why so many surgeons are divorced — they put everything into their work and neglect their families. The same can be true among Christian workers who, in the pursuit of excellence, ignore their families, don't take a weekly Sabbath rest, and burn themselves out — which is certainly not to the glory of God. We need to be lining up our standards with God's and letting His prevail. Forgiving ourselves as He has forgiven us is one way to live by His values.

Dave versus Jack on Excellence

When Dave arrived, Jack was out in the yard working on trimming the hedge. His hurt hand was still bandaged, and Jack was having a hard time holding the trimmer level. Dave noticed that the hedge didn't have its usual straight edge.

"Hello, Jack," Dave greeted him

Jack turned and saw Dave. He shut off the trimmer. "Well, hello Dave, good to see you. Let me just finish this last section, and then we'll go in for our lesson." Jack paused, catching a look of concern on Dave's face as he looked at the hedge. "Something wrong with the hedge, Dave?"

"No . . . well . . . ah . . . , it's not as straight as usual," Dave stuttered.

Jack laughed, "You're right! With this bandaged hand, I'm having a hard time keeping the clippers straight. But there's a saying, 'If it's worth doing, it's worth doing badly!'"

Dave looked startled. "That's not how I remember it," he said. "It's 'If it's worth doing, it's worth doing right!'"

"You're right, Dave, that is the original saying, and there is truth in that. We should try to do things well. But when we start out, often we can't do it well. It's better to start and try than not do it at all.

"I'd rather have the hedge clipped a bit crookedly than not clipped at all. I can make corrections when I clip it the next time; by then my hand should be fully recovered."

Dave looked a bit doubtful. "Won't it bother you in the meantime? I mean, seeing that it's crooked?"

"It would bother me more to have it unclipped. At the same time, this is a small thing on the radar screen of life. I need to evaluate how important something is before I let it bother me."

Jack turned on the clipper, ran it over the last part, and stood back to survey his work. "Well, that's as good as I can get it, so let's go in for our lesson."

Study Guide questions for Chapter 25: "The Breastplate of Righteousness"

1. What relationship does the breastplate represent? (215)
2. Describe "forgiving myself." (216-217)
3. What does the grief cycle have to do with forgiving myself? (216)
4. How can you go about forgiving yourself? (218-219)
5. How does perfectionism torpedo forgiving of myself? (220-221)
6. What do you need to forgive yourself for right now?

CHAPTER 26

The Shoes of Peace

Truth #8: Forgiveness Brings Freedom

Once we have put on the belt of truth (our relationship with God is in place, with no unconfessed known sin) and have the breastplate of righteousness attached properly (our relationship with ourselves is at peace, having forgiven ourselves), then we can put on the shoes of peace. Ephesians 6:15 commands, "[Stand firm] with your feet fitted with the readiness that comes from the gospel of peace."

Fig. 26.1. The shoes of peace

This third piece of armor speaks of our relationships with others. As we have been forgiven by God, we need to forgive others — something easily said, but not so easily done.

God had to teach me this lesson of forgiving primarily by using my German mother-in-law. Omi ("Grandma"), as we call her, was a hard-working, talented woman who had very definite ideas about what was right and wrong. She was somewhat dismayed when her daughter married me, a foreigner, an American.

Whenever we visited her home, inevitably there would be a blowup between us. She was constantly working on remaking me into a German. She would reach over and button the top button on my shirt (that's the way men of her generation dressed). She strongly disapproved of how little butter I put on my bread. She was critical of how fast I ate, how quickly I made decisions, and how I disciplined the children. She corrected me a thousand times every day.

To give her the benefit of intent, she felt, I believe, that she was graciously coaching me on how to be a man of culture — her culture. I, however, failed to grasp her good intent and struggled with what felt like a constant barrage of criticisms and put-downs. I was glad she lived 3,000 miles away from our home and that we saw her infrequently!

My wise wife told me several times that God had given me two ears for a good purpose, but I wasn't using them correctly. "Let my mother's words go in one ear and out the other!" she would say. But Omi's hurtful words kept getting stuck in the emotions between my two ears!

One time while preparing a message on forgiveness, I sensed a question directly from the Holy Spirit, "So, have you forgiven everyone?"

"I think so!" I answered.

There was a pause, then, "What about your mother-in-law?"

"Oh . . . my mother-in-law!" I sighed. It was clear that the finger of the Lord was on a sin in my life. "You are right, Lord. But what should I forgive her for?" The answer immediately came to mind: "For not accepting you as you are."

I bowed my head and heart, "You are right, Lord, I must forgive her for not accepting me as I am. I am wrong in fighting her; forgive me for not listening more carefully to you! As you have forgiven me, so I forgive her for not accepting me for what I am."

It was simple as that for the start. Shortly after that interchange we went to Germany for a visit, but this time it was different. I found that forgiving my mother-in-law had freed me emotionally, and now I could begin to let her comments go in one ear and out the other.

Then an amazing thing happened: as I changed in my attitude, she began to change in hers — even though I hadn't said anything to her about forgiving her! It seemed that my forgiving her in my heart opened the way for God to work in her and change her attitude toward me!

You might ask, Why didn't I tell her that I'd forgiven her? The answer is, she could never have understood that — in her mind she had done nothing wrong! This business of forgiving at this point was just between God and me; with that transaction taking place in the vertical relationship, I was able to then act freely and lovingly in the horizontal relationship.

As God took me through the application of forgiveness with my mother-in-law, I took the time to write these lessons down in my journal, thinking them through. That was especially helpful in applying them to new situations.

The Principle of Forgiveness

Forgiveness is, I believe, the highest form of obedience, for it is a most unnatural thing to do: the more hurtful the offense, the more unnatural it becomes. Forgiveness is of great importance in God's eyes, though, being the second major message of the Bible, coming only after the message of His love.

Here are some major points about forgiveness to help in understanding and applying it.

- Forgiveness is a process. It starts with a definite act of the will in forgiving the other person. Then it continues on. Every time the offending person comes to mind, I need to reaffirm my forgiving, "Lord as you forgave me, so I affirm my forgiveness of this person." As Jesus said in Matthew 18:22, we are to forgive a person seventy-seven times (or seventy times seven, NIV margin); that is, we have to persist. When we make this repeated choice, it slowly but surely penetrates and transforms our emotions and sets us free. With one person who had hurt me deeply, I had to choose to forgive every morning for over eight years before my emotions came up to "zero," and then for a couple more years until my emotions were at a healthy "plus."

- Forgiveness is not based on the other person's changing or being punished or asking for forgiveness. Rather, it is based on Christ's death and resurrection; my sin and this other one's sins have both been paid for.

- As God has forgiven me an immeasurable amount of sin (see the Matt. 18 story of the unforgiving servant, explained below), so I can and must forgive my fellow believer. (Note Col. 3:13: "Bear with each other and forgive *whatever* grievances you may have against one another. *Forgive as the Lord forgave you.*") The more we know of our own depravity and cleansing, the more easily we are able to forgive others.

- Forgiveness, as I am using it, is most importantly between God and me; rarely have I gone to the other person in the midst of a conflict and said, "I forgive you." The emotional state is usually such that the other person could neither hear nor comprehend what I might say. No, at this point it is first between God and me. Later, as the person sees his or her part, I can gladly offer forgiveness, especially if the person asks for it.

- Forgiveness is not letting the other person off the hook. It is getting out of the way and letting God deal with the person instead of me trying to do it with my wrong motives and feeble efforts (see Rom. 12:17-21). When we forgive, we have basically given God a free hand to work in that person's life. When we forgive the other person, he or she is then freed to change, even though we have not personally told him or her of our forgiveness.

- God never says, "Forgive and forget." He Himself forgives and then chooses not to remember. We weak humans can never fully forget, especially hurtful happenings — they are burned into our memory and emotions — but we can "forgive and rewrite," that is, look at the person and the hurt to see how God has used that one to shape and mold us into the image of His Son.

Let's expand a bit on this point. Jesus Himself went through difficulties to make Himself a complete Savior: "Although he was a son, he *learned obedience* from what he suffered" (Heb. 5:8). He looked at his difficulties as they fit into God's plan, not from a human viewpoint. So as we go through such things, we can strive to see them from God's point of view, rewriting the event as He sees it.

When we rewrite the event from God's perspective, the hurt then becomes an impetus for thanksgiving as we see God's wisdom unfold (1 Thess. 5:18). We need to trust God to use all that He allows for our good and His glory.

In the rewriting process, it is important to get your feelings out before God, lifting your soul to Him, preferably by journaling: tell Him you are angry at the other person, angry at God for allowing this situation, angry at the situation, the hurt, the turmoil. Then go with Him through these feelings, measuring them against the Word.

> Yes, Lord, I am angry at you, but this is presumptuous on my part, it is wrong. I believe I understand better than you, but this is not true. I confess my inadequacy, my smallness, and reaffirm my faith in you, in your wisdom and your love in bringing this difficulty into my life to shape and deepen me. As you worked in Joseph's life and in Christ's life, so you are working in mine, and I praise you for it.

Here, then, are six more points on the meaning, significance, practice, and personal value of forgiveness:

- I forgive, not for the other person, but first for God (it gives Him great glory) and second for myself so I can be free to serve God.

- If I don't forgive, the one who has offended me will control me: every time I think of that one, or see or hear of him or her, I will get uptight. Without the offender knowing it, he or she has hold of my emotions in a painful, powerful way. This can lead to problems for me in every area of life: psychologically (control by negative thoughts), emotionally (fear, anger), physically (ulcers, tensions, illnesses), relationally (anger spilling over), and, most importantly, spiritually (hampering my relationship with God). To forgive the offender sets *me* free, although often not immediately.

- If I don't forgive, I have sided with Satan, asked to be turned over to the torturers (see Matt. 18:34-35), and will be limited in my usefulness to

The Shoes of Peace

God, for I have "shut off the faucet of grace" (Matt. 6:14-15; James 4:6).

- If I don't forgive, I have, in a twisted way, put the offenders in God's place: I am expecting from them what only God can do, namely, always demonstrate perfect actions, perfect love, perfect fellowship, perfect motives, and perfect acceptance. By forgiving the offenders, I am removing them from this place of exalted expectations and again focusing on the living God, who alone is perfection.

- Forgiveness is a promise, giving my word to God not to take revenge (which rightfully belongs only to God — see Rom. 12:17-19) but to cooperate with God in giving glory to Him in whatever way this may require. It is a promise that I will not gossip about the one who hurt me, that I will not use the offense to attack him or her but will work for it to be a blessing to the offender.

- Forgiving offenders in your heart does not preclude your confronting them (or perhaps a better term is *care*-fronting them). To forgive takes care of the legal issue — you have given up the right to get revenge, be it ever so mild as talking about the persons to others. It does not, however, eliminate practical issues, such as whether or how to confront them, or how much contact to have with them in the future.

If a person has seriously sinned against you (meaning that it is not something simply to overlook), Matthew 18:15-17 commands us to go and talk with him or her about the offense for the purpose of helping that one, winning back him or her. Forgiving the person in our heart before going to talk with the offender is what makes the "care-fronting" possible and powerful. Then it is not the anger of personal hurt that drives us but godly concern for the individual and our relationship with him or her.

Galatians 6:1-2 talks more generally about confronting a sin directly: "Brothers, if someone is caught in a sin, you who are spiritual should restore him gently. But watch yourself, or you also may be tempted. Carry each other's burdens, and in this way you will fulfill the law of Christ."

When we forgive, we can pray more effectively for the other person, having removed the emotional barriers that we had erected against him or her. When we reach the point where we can pray for God's blessing in the offender's life, asking that God bless that one as much or more than me, then we are well on the way to healing and a godly balance.

Forgiveness in the Light of Matthew 18

Matthew 18:21-35 is Jesus' story of an unforgiving servant. This passage teaches the foundational issues of forgiveness.

> Then Peter came to Jesus and asked, "Lord, how many times shall I forgive my brother when he sins against me? Up to seven times?"
> Jesus answered, "I tell you, not seven times, but seventy-seven times [*or,* seventy times seven]." (vv. 21-22)

Note here that Peter thought he was being really generous to forgive 7 times. However, Jesus jacked the number up considerably to 77 times (or, as some older translations have it, 490 times). Does that mean Peter should keep a notebook of how many times he'd forgiven one person? No, it means we should forgive as much as is necessary, without putting our own limits on it.

Jesus now begins to tell a story that is meant to open up Peter's (and our) understanding of forgiveness.

> Therefore, the kingdom of heaven is like a king who wanted to settle accounts with his servants. As he began the settlement, a man who owed him ten thousand talents was brought to him. Since he was not able to pay, the master ordered that he and his wife and his children and all that he had be sold to repay the debt. (vv. 23-25)

This servant owed a huge amount. The Greek word used here, *myrias,* means 10,000, or "countless thousands" — that is, "an incalculable amount." Jesus was saying, "the very biggest debt you could possibly imagine." It was an impossible amount to repay, equivalent to millions of dollars — a hopeless situation!

> The servant fell on his knees before him. "Be patient with me," he begged, "and I will pay back everything." The servant's master took pity on him, canceled the debt and let him go.
> But when that servant went out, he found one of his fellow servants who owed him a hundred denarii. He grabbed him and began to choke him. "Pay back what you owe me!" he demanded. (vv. 26-28)

Consider the second servant's debt. A denarius was about one day's wage for a laborer. This is a manageable debt, in contrast to the one that he had just had canceled. With time and discipline, the second servant could pay it back.

> His fellow servant fell to his knees and begged him, "Be patient with me, and I will pay you back."
> But he refused. Instead, he went off and had the man thrown into prison until he could pay the debt. When the other servants saw what had happened,

The Shoes of Peace

they were greatly distressed and went and told their master everything that had happened.

Then the master called the servant in. "You wicked servant," he said, "I canceled all that debt of yours because you begged me to. Shouldn't you have had mercy on your fellow servant just as I had on you?" In anger his master turned him over to the jailers to be tortured, until he should pay back all he owed." (vv. 29-34)

In this parable, the king certainly represents God, while you and I are the first servant. As believers, we have been forgiven our huge debt of sin by our King. The other servant represents someone who sins against us.

Consider the contrast between these two debts: the equivalent of half a lifetime of work versus three months' of work. The first debt represents our sin against God and how much He has forgiven us: an incredible, unimaginable amount! In comparison, the debt of the one who has sinned against us is miniscule. If I have been forgiven such a virtually unlimited amount, how can I possibly find it too hard to forgive such a relatively small amount?!

Note what the king did to the unforgiving servant in the end. He didn't just put him into prison, he turned him over to the *torturers*! Then comes the shocking last verse in this passage:

This is how my heavenly Father will treat each of you unless you forgive your brother from your heart. (v. 35)

So how will God treat us if we don't forgive? He will turn us over to torturers! Is that possible for a loving God to do?

Think of it this way. I'm sure you have had someone hurt you badly. The next time you saw that person, how did you feel? You probably wanted to avoid him or her. And how was your stomach? When you saw that person, didn't you experience a tightening in your stomach, a tension? That tension will remain, and the stress will grow, if you do not forgive the one who hurt you. You will seek to avoid the person, but that won't work, for whenever he or she comes to mind, so will the physical and emotional discomfort. This discomfort is part of the torture that God will turn us over to.

If the situation goes on festering, it can result in physical damage, maybe an ulcer, a nervous condition — certainly unhappiness that can bring depression. This can lead to relational difficulties as you get irritable, short tempered. This could lead to loss of your job, economic problems, and more.

I have a believing friend who, before I knew him, treated his wife like a slave. (He blissfully thought he was following the instructions in Ephesians 5!)

His wife was so negatively affected that she could not forgive him, and she ended up an invalid, unable to walk.

When my friend was convicted of his wrong viewpoint and actions, he asked his wife's forgiveness, and she forgave him. Shortly after that, she recovered fully. That's the power of hurt, of unforgiveness, and then of forgiveness. This couple went on to become effective missionaries in Ethiopia in their late fifties! This was because the husband was willing to admit his wrong and ask for forgiveness, and she was willing to forgive.

We can surmise both from Jesus' statements and from this couple's story that God's willingness to use such drastic means to get our attention means that forgiveness is really important to Him! Look at Matthew 6:14-15, where Jesus makes a comment on the prayer He had just taught to His disciples: "For if you forgive men when they sin against you, your heavenly Father will also forgive you. *But if you do not forgive* men their sins, your Father will not forgive your sins."

This comment on forgiveness is the only one Christ gives us on His prayer. That means it is important! Our forgiving or not forgiving powerfully affects our relationship with God. Unforgiveness effectually shuts off the faucet of grace in our lives. This is a serious thing, making us useless to God, a detriment to His work.

The question for us is, Which power will we tap into: Satan's power in unforgiveness, or God's greater power in forgiveness?

Forgiving and Rewriting

Rewriting a hurtful event from God's point of view, as mentioned above, is another powerful way to get out of the resentment, self-pity, and anger that accompany the painful experience of being sinned against.

The story of Joseph in the Old Testament is a great illustration of this. When Joseph was sold by his brothers as a slave, he had plenty of reasons to be angry. Betrayed by his own flesh and blood, left without defense, having no hope, facing a life of oppression and probably an early death, Joseph trudged over the sands to Egypt, the sun beating down on him, the shackles on his ankles cutting into his skin. Yet, when he arrived in Egypt, he seems to have forgiven his brothers. The Bible does not tell us this directly, but there are strong clues that point to Joseph's having forgiven those who betrayed him, leaving him for as good as dead.

In Genesis 39:2-4 it says, "The LORD was with Joseph and he prospered, and he lived in the house of his Egyptian master. When his master saw that the

The Shoes of Peace

LORD was with him and that the LORD gave him success in everything he did, Joseph found favor in his eyes and became his attendant. Potiphar put him in charge of his household, and he entrusted to his care everything he owned. "

Think about what a bitter, unforgiving person is like. The ones I've known are crabby and unpleasant. And they are often not very hard working — they feel the world owes them a living. Joseph was exactly the opposite of this pattern: it seemed he was pleasant, hardworking, willing to make his master successful, and enjoyed his work. Plus, it says that God was blessing him. Bitterness cuts us off from God's blessing. All indications point to Joseph's having made his peace with God; with trust in God, Joseph had forgiven his brothers.

This conclusion is further supported by Joseph's attitude when, after being unjustly accused, he found himself locked up in prison. When two of his fellow prisoners, officials of Pharaoh, had perplexing dreams that made them unhappy, Joseph noticed this and asked what was wrong. A bitter, self-centered person is not likely to do that. People who see themselves as victims rarely think of others.

The real proof comes in Genesis 50:20, where Joseph says to his fearful, conniving brothers, "You intended to harm me, but God intended it for good to accomplish what is now being done, the saving of many lives."

Here Joseph is looking at the event from God's eyes, rewriting it to see the greater purpose God had, not just for Joseph, but for many, many others who lived because Joseph had been willing to trust God and forgive his brothers. And Joseph not only saved the people of Egypt and his family. What he did ultimately saved you and me: by his obedience to God, Joseph preserved the line of Israel through Judah, from whom came the Messiah, who saved us through His death and resurrection. God works huge things through seemingly small events.

As stated above, I believe that Joseph had begun to have this perspective even before he arrived in Egypt, even before he saw what God would do. I believe he trusted God to be using his suffering for good. Later he could look back and see that what was later written as Psalm 23:6 was true, "Surely goodness and love will *follow me all the days of my life.*"

When we are going through some difficulty, especially what could be called a valley of the shadow of death, we probably won't perceive God's goodness and mercy. At that point we have to trust Him by faith that His goodness and mercy are at work, which gives us the perspective to forgive those who hurt us. Afterward, however, we may be able to look back, as Joseph did, and see the goodness God was working on in our lives through the difficulties.

Personally, I've had plenty of opportunity to practice this principle of forgiving others and trusting God to work things out for better ends in my own life. I'll give you just one more example here.

Early in our time in the Middle East I wanted to purchase a video player, thinking it would be a great tool for evangelism. These players had just come out on the market, and all the locals were buying them. My teammates, however, strongly urged me to wait and do more research. I really was unhappy with this and resented their butting into what I viewed as a personal decision.

However, knowing that God wants us to work in unity, to take advice, and to be patient, I chose to trust God to work through what I thought to be my teammates' shortsightedness. I forgave them for their lack of faith and waited.

Not long afterward, my supervisor at the university where I worked asked me to take a course on making videos. As part of the course, the instructor gave us recommendations on what was the best equipment on the market. It was definitely *not* what I'd planned to buy! When I talked with my teammates about what I'd learned, they all agreed that buying the recommended player was a good idea. I did so and was able to use it for years, making some good videos, one of which ended up being widely used. If I'd followed my own ideas and timing, the outcome would not have been anywhere near as good.

In the midst of this example, before I understood what He was doing, God enabled me to rewrite my teammates' resistance as something He was going to use to give me better direction — and that's exactly what He did!

Cooperating with God in Forgiving

There is a very prevalent belief that if I forgive someone who wronged me, I'm letting that person off the hook. This perspective can actually be the desire for revenge (often disguised as a desire for justice). When we don't forgive those who offend us, we desire to get revenge on them, to make them hurt as they have hurt us. This is standing in the place of God, who says, "Vengeance is mine" (Rom. 12:19 KJV). Let's look at the whole passage that speaks of this.

> Do not repay anyone evil for evil. Be careful to do what is right in the eyes of everybody. If it is possible, as far as it depends on you, live at peace with everyone. Do not take revenge, my friends, but leave room for God's wrath, for it is written: "It is mine to avenge; I will repay," says the Lord. On the contrary:
>
> "If your enemy is hungry, feed him;
> if he is thirsty, give him something to drink.

The Shoes of Peace

In doing this, you will heap burning coals on his head."
Do not be overcome by evil, but *overcome evil with good.* (Rom. 12:17-21)

When we are trying to play God by getting revenge, we cannot obey the commands in this passage: living at peace, feeding and giving our enemy to drink, overcoming evil with good. Instead, we are getting in the way of what God wants to do.

In contrast, when we forgive and begin to bless our former enemy (whether they have repented and changed or not), then God is freed to work through us and through others to bring conviction and change in this person's life.

As I mentioned, this is what happened in my mother-in-law's life, and I have seen it happen in a good number of other situations as well. When I forgive, I become a channel of grace to the other person, allowing him or her to be changed. This is right in line with the command to do good to those who persecute us (Matt. 5:44 and Luke 6:27-28).

Going Further: Confronting/Care-Fronting

It bears repetition: forgiving is the highest form of obedience because it is so unnatural. Confronting others with their sin and doing it biblically, with right motives, is a close second. It is so human to avoid confrontation, unless you are a fighter by your old nature, which means automatically that your motives in confronting will be wrong.

When I have forgiven the person who hurt me, I need to evaluate whether it is necessary to confront him or her. Was this offense a sin? Does it fall under the instructions of Matthew 18:15-17? Or is it something I should overlook? In my mother-in-law's desire to remake me, it was not a clear sin; it was something I could forgive, overlook, and let go of. At other times she said or did things that were clear violations of Scripture, and I did talk with her about them. Her reactions were generally not what I wanted, but we worked it through to a better situation than before.

A counselor once told me, "People are monsters only because we allow them to be." It is sometimes necessary to put down boundaries for those who don't have a sense of what personal boundaries are.

It may be a scary thing to confront a strong person, but once we have forgiven him or her and are willing to confront for the right reasons (first to please God, second for the sake of that person, and third to make ourselves more effective for Him), confronting takes on a different color.[42]

As noted, this process could be called care-fronting, rather than confronting. That is, we are doing this "for" the person, rather than against

---

42. For good guidance in confronting difficult people, see the excellent book *Boundaries,* by Henry Cloud and John Townsend (Grand Rapids: Zondervan, 1992).

("con-"). Our job is to speak up in love, not to force change in the person.

We need to pray about it first, purifying our motives before God, asking Him to prepare the one we will speak with, and praying for wisdom in how to approach the person. It is good to prepare your words, making your statement short, to the point, and clear. Like, "The way you spoke to me yesterday was painful because I felt it cut me down. I would ask that you not use name-calling in our talks together."

The person may not respond positively, but you have done your part until the next offense, and you can leave the offender for God to work on. It may later be necessary to go to the next step in Matthew 18:15-17, "care-fronting" the person with someone else if he or she chooses to ignore your personal care-frontation.

My comments here make the process sound reasonably neat and easy, but in my experience it is more often quite messy. Dealing with people is rarely nice and neat! However, the preparation of forgiving the person in your heart (of rejecting wrong motives, acting out of right ones), plus having your words prepared, can avoid a lot of the messiness.

Let me give you an example of care-fronting. While talking with a friend recently, he uttered some words of disapproval for what I'd said, and then added a couple of zingers about my manhood to emphasize the point.

I had three choices: (1) to bow my neck to his thoughts and say nothing, stuffing my hurt; (2) to reply in kind; or (3), remembering who I am in Christ, to deal graciously with the issue without attack or anger.

Because the Holy Spirit had been working with me on this issue of care-fronting, setting me free from the trap of fear, I could process and let go of my anger, hold onto the truth that I am safe in Him, and rise above the events. I forgave my friend in my heart, then asked him if the same things could be expressed without resorting to "zingers." The rest of the talk went much better.

Care-frontation is one way of truly loving the person. As one strong personality I worked with said to me after I had done a care-frontation, "You are one of the few who love me enough to confront me!" Let us love one another enough to speak up in love.[43]

43. Here is another example of confronting. In one organization I worked in, the leader asked me to help him with interpersonal problems that kept bubbling up in the office, making for a poor work environment. After interviewing all thirty people in the office, it became clear that one big source of discontent was the way the leader himself was interacting with his people. So, though he was my boss, I had to care-front him. Fortunately, he had told me earlier that he liked the "sandwich method" of confrontation: first complementing him on things done well, then confronting on changes needed, and finally encouraging him on good past performance.

So, I carefully prepared what I had to say, writing it all out before going to see him. He took it well (showing his spiritual maturity), and I left him with a copy of the

The Shoes of Peace

Dave and Forgiveness

"So, Dave, anything to report on opportunities to apply the lesson on forgiving others?" asked Jack.

Dave settled back into his chair. "Yes, as usual, the Lord gave me another tailor-made lesson using what you've taught me. This past weekend I was home alone the whole time, Friday morning through Sunday night, working on a big paper. I'd spent Thursday with a good friend whom I've been sharing with about Christ. We agreed to get together to watch a video on Intelligent Design over the weekend. I made it clear that it was up to him to call me, as I didn't want to impose on him and his family."

"So what happened?" asked Jack.

"Nothing! I waited all weekend for a call, but not a peep. A number of times I felt sorry for myself, being forgotten and left out. I struggled with resentment. But then I remembered what we had talked about on forgiving others, so I decided to forgive my friend for forgetting me.

"Did that help?" Jack asked.

"Well, it did, although it was a struggle. I had to go to my journal and write out my feelings and process them: self-pity, resentment, and hurt pride were the primary ones, it turned out. When I confessed these and then forgave my friend as God forgave me, then there was some release from my emotional turmoil.

"Anything else in this? What about rewriting the events from God's point of view?" asked Jack.

"Yes, that was another factor. As I thought about it, it became clear that God knew I really needed to get that big paper done and gave me a weekend without interruption that made it possible. Plus I had time in between to relax. I probably wouldn't have had time for all that if my friend had called.

"Another 'rewriting point' came to my mind as I prayed about it. God probably knew that this wasn't the optimal time for more input for my friend, and when the appropriate time comes, he will give us opportunity to view that video. I was probably pushing too hard to share with my friend, and God helped me back off."

"Well, done, Dave. You probably also recognize the attacks of the enemy in all this, trying to drive a negative emotional wedge between you

---

care-frontation I written out so he could review the positives to encourage himself, while considering the negatives. He accepted what I suggested, and things began to improve.

There were two other people in that setting who were greater causes of disruption. They were both unwilling to respond to care-frontation. In God's providence, however, in response to prayer for God to bring about a solution, both committed blatant violations of policy and ethics, bringing out into the open what had been going on under the surface. As a result, they were both legitimately released from work, resulting in a much better situation both for us and for them.

DEEPER THOUGHTS ON PUTTING ON THE ARMOR

and your friend. We'll talk in the next lesson about how to follow up on forgiveness with holding up the shield of faith. So read chapter 27 before you come next week."

Study Guide questions for Chapter 26: "The Shoes of Peace"

1. What relationship do the shoes represent? (223)
2. Why is forgiveness the "highest form of obedience?" (224)
3. Which of the forgiveness principles do you find hard to accept or understand? (225-227)
4. In the parable of the unforgiving servant, who is the King, who is the unforgiving servant, who is the servant who was jailed? (229)
5. How much has God forgiven you? How does this help you forgive others? (228)
6. What are the consequences of not forgiving? (229)
7. What does it mean to "forgive and rewrite?" (230-232)
8. How does forgiving someone allow God to deal with them? (232-233)
9. What is "care-fronting" and how is it connected to forgiveness? (233-234)
10. How will this chapter bring more freedom into your life?

CHAPTER 27

The Shield of Faith

Truth #9: Offering the Sacrifice of Thanksgiving Honors God

The soldiers were tense, waiting for the order to attack. Standing in rows, each rested his shield on the ground in front of him. Every man's eyes were on the commander standing on the hill above them, the ensign of Rome flapping in the wind from the pole behind him. His eyes were on the forest's edge, where the enemy was massed, working up their courage to attack.

A shout rose from the woods, beginning in one throat, then a dozen, then rising from five thousand. The enemy began to advance.

"Take shields!" shouted the officer. Each man lifted his shield in his left hand. Then "Take swords!" came the order. Each man drew his sword, holding it behind his shield.

"Close ranks — advance!" the officer commanded. The lines of soldiers shifted, each man moving to touch his neighbor's shoulder, his shield covering his own chest, plus part of his neighbor's to his left. The ranks began to move as one man, marching to the beat of a large drum.

As they came within 100 yards of the enemy, the officer barked, "Double time!" The drum beat faster, the soldiers broke into a trot, keeping in step, each man's shield in place, covering himself and his neighbor. The enemy, too, began to run, shaking their small round shields, waving their swords. Their shouts grew louder. The Romans ran silently, keeping their swords behind their shields.

"Triple time!" bellowed the officer, and the drum responded with a faster beat, quickly matched in the faster stride of the soldiers. The two lines crashed into each other, the enemy slashing with their swords. The Romans, however, kept their discipline, maintaining their lines, holding their shields in place and using them to push the enemy back, knocking them down, then stabbing them on the ground, moving to the next in line to push them back too.

As the battle progressed, the Romans' lines broke up, and it was each man on his own, but the initial clash had left many of the enemy on the ground for good, defeated by the disciplined use of the Roman shield.

The enemy soldiers began to retreat, their strength broken. "Roma victa!" shouted the officer. "Roma victa!" echoed the soldiers, lifting their shields.

DEEPER THOUGHTS ON PUTTING ON THE ARMOR

Fig. 27.1. The full armor

The Roman soldier is what inspired Paul in his description of the armor in Ephesians 6. As seen in the passage above, the Roman soldier's shield was his primary weapon of offense, used to knock the enemy down so the soldier could effectively use his sword, his secondary offensive weapon. But just having a shield wasn't enough; he had to know how to use it, both with his fellow soldiers and individually.

Think about Paul's command to us in Ephesians 6:16: "In addition to all this, take up the shield of faith, with which you can extinguish all the flaming arrows of the evil one." The little phrase "in addition to all this" is very important in the use of the armor. "All this" refers to the first three pieces of armor: the belt of truth, the breastplate of righteousness, and the shoes of peace.

Can you imagine what it would be like for a Roman soldier to show up for battle without his belt, breastplate, or shoes, having only his shield and sword? He'd be much more vulnerable and much less effective. He'd have nothing to hang his sword on, every step would be a potential wound to his foot, and his whole chest would be totally open to any attack that came along.

As we have seen, the first three parts of the armor each represent a relationship: the belt of truth speaks of our relationship with God, the breastplate speaks of our relationship with ourselves, and the shoes of peace refer to our relationship with others. We must have these relationships in place in order to effectively take up the shield of faith.

The Shield of Faith

Practically speaking, this means that everything must be clear in each relationship: that with God I have no unconfessed sin, that I've forgiven myself, and that I have forgiven anyone who's sinned against me. When we have peace with God, with ourselves, and with others, then we are free and ready to live in praise, trusting God. Otherwise we are unprepared, unprotected, and unable to effectively use the shield of faith — and usually also unwilling to do so!

Taking Up the Shield

Raising this shield is relatively simple: we lift it up by praising God, which is a clear expression of our faith. When we praise God no matter what comes, we are declaring our trust in Him.

As we have seen, if I am having trouble in any of the three relationship areas, it will be harder to trust God when something difficult comes along. I would tend to be hiding from God or mad at myself or fuming about someone else. Not forgiving shuts off the faucet of grace and makes it harder to praise when I can see no reason for it.

Consider a person in the Bible who was good at using the shield of faith: Job. Look at his response to the great losses he suffered in chapter 1 of his book: gone were all his children, many of his trusted servants, and all his oxen, donkeys, sheep, and camels. Verses 20 and 21 say that, after hearing all he'd lost, "Job got up and tore his robe and shaved his head. Then he fell to the ground in worship and said: 'Naked I came from my mother's womb, and naked I will depart. The LORD gave and the LORD has taken away; *may the name of the LORD be praised.*"

Personally, I stand in awe of one who could make that his first response! Just look at what he did: with everything pushing him away from praise toward complaining, anger, despair, and depression, he made the decision to worship.

He declared some hard truths: in reality he owned nothing, and God had the right to give and take as he saw fit. Job chose, against all human reason, to praise God with clenched teeth, raising the shield of faith against the onslaught of natural thought, of the world's values, and of Satan's flaming arrows of doubt.

The question we should ask ourselves is, "How could a man come to this point of maturity?" It is obvious that Job knew the character of God well and had surrendered himself to Him. This would indicate that he spent time with God, learning to think as God did.

A comment in the next chapter of Job gives us a further clue. After Satan was allowed to strike Job with sores, we hear the reaction and advice of his wife:

> His wife said to him, "Are you still holding onto your integrity? Curse God and die!"
> He replied, "You are talking like a foolish woman. Shall we accept good from God, and not trouble?" (2:9-10)

Job's wife obviously did not share his view of God, nor did she share Job's integrity. She knew he lived by what he said he believed. However, in her bitterness of soul, having lost so much and now having a sick husband to care for, she was living according to her feelings and did not think it was worth living by truth.

Her prescription to curse God and die flowed from a very human view of the situation, with all its hopelessness. No faith is evident. She is probably striking out in her own hurt, very conscious of her own losses and of her husband's terrible suffering.

Humanly speaking, it is understandable that she was angry at God for allowing these losses, angry at Job for not grieving with her, angry at those who had robbed and killed. She evidently did not have the first three parts of the armor in place, and so could not hold up the shield of faith.

Note Job's response: he does not react in anger or scorn because of her hurtful words, nor does he put his wife down by calling her foolish. Instead, he gently rejects her foolish thinking and gives her the bigger picture of life. In a sense, he tries to raise the shield of faith for her to protect her from Satan's fiery darts.

One important thing is pointed out by Job's responses: he had the first three parts of the armor on. His relationship with God was close and trusting, he did not blame himself unnecessarily, and he was loving and forgiving toward his wife. That made him ready to take up the shield of faith.

We know that the rest of Job's book has to do with his wanting to know why God brought this suffering into his life. God never gives him a direct answer to this question. Instead, He reveals more of His greatness to Job.

Job's response to God's revelation comes in 42:3, "Surely I spoke of things I did not understand, things too wonderful for me to know." Then he adds this revealing point: "My ears had heard of you *but now my eyes have seen you.*"

Job's initial response of raising the shield was based on a faith stemming from what he'd *heard* of God. His suffering, however, became the opportunity for him to *know* God more, which brought him to a deeper surrender. We could say that it brought him to a deeper faith, or a position where he could better hold up the shield.

Job's example shows us two truths to implement when we encounter difficulties. First: suffering brings opportunity for growth in faith, if we respond with praise. Second: if we hold up the shield of faith in one situation, it helps us to make the same decision in a harder situation.

The Flaming Arrows of the Wicked One

What are these those flaming arrows mentioned in Ephesians? I believe they often have to do with thoughts, fears, and words, both of others and our own words to ourselves — they are usually lies in the form of half-truths. In my life these are most frequently thoughts of self-pity or self-accusation. They can also be worries or fears that lead to anger, remorse, and unwillingness to forgive myself or others. And they can be events that push us to think these negative thoughts.

Satan, "the father of lies" and "the accuser of our brothers" (John 8:44; Rev. 12:10), is skillful at shooting these fiery arrows at us. Very often they have to do with our emotions, which in themselves are untrustable; they need to be measured by the Word. For example, when we hear of an old friend who has been very successful in his or her work or ministry, Satan can throw a dart of jealousy at us. In order to ward off these flaming arrows, both to protect ourselves and to extinguish the flames, we need to hold up the shield of faith by responding in praise.

Different Types of Arrows

As I meditated on this concept of the shield extinguishing all the flaming arrows of the evil one, a thought came to mind. There are three categories of flaming arrows. First, there is the everyday, normal-sized arrow. Events like being late, having people treat us unjustly, or a fender-bender bring this type of arrow, or may be arrows themselves.

The second type is a telephone pole–sized arrow: loss of your job when you have a big mortgage, a broken relationship, a serious accident or illness can bring on such arrows.

The third type is like a nuclear-tipped arrow: the unexpected, early death of a loved one, becoming a quadriplegic, getting terminal cancer, having your spouse leave you. These traumatic events can bring on all kinds of fears, negative feelings, and despair.

The shield of faith, however, is sufficient to extinguish each one. With the shield we can counter the lies of the enemy, the fears of the flesh, and the terrors of the world, all of them the arrows of Satan. God has given us what we need to ward them all off.

Learning by Failing

An instance of failure in my life to hold up the shield of faith shows how important it is to praise instead of complaining. I had applied for a seminar for my son. When he was rejected, in the split second after getting this news, I consciously rejected the privilege of praise and chose to complain instead.

I went through the rest of my day in minor emotional turmoil. That evening I journaled and tried to deal with it, even praising God for the event and my disappointment, but the turmoil continued and was soon accompanied by a pain in my abdomen.

The next day was more of the same. I tried everything I knew, but to no avail. Before bed that night I prayed, "Lord show me what to do." The next morning, before fully waking up, it came to me: I was wallowing in self-pity! That may have seemed like the obvious, but when you're in the midst of it, often the culprit is not clear.

Labeling our sin makes it possible to deal with it. As soon as I woke up, I confessed my self-pity to God. Within minutes the pain in my abdomen began to subside, and my whole outlook brightened. I could now hold up the shield of faith again.

What had happened? I was angry at God and at the people who had rejected my son. Two of the first three parts of the armor were not in place, so even when I tried to hold up the shield later, it was not effective. Once I confessed my sin of self-pity, I could bow to God, forgive the others, and be ready to take up the shield of faith to quench those fiery arrows.

Note that there is often a split second in which we choose to praise or complain. The more we practice praising, the easier it becomes to make the right choice at that critical moment.

At times I've been discouraged that my first response to difficulties or disappointments has not been like Job's. But I later realized that the important response is not necessarily the first one, which is usually our natural, automatic one, but the second one, correcting my first response and bringing my thoughts and actions in line with Scripture. Of course, the more we make the correction right away, the more often praise will be our first response. Job had evidently been practicing holding up the shield of faith in his life, so when the big challenge came, he was ready.

Earlier we talked about surrendering everything to the Lord regularly. This is an excellent preparation for holding up the shield of faith as Job did. He had grasped that all belongs to God and that, in His wisdom and love, God has the right to do what is best: "the Lord gives and the Lord takes away. Blessed be the name of the Lord."

How It's Done

Here's a specific example of how I pray to hold up the shield of faith when I am tempted with thoughts of fretting or fear.

> Lord, I am beginning to worry here. I am afraid of what might happen, and I am not trusting you. Forgive me. I want to praise you that you are in control. You are the Most High, who rules over all with wisdom. You are the Almighty, whose power controls all and guides all. I *can* trust you in this situation to care for us in whatever you allow, so I praise you now for what you are going to bring, for what you are going to do, for what you are going to allow, for how you are going to protect me from evil. I praise you for your goodness!

You might recognize that this is "journaling in prayer," the same truth applied a bit differently. In this prayer I am laying out my wrong thoughts and feelings and then proclaiming the truth about God and surrendering to it, thereby extinguishing the flaming arrows of fear and worry and overcoming the negative of Satan's attack.

Of course, I could also pray much more simply: "Lord, I'm beginning to worry here. I repent and praise you now for how you are going to work out this situation! Amen."

Psalm 91:1 has given me more understanding of this concept of God's protection: "He who dwells in the shelter of the Most High will rest in the shadow of the Almighty." God's shelter is His precepts, principles, and promises, as well as His presence, all of which are to keep us safe from Satan's attacks.

When we walk in obedience, staying within His guidelines, we are safe from unwarranted attacks; we can rest in assurance. Not that we will be free of suffering and difficulty, but that He will protect us from what is evil, that is, what will harm us spiritually. However, if we wander outside of His guidance in the Word, we get off into the fields of Satan, where, like a wild bull, he is free to attack and harm us.

DEEPER THOUGHTS ON PUTTING ON THE ARMOR

If we obey God, we stay in His provided protection. When we use praise to hold up the shield of faith, we are sheltered. This is the concept of a shelter provided by "the Most High," the final authority, who can never be conquered. The question is, Am I going to get in the shelter and stay there, or will I wander about in the open where Satan can attack me?

Sources of Learning to Praise

The Lord used three major factors in my life to teach me about lifting up the shield of faith. The first was reading a book called *Prison to Praise*, by Merlin Carothers, an inspiring story of a man who learned to praise God in all things.[44] It gives specific examples that I have been able to grab hold of and apply in my own life.

Second was the teaching of Bill Gothard on taking Scripture seriously, taking God's Word at face value. He applied this particularly to verses like 1 Thessalonians 5:18 ("Give thanks in all circumstances, for this is God's will for you in Christ Jesus") and Colossians 3:17 ("And whatever you do, whether in word or deed, do it all in the name of the Lord Jesus, giving thanks to God the Father through him"). He taught about linking this attitude of praise with meditation on Scripture, helping me to internalize these truths. (See chap. 30 below, "Meditation.")

A third help was continual reading through Scripture, doing a chapter each morning in the New Testament, and one in the evening from the Old Testament. This provided me with more understanding of the reasons and importance of giving praise in and for all things.

The familiar words of 2 Corinthians 12:9-10 have been especially powerful in propelling me forward in praise. Paul wrote concerning his thorn in the flesh, "But he [God] said to me, 'My grace is sufficient for you, for my power is made perfect in weakness.'" It is very liberating knowing that, when I am weak, unable to resolve the events and problems cascading into my life, my time of weakness is exactly when God can work most powerfully in and around me. I cannot trust in myself, but I can trust in Him who is the Most High.

Paul goes on, "Therefore I will boast all the more gladly about my weaknesses, *so that Christ's power may rest on me.*" Paul's response is one of positive reality, seeing his weakness as a vehicle that Christ can use. When he praises God for his weakness, *then* the power of Christ could come into his life. The opposite is also true: if Paul did not praise God, power would *not* come into his life.

Paul's next statement continues to be a huge challenge to me: "That is

---

44. Merlin R. Carothers, *Prison to Praise* (Plainfield, N.J.: Logos International, 1970).

why, for Christ's sake, I *delight* in weaknesses, in insults, in hardships, in persecutions, in difficulties. For when I am weak, then I am strong."

To delight in such tribulations is so unnatural, so supernatural! It is another example of the "right-side-upness" of God's kingdom, just the opposite of the human viewpoint. When we have learned to "see" enough of God's character, we can be expectantly poised to see how He's going to use this difficult, unpleasant event for good. This approach is so different from the world's living by sight — in fact, it is truly living by faith.

I can imagine Paul, as another trial descends upon him, raising his hands in praise and saying, "O boy! Another chance to see God at work; I wonder how He is going to solve this one and display His glory in it. Lord I praise you for this; help me to cooperate with you!"

Personally I am not there yet, but I certainly am working on moving in that direction by practicing praise, especially when I don't feel like it.

More Foundations for Praise

Psalm 50:23, one of my favorite verses, illustrates further the truths of 2 Corinthians 12: "He who sacrifices thank offerings honors me, and he prepares the way so that I may show him the salvation of God."

Giving thanks when we don't feel like it is a sacrifice, and doing so honors God in a way that we can't do otherwise. By obeying in faith before the unseen hosts of angels and demons watching us and before the people around us, we can give God the great honor of trusting and praising Him when we normally would be complaining and whining. People notice that! So do the unseen hosts!

Giving God praise in such circumstances is also cooperating with Him in opening the way for Him to work in the situation, bringing whatever salvation He has for us in this. Then we will experience the truth of Psalm 91:4: "He will cover you with his feathers, and under his wings you will find refuge; his faithfulness will be your shield and rampart."

All of this has led me to the powerful sentence that is the title of this book: "Knowing Jesus is enough for joy, period!"

Having a relationship with our God — the eternal, all-sufficient, all-knowing, all-present, all-loving, all-wise God — is all we need for joy. This relationship raises us up out of the mire of the mundane onto the Rock of our Redeemer. When we have an intimate relationship with the Architect of the universe, the Lord of history, the God of Righteousness, how can we give permission for the chains of hurt, disappointment, and anger to hold us down to earthly thinking?

Anything we think is necessary for our happiness is actually an idol; all we actually need is God. As Paul wrote when he was in prison in chains, facing an uncertain future: "Rejoice in the Lord always. I will say it again: Rejoice!" (Phil. 4:4).

Every time I find myself being unhappy, it turns out to be because I have elevated a desire, legitimate or not, to the level of an idol. In effect, I am thinking that if my desire isn't fulfilled, I can't be happy. Letting go of it and looking to God brings me back to the source of joy. I need to hold everything with an open hand so God in His wisdom can take and give as He, in His wisdom and love, knows best, just as He did with Job.

This is not to say that we will never be sad or grieve. In the midst of sadness and grief, however, our joy can remain strong as we work through things, honestly processing our thoughts and emotions. This is true if we make the Lord our source of joy.

Asaph, the author of Psalm 73 (which we considered in chapters 5 and 20), found this to be true as he wrestled through his jealousy and anger at the prosperous evil men of his time. He concludes the lifting of his soul by admitting:

> When my heart was grieved
>   and my spirit embittered [these are his negative emotions],
> I was senseless and ignorant;
>   I was a brute beast before you [thinking only in natural terms,
>   not spiritual ones].

But now he turns his eyes of faith to God:

> Yet I am always with you;
>   you hold me by my right hand.
> You guide me with your counsel,
>   and afterward you will take me into glory.

Asaph's conclusion is to find his joy in God, who is trustable, who is with him, who is taking him to heaven.

> Whom have I in heaven but you?
>   And earth has nothing I desire besides you.
>   [God is his source of joy, he has let go of what he thought was
>   so valuable on earth]

The Shield of Faith

> My flesh and my heart may fail,
>> but God is the strength of my heart
>> and my portion forever.
>> [Asaph has taken the long-range view, looking to eternity].
>>> (Ps. 73:21-26)

Who remembers those prosperous, selfish, rich men Asaph was jealous of? No one but God. In contrast, Asaph, who found his joy is God, has stood as a beacon of hope through thousands of years to all of us to follow him in praise.

Application Brings Deepening

Another source of learning this lesson of "praising in all," of holding up the shield of faith, was the challenge of applying these truths in our time in the Middle East. We were frequently encouraged by the Holy Spirit to act on the Scripture we knew by praising Him when things looked bleak.

On one trip to the East of our country in a small Volkswagen station wagon with ten people in it, the driver went over a large stone in the road, which hit the transmission. Although we could see no damage, it was cracked, and after another seventy-five miles, all the oil had run out, and the transmission froze up, leaving us stranded beside the road in the middle of nowhere. It was desolate country: no villages, no fields, just wilderness.

The local fellow accompanying us decided to hitchhike to the next village to get help. In the meantime I took a walk. I was angry: angry at the driver for not going around the rock, angry at myself for not paying more attention, angry at God for allowing this to happen. It was inconveniencing me, hampering my plans!

As I walked, the Holy Spirit nudged me, "I want you to praise me for this."

"No way!" was my reply. But the Spirit kept prompting me, helping me to think truth. Finally I agreed, against all my feelings, to thank Him for this situation. My mental and emotional state improved after that. But more importantly, God went on to use this "accident" for much good, including bringing us into contact with people who would probably never have otherwise heard the gospel. But that's another story you can read in my next book.

Truly, learning to hold up the shield of faith is an ongoing saga, with ever greater challenges and ever greater joy in trusting Him!

Spiraling Parable

Here's a vision of what the joy and discipline of lifting the shield of faith by praise does in our lives. Our spiritual life is like a golden spiral staircase reaching up to heaven. When we become believers, there are a number of steps in the staircase, each one made of clear crystal. We race up these in our eager growth with God, but then we come to the last step and have to stop. The framework of the staircase goes on up, but without steps we cannot continue.

"OK, Lord, what next? Give me some more steps to climb higher," we pray.

Suddenly a big, black burden, an unwanted problem, appears on our shoulder, weighing us down. "What's this, Lord? I asked for a step up, not a hindrance!" we protest.

God replies by patiently teaching us about praise. When we begin to obey by lowering this burden before the Lord in praise, it is transformed into the next crystal step! The burden becomes the next step up! Its usefulness in our lives is determined by our response: praise glorifies God and opens the way that He may show us the salvation of the Lord (Ps. 50:23). Complaining and thanklessness means we stay where we are until we learn the lesson.

Dave and the Shield of Faith

Dave leaned forward, tapping his fingers on his knees. "Holding up the shield of faith sounds easy when we talk about it, but I don't find it easy in everyday life."

Jack nodded, "You are right. There's a lot of opposition to it: our own negative thinking, our tendency to self-pity, all the messages the world gives us every day about our right to be happy, plus Satan's pressure to complain. But when we know God, then we can rise above all this opposition like a mighty warrior rising above the clash of battle, and we can raise that shield."

"Sounds good, but I have trouble remembering that when I begin to complain!" replied Dave.

"Do you remember in the Bible where David was living among the Philistines, hiding from King Saul? When the Philistine king went up to fight against the Israelites, the Philistine nobles did not trust David, so the king sent him back home.

"When David arrived with his men in their town of Ziklag, they found that it had been raided and burned; all their goods and families were gone. David's men were angry to the point where they were talking of stoning him. Do you remember what David did?"

Dave shook his head.

The Shield of Faith

"Let's look at the passage," said Jack. "It's in 1 Samuel 30. Here, read verse 6."

Dave took the Bible and read, "David was greatly distressed because the men were talking of stoning him; each one was bitter in spirit because of his sons and daughters. But David found strength in the LORD his God."

Jack nodded. "Notice that David's men were wallowing in self-pity and anger, but David went to God and found strength. The King James Version says, 'He *encouraged himself* in the LORD.' He went to God and got his relationship there straight before proceeding. He certainly did some lifting of his soul and worked on getting up the shield of faith. Now read verse 8."

Dave found the spot and read:
And David inquired of the LORD, "Shall I pursue this raiding party? Will I overtake them?"

"Pursue them," he answered. "You will certainly overtake them and succeed in the rescue."

Jack took his Bible back. "Because David had his mind, will, and emotions submitted to God, he could hear God's direction. Then David could set off in faith with his men and was able to defeat a much larger force, getting back all of the women, children, and goods unharmed. He trusted God and as a result was able to redeem the situation for his men.

"So the key for us is to strengthen ourselves in the Lord every day, and then when difficulties come, to flee to Him. With daily preparation we will more readily lift up the shield of faith and ward off those flaming arrows of Satan. And also, then we can hear God's voice as He directs us."

Dave finished making notes in his book and looked up. "It's the same story: walk with God, win with God!"

"Well put, Dave, although it may not always work out so neatly!" replied Jack.

Dave put his notebook back into his pack. "I would guess that my assignment is to read the next chapter, right?"

"Yes, that's it," replied Jack. "See you next week."

Study Guide questions for Chapter 27: "The Shield of Faith"

1. What is needed before you can get up the shield of faith? (238)
2. How do you raise the shield? (239)
3. What are the flaming arrows the devil shoots at us? (241)
4. Why is it important to "label our sin?" (242)
5. How is journaling helpful in getting up the shield? (243)
6. What is the best source for learning to praise? (244)
7. What is an "idol?" What are some of yours that keep you from praising? (245)
8. What's the best way to learn to get up the shield, to praise in all? (245)
9. How does praise open the way for growth? (247)
10. How will you move forward to up your "paise quotient?"

CHAPTER 28

The Helmet of Salvation

Truth #10: Our Significance and Security Come From God

As with the other parts of the armor, the helmet of salvation is a gift for us to take up and use. It refers, I believe, to the fact that our salvation is rooted, not in our obedience or performance or consistency, but in the very character of God.

Fig. 28.1. The helmet of salvation

The first promise of a coming savior is spoken in Genesis 3:15:

> And I will put enmity
>   between you and the woman,
>   and between your offspring and hers;
> *he will crush your head,*
>   and you will strike his heel.

God promised this because He "wants all men to be saved and to come to a knowledge of the truth. For there is one God and one mediator between God and men, the man Christ Jesus, *who gave himself as a ransom for all men* — the testimony given in its proper time (1 Tim. 2:4-6).

The point in these and other passages is that salvation is secured by God and given to us. Our performance has nothing at all to do with securing it or prolonging it. We are saved through faith by His power. Period! We can live far

The Helmet of Salvation

below what He desires, and then He will discipline us (Heb. 12:4-11), but we can neither add to nor subtract from our salvation. Our response to God's grace is critical (see Rom. 8:13, Heb. 12:14, and other passages), but ultimately even our response is dependent from start to finish on the character of God.

This should give us great assurance and peace; it should also encourage us to love God as He has loved us, to reject the natural, sinful human tendency to think, "Well, I'm saved, so I now can live as I please."

Maybe that's why the helmet comes where it does in the list, after having our relationships correctly in place and living a life of praise focused on God. Then we can rest in His peace and walk in obedience. This progression has to do with ongoing heart-level transformation.

Our Deepest Desires

Our salvation has two important aspects: security and significance. We crave both of these, but we often seek them in the wrong places. The desire for security and significance is so strong that people will even fight and kill for them. They will give everything they have to get them.

This is exactly what James tells us in 4:1-3

> What causes fights and quarrels among you?
> Don't they come from your desires that battle within you?
> You want something but don't get it.
> You kill and covet, but you cannot have what you want.
> You quarrel and fight.
> You do not have, because you do not ask God.
> When you ask, you do not receive,
>   because you ask with wrong motives,
>   that you may spend what you get on your pleasures.

These verses, of course, refer to many things in life that we want, but they definitely include the foundational, emotionally held desire for significance and security.

The most important statement in these verses is "You do not have, because you do not ask God." We spend all our time looking in the wrong places for significance and security. So let's look now in the right place!

Significance

Where do we get our significance from? Most of us seek it from our environment, following what could be called "Satan's formula":

my performance + others' opinions of me = my significance[45]

This is a formula for failure because every day we are obliged to perform again, and every day people react differently to us. As one friend who is an electrician in a factory likes to say, "One day I'm a hero for solving everyone's problems, the next I'm a villain because I am unable to get things going."

Seeking significance in this way can be very painful because all those around us are sinners who are also seeking significance. This leads to intense competition. One common way of seeking significance is to cut others down. Others seek it by being distant or abusive fathers, overcontrolling mothers, demanding teachers, and unrealistic bosses, all giving us negative messages about our significance. And the world of advertising tells us constantly that we can be significant or secure only if we have this product or that position. Ads also tell us subtly that we are important only if we are beautiful, rich, or highly educated, setting standards so lofty that few can claim to reach them.

All of this produces much insecurity, poor self-images, and lots of competition for significance on the streets of life. Even those who have reached pinnacles of achievement find that it's never enough.

Thinking in terms of confession in layers, here's how it can look:

anger/fighting/touchiness
using people
competition
selfishness
rejection of Scripture
pride
seeking significance and security in the wrong place
unbelief/rebellion

Another Way

Fortunately God has a different formula for significance, one based entirely on Himself:

God's character + His provision + His promises = my significance

This deep desire for significance and security is actually built into us by God. It is part of His plan to provide for us richly in the deep and wonderful rela-

---

45. Robert S. McGee, *The Search for Significance* (Nashville, Tenn.: Word Publishing, 1998), p. 22.

The Helmet of Salvation

tionship He desires to have with us. And He has already supplied all the significance we could possibly need. He articulates this many places in Scripture. Think about it: He declares that we as believers are:

- made in the image of God (Gen. 1:26)
- chosen before the creation of the world (Eph. 1:4)
- redeemed by the blood of Christ, the Lamb (Eph 1:7; John 1:29)
- adopted into the family of God (Eph. 2:19; John 1:12)
- commissioned for special service (Eph. 2:10)

The wonderful thing is that none of these great privileges has anything to do with our performance or our position in the world. They are what *God* has provided. This is God esteeming us — "God-esteem." We don't need self-esteem when God already gives us all that we could possible need.

In my opinion, the first part of Colossians 3:12 best summarizes the incredible significance we have with God, our Father:

Therefore, as God's chosen people, holy and dearly loved. . . ."

First, we are His because He chose us. It was not that we were special, for He chose us in spite of what we were: His enemies, dangerous, harmful, and a detriment to His plans. He chose us because He is love. He would like all people to come to Him, having made provision for them (Christ Jesus "gave himself as a ransom for *all* men," 1 Tim 2:6; see also 1 John 2:2), but He does not override the privilege He has given us of choosing to come into His family — or not.

We who are believers belong to Him. He wanted us, He bought us at a high price, He says we are valuable to Him — that gives us great significance.

Second, we are holy. This means that, although He called us as we were, He did not accept us as we were. He actually transformed us, making us new creatures, cleansing and forgiving us. It means that now we are holy in the sense of being righteous in Christ, accepted in Him. We have a pure legal standing before Him.[46] All this grants us significance in God's eyes — and we must accept that what He thinks is true.

Holiness has another aspect to it: that of being set aside, selected for special service to the King. He has commissioned each of us to special tasks.

---

46. Our legal standing of holiness is granted at conversion. Our practical holiness is then developed throughout our lives as we cooperate with the Holy Spirit in being transformed on the basis of the holiness granted to us. See Hebrews 12:7-11, especially verse 10, "God disciplines us for our good, that we may share in his holiness." He is building practical holiness into our lives through discipline.

Each of us has important work to do for the kingdom, work appointed just for you and for me.

God says, "This is what I want you to do to help me. Your help is important to me." This also gives us significance. Not because we do the work, but because we are selected to do it.

If we do our work well, that will give us satisfaction (which is different from significance — we often tend to confuse the two.) This also gives us joy in having done what is right ("The precepts of the Lord are right, giving joy to the heart," Ps. 19:8) and in giving pleasure to our King Jesus.

Then *third,* we are dearly loved. This includes the fact that we are adopted into the family of the King. If that is true, then we are princes and princesses. Also we are ambassadors of God's grace to others, given position and honor in God's kingdom. In addition, we are not just a son or daughter, we are a *dearly loved* child, one whom God delights in and desires to spend time with.

This whole concept is wonderfully touched upon in Psalm 103:4, which states that the Lord "crowns you with love and compassion."

Fig. 28.2. The Lord crowns us

Think about what it means when someone is crowned. He or she is chosen for a special task, trained for it, equipped for it, given recognition, and entrusted with authority and power.

Here we are crowned with God's love. Just imagine God lowering a golden crown on your head, looking at you with great compassion, saying, "My beloved child, you are the one I love especially because I am love itself. I chose you to be my child. Enter into my love. I give you authority — and I strongly encourage you — to come to me at any time, to ask for anything in my name, and to represent me to all those who live around you. Live in my love, be my channel of love to all who come into your life. Know that you are fully accepted by me, for you are a new creature, holy in Jesus, redeemed from the kingdom of darkness. You are now a member of the kingdom of my beloved Son, for I have made you qualified to come to me, my dearly loved one."

This is what every human being deeply desires: *to be loved unconditionally, deeply, continually, forever.* And we *have* this in Christ!

Why do we persist in looking for significance from others, when that never works for long? One major reason we persist in looking for it in the wrong place is that we have not internalized this truth of what God has given us; we have given intellectual assent to it, but we have not had a heart-level grasp of it that brings inner transformation. (In the next chapter, on the sword of the Spirit, we talk about how to internalize Scripture to bring heart transformation.)

Personally, as I put on the helmet of salvation each day, I remind myself of how my significance comes from the unshakable Rock, the Lord Jesus Christ, and of how I don't have to defend my significance or fight for it in any way.

Security

Our true, unshakable security can be found only in God, not in our circumstances. Life is very tenuous: we can die any minute. All it takes to change everything is one virus or one drunk driver or one misstep on the stairs or one drug addict after money.

Our situation in life can change quickly too: we can lose our job, or have the stock market drop and lose most of our money, or go bankrupt, be robbed, or lose close family members. Life on a sin-riddled planet has very little real security.

We know this down inside; our response is to work hard to make ourselves secure. One common way of getting security is to control as much of our environment as possible. This leads to compulsive, controlling mothers, bosses, teachers and friends. They may have some security, but the rest of us are driven nuts!

Unfortunately for them, the more controlling people are, the more easily things get out of control because they tend to focus on more and more tiny details. They also drive others away from them, damaging relationships.

Some try to find security in money, power, and position. But the more you have of any of these, the more vulnerable you become to circumstances and competition.

The only true security is in God Himself — the question is, do we seek it in Him? As you know by now, Psalm 62 is one of my favorite passages, partly because it speaks to this need we have for security.

> Find rest, O my soul, in God alone;
> my *hope* comes from Him.
> He alone is my *rock* and my *salvation;*
> he is my *fortress,* I will *not be shaken.*
> (vv. 5-6)

In the Lord Jesus there is genuine security:

- In Him we can find true, continual rest.
- From Him comes what I hope for, but not from my efforts, from others, or from circumstances.
- He is my rock, the unshakable eternal One, always loving me.
- He is my salvation, both for eternity and for everyday needs.
- He is my fortress, protecting me from what is truly evil.
- In Him I will never be shaken — I am always secure if I remain in Him, trusting Him, thinking His truth.

Jesus Christ is the mighty One who has never been defeated. He is the Most High, who is the final authority. He is the all-knowing One, who is never surprised. He is the all-loving One, who cares deeply for us. Do we know Him like this?

With such a God, we can be secure in the powerful and faithful One.

Do we believe it? Do we live it? The mother of a woman who worked in an all-male maximum security prison in South America was asked, "Don't you fear for your daughter when she gets locked in there with all those violent murderers, drug dealers, and rapists?"

"Oh no," answered the mother. "I know that safety is not the absence of danger but the presence of Christ!" She knew where true security comes from, as did her daughter, who had led many to Christ, resulting in a church being formed right in that prison.

I want to be very clear that having such security does not protect us from trials and difficulties — these are both a part of life in a sinful world and part of the training/maturing plan that God has for us. Security in Christ, however, can protect us from unnecessary misery flowing from poor choices, self-pity, complaining, and negativism. It allows us to respond with praise to difficulties and to live in the truth that "knowing Jesus is enough for joy, period!"

The Helmet of Salvation
Benefits of Putting on the Helmet

One day my wife offered to straighten out the files in my office. Since I am not a very orderly person, I gladly accepted her help. While she delved into those file drawers, I worked on some difficult correspondence.

My wife kept talking to herself, making comments like, "What is this doing in here? This isn't the right place!" and "Whoever put this here, that's wrong!" Plus, she was saying these things in what I call her "teacher voice," which communicated to me that she was looking down on the poor ignorant fool who had made such a mess of filing. And that was me!

After about half an hour of hearing this, I blew up at her. She was disturbing my concentration, but much more significantly, in my sight, she was criticizing me, making me feel like a fool. I'm the one who put all those things in the "wrong" place!

I felt that she had been striking at my significance. The problem, though, was not what she said or the way she said it; the problem was my insecurity and wrong sense of what gave significance. Actually my more foundational sin was that I had been expecting from her what only God can give me: unconditional love, recognition, nonstop approval, and unending affirmation of my significance. She, of course, being human, failed to meet these unrealistic desires, and I reacted in anger.

After meditating on Colossians 3:12, with God's help I was able to see the real struggle going on in my heart. Then the Holy Spirit enabled me to turn from my unreasonable desires and resulting anger, to thinking truth and being set free — which included apologizing to my wife! He began to teach me to draw my significance from the great unfailing One.

On a winter weekend shortly after this incident, my wife and I went to Maine to speak in a church. We arrived in the town early in the afternoon and had an hour to spare before anything started, so my wife suggested we go for a walk by the sea.

We parked and walked along the road overlooking the beach. When we came to a set of stairs leading down, knowing that my wife really likes walking on the sand, I suggested we go down to the beach. She rejected my suggestion. I then made two others, both for things she likes, which she also rejected.

I found myself getting angry: because my good suggestions were rejected, I felt like a fool (always a big red flag for me that my significance is in danger). But before I blew up, I heard the Holy Spirit say to me, "And where does your significance come from?"

"Oh, right," I replied, "I am chosen before the foundation of the world, redeemed by the blood of the Lamb, and adopted into the family of God. So my wife's rejection of my suggestions doesn't matter." And with that, my anger melted away.

The rest of the weekend went really well, in spite of some difficult situations, as I was now open to the Spirit's leading and could ignore those urges to get significance from people and activities.

In my work of helping people in many countries, I have seen such conflicts played out often. I have come to realize that at the bottom of every conflict is either a desire for significance or for security, or both. Knowing this has been a big help to me in learning to avoid conflicts and in helping others solve their conflicts.

If we would just believe that God has given us all the significance we need for eternity, we could quit scrabbling on the streets of life for the few crumbs of significance available in the marketplace. We would go directly to the whole warehouse full of significance God has already given us. If only we would believe and avail ourselves of it, we could avoid a lot of conflict and no doubt could resolve the rest.

Stopping conflicts cold. One major benefit of having on the helmet of salvation is that we can learn to recognize the signs of a struggle for significance/security before it really gets going and stop it. Here are several signs that are important for me to note, and maybe for you, too.

First is frustration with another person for not "giving me what I want." This could be affirmation, encouragement, support, respect, or saying "yes" to all my plans. It is a warning to turn to God for these things and to reject the fear of man.

Second is feeling that someone has snatched away my dignity. People have a way of speaking to us in a manner or tone that lets us know how wretchedly incompetent we are. Comments like "Why did you do it that way?" are followed by an unspoken but clear "You dummy!" I sometimes say things like that to myself. It is the accusation that we are incapable and great bunglers, which takes away any sense of our dignity.

Third is feeling like a fool, whether because of a mistake I made or because of what someone else has done or said to me. For instance, one thing I despise is being overcharged when I buy something — that really makes me feel like a fool, like I'm being taken advantage of. Once the Lord showed me the source of my anger over being taken advantage of, I was able to let go and forgive the other person, living in the truth that this event hasn't altered my significance one bit!

The Helmet of Salvation

In every such situation I have to make a choice: will I react like a fool or like a wise man? "A fool shows his annoyance at once, but a prudent man overlooks an insult" (Prov. 12:16). If we know who we are in Christ, such comments are easily blocked and rendered harmless by holding up the shield of faith and keeping on the helmet of salvation.

More effective ministry. Another major benefit of keeping on the helmet of salvation is that it makes our ministry more effective. As noted earlier in this book, all of us serve God for a variety of reasons and motives. We rarely take the time to examine these because the most obvious one is usually one that appears to be good. However, since the motive or desire for significance and security is held on an emotional level rather than an intellectual one, we are mostly unaware of how this influences what we do.

When we minister out of a motive to get significance or security, we are giving to others with the goal of getting. It is like a person who invites friends for tea but then goes around and eats the majority of what is on each person's plate. How do the guests feel? Cheated, perhaps used, and certainly not loved!

So it is in real-life ministry. If we don't lay aside the motive to be significant or secure, we will end up using those we are supposedly helping so that we get significance and security for ourselves. They will sense that they are a project in our eyes and heart and will correctly discern that we don't really love them. And if they don't "perform" as we desire, our angry reaction will clearly show them we don't love them; we only love the result of their proper performance, which makes us feel significant.

An opposite example is Jesus washing His disciples' feet. This was the task that the lowest slave normally performed in the household. On this occasion, "Jesus knew that the Father had put all things under his power, and that he had come from God and was returning to God; so he got up from the meal, took off his outer clothing, and wrapped a towel around his waist. After that, he poured water into a basin and began to wash his disciples' feet, drying them with the towel that was wrapped around him" (John 13:3-5).

Note that Jesus did not do this humble act in order to get significance, but He did it out of His own significance, knowing three things: (1) the Father had given everything into His hands, (2) He had come from God, and (3) He was going back to God. He knew who He was, and on this basis He was able to do the lowest possible task without it touching His significance. We can do the same.

One way to check how much "significance hunting" goes on is to read prayer letters of missionaries. When we read about "my church" or "my ministry" or "my converts," we may be encountering an underlying motive of wanting to be significant, of extolling all that we have done. This type of letter often does not mention struggles and difficulties. That would make us look weak, something the significance hunter wants to avoid. I have been guilty of such attitudes! I do praise God, however, for the Holy Spirit's patient work with me.

Another way of spotting this desire for significance is to look at conflicts in churches or among missionaries. At the bottom there is always a desire to be significant or secure.

One conflict I had to deal with was between two couples working in a rural area in Asia. They had had a very good relationship for ten years. Then the younger couple suddenly began to emphasize a specific doctrinal teaching; this put a wall between themselves and the older couple, who couldn't accept this "new" teaching.

In trying to solve this theological conflict, it came out that the older couple had from the beginning acted like parents to the younger ones. After ten years of playing the role of children, the younger couple had had enough — now that they had the language, knew the culture, and had experience, they wanted to be treated as equals. Here was the significance issue.

However, because the older couple was so competent in every area of life, the only place the younger couple could find to take a stand was this theological issue. When we were able to deal with the significance issue — helping the older couple change their style of leadership and the younger couple to see what was driving them — the theological issue largely disappeared.

We need to check our motives regularly. Am I ministering to give God glory, joining Him in what He's doing and seeing prayer as His invitation to join Him, or am I using ministry as a way to make myself feel good, look good, and gain the admiration of others? Keeping on the helmet of salvation will protect us from such wrong thinking and keep us ministering for the right reasons, giving God glory.

God's Love Gives Us both Significance and Security

In chapter 21 we looked at Eph. 3:17-19: "I pray that you, being rooted and established in love, may have power, together with all the saints, to grasp how wide and long and high and deep is the love of Christ, and to know this love that surpasses knowledge — *that you may be filled* to the measure of all the fullness of God." (See fig. 21.2.)

The last phrase, about being filled with "all the fullness of God," certainly

The Helmet of Salvation

gives us the basis for a deep sense of unlimited significance and security! And what is the one condition for being filled with all this fullness? Simply knowing how much Christ loves me. The more I grasp that, the more I grasp the significance and security I have in Christ, and the more He will be able to fill me to the fullness of God.

Just think what the effect would be on the ministry God has given us if we have this fullness and minister *out of* it, rather than ministering *to get* significance and security? These verses are a good prayer to pray for yourself and those you regularly intercede for.

I pray that my teammates and I, "being rooted and established in love, may have power, together with all the saints, to grasp how wide and long and high and deep is the love of Christ, and to know this love that surpasses knowledge — that we may be filled to the measure of all the fullness of God."

Dave's Struggle with Significance

Dave tapped his pen on his notebook. "This stuff on significance really strikes home to me," he said.

"In what way?" asked Jack.

Dave was quiet before answering. "I realize now that my wanting significance is the source of a lot of uncertainty in my life. I have a number of relationships where I am not sure of how I stand. Do people like me, or do they just tolerate me? Are they cultivating a friendship for what they can get out of me, or do they really care for me?"

Jack nodded. "I can identify with that. Tell me how putting on the helmet of salvation is going to change things for you," he said.

"Well, if I begin to live in the truth that my significance and security are rooted in Christ, then whether these people really like me or not becomes a lot less important," answered Dave.

"I also see that in my insecurity, I've been trying to get from these people what only God can give. As you said, I have treated these as 'taking relationships' rather than ones of 'give and take.'"

"So, what will you do differently?" asked Jack.

"Well, obviously the first thing is to spend some time journaling about this, laying things out so I can better see the big picture. Then confession of where I've been barking up the wrong tree. And then I need to memorize some of those passages in Ephesians we looked at, especially in chapter 1, so the Holy Spirit can be doing some deep transformation in me. And last will be to consciously reject the emotional drive for gaining significance when it comes up and I'm tempted to fall into fear or to manipulate people."

Jack smiled. "You are learning well, Dave. I agree that a change of motive from getting to giving is going to free you up a lot. It will also give you more joy as you think on how much Jesus loves you — and loves to affirm the significance he has given you so you can serve others out of it.

"As you change your motives, God is going to use you to change a lot of relationships and people!"

"Oh," exclaimed Dave, "there's another good motive for drawing my significance from the right source — I can help other believers find the same freedom! I like that!"

"Good," said Jack. "Now we'll add to that the sword of the Spirit. Read chapters 29 and 30 for our next meeting."

Study Guide questions for Chapter 28: "The Helmet of Salvation"

1. In what is our salvation rooted? How does that affect my behavior? (250)
2. What two important provisions does God give us in our salvation? (251)
3. How does God give us significance? (251-255)
4. How will understanding this help change your interaction with the world? (255)
5. How does God give us security? (255-256)
6. What are the benefits of putting on the helmet? (257-260)
7. How will you use this new knowledge?

CHAPTER 29

The Sword of the Spirit

Finally we come to the last piece of armor, the sword. This is the part of the armor we all want to use first! But God has a definite reason for putting this last. Without the other parts of the armor being in place, the sword is not that effective — in fact, it will probably get us into trouble. We can wade into a situation swinging the sword left and right, but having no other armor on, we would be completely exposed to the enemy's attacks.

In addition, without having the first three pieces of armor in place — covering our relationships with God, with ourselves, and with others — we can do a lot of damage, fighting the wrong enemy. We won't be listening to the Spirit, we will tend to act out of wrong motives, and we will be hampered by broken relationships, anger, and unforgiveness. In such cases we tend to attack our brothers and sisters with the sword rather than the real enemy, Satan. Instead of serving God, we will be assisting Satan, who is busy inciting us to struggle with others.

Once we have the other parts of the armor in place, having brought all our relationships to a good level, practicing praise in an ever-increasing way, and thinking the truth of who we are in Christ, then the sword becomes an effective weapon against Satan and a tool of healing for others.

Overall, we need to ask ourselves two questions in relation to the Word of God: how well do we *know* it? and how well do we *live* it?

Reading the Word

A Middle Eastern proverb says, "A lake is made drop by drop." As we read God's Word continually, drop by drop our reservoir of knowledge and understanding will fill up, so that when we need to draw from it, the supply will be more than adequate. Learning drop by drop in our daily lives also has the advantage that we are able to apply things as we progress in our knowledge.

In contrast, learning only in an academic setting often stuffs our heads with lots of facts, but there is rarely ample time to live out this knowledge. I would encourage people to attend Bible school, if that's the direction God leads, but would add that it is no substitute for continual personal input from the Word, along with consistent application.

A regular quiet time is a powerful discipline to help us grow in our knowledge of God's Word. The Lord led me to begin at the age of nine to read a chapter a day. I started in the Old Testament and found it pretty hard going in Leviticus and Deuteronomy (and was questioning whether I should be eating pork!), but in persevering I picked up a lot of truth.

Daily reading continues to be my practice. Each morning I read a chapter of the New Testament, which means that every nine months I read through the whole of it. In addition I work my way through the Psalms, using them for worship each morning. It may take me a year or longer to make it through them all, but there is a continual review of truth. And each evening I read a chapter in the Old Testament; at this rate, it takes twenty-six months to read through all the Old Testament (not counting the Psalms).

You should find a plan of reading that takes you through Scripture regularly, whether it is a plan of reading through the Bible in a year, or the chronological Bible, or something else. Regular reading is important.

Benefits of Regular Reading

The continual review of the Bible by reading gives us three benefits. *First,* it gives an overview of Scripture, helping us to think "in context." This is really helpful when encountering new ideas in life or evaluating a sermon or reading a book or debating about a theological system. A statement made (including my own!) can quickly be discerned as unbalanced when put up against the bird's-eye view of Scripture gained in regular reading.

For instance, in one book I read the statement, "God is never disappointed in us." Is that really true? What about God's many statements in the Old Testament of His anger over Israel's sin, with the resulting discipline (Judg. 2:20; 1 Kings 11:9; Isa. 47:6)? This anger is part of God's love for us because He desires better for us, and His discipline is the outworking of His love, as seen in Hebrews 12. Notice also that Paul warns us about not *grieving* the Holy Spirit (Eph. 4:30).

No, the author was wrong, or at least misleading, which a broad knowledge of Scripture immediately makes clear. The author's basic intent was to show that God loves us unconditionally, which is correct; he just carried it too far in making his point.

Second, reading helps to make connections between passages. Often as I read, a concept or truth will trigger the memory of a similar statement elsewhere. I look it up and put a cross-reference note by each verse. The next time

The Sword of the Spirit

I read through the passage, I sometimes look up these cross-references and find that I have an enriched understanding of what I'm reading.

Third, reading brings a continually deepening understanding of Scripture, of the character of God, of His plan, of our situation, and of wisdom. There is just no end to the wonders the Holy Spirit is waiting to share with us as we spend time in the Word. A one-time or infrequent reading will not lead us into this richer understanding.

In a very clear sense, our interaction with the Word shows what we really believe. Adrian Rogers was quoted as saying, "We do what we believe; all the rest is just religious talk." If we are not spending time in the Word, then we really don't think it is all that important. Instead, we think that we are wise enough and capable enough to handle life on our own. We may give a little room to God — maybe a few minutes on Sunday, maybe a meeting in the week — but the majority of our life is up to us. Such poverty of thought leads to poverty of life. The Word should be central in all we do.

Study of the Word

Reading is good and necessary, but alone it is not enough. It should lead to *study* of the Word, and then on to *meditation.* (See chap. 30.)

As I read through Scripture, certain things catch my eye and may lead me to look up a word in Greek or Hebrew. (I know neither, but there are resources to help us, such as *Strong's Concordance,* which gives us the meanings of each word.) Or they will lead me to look up other passages that speak of the same subject, using a concordance or cross-references listed in my Bible. After digging out what I am able to find, I may turn to a commentary for some further input — but *only after* I've done my own homework. Our thoughts and insights should come first from the Word, not primarily from someone else's teaching.

Speaking of teaching, teaching others is a great way to motivate yourself to study. Taking a passage, preparing an inductive study or a lesson to present, can lead us into a deeper grasp of those verses. In preparing and giving a lesson, a good teacher always learns more than his or her students.

My teaching must be coupled with application of what I'm learning in my own life, not just some theory I'm passing on. In fact, when teaching the lesson, if I can share my own struggles and victories in applying this passage in my own life, the students are much more likely to apply it in their own lives.

Study Guide questions for Chapter 29: "The Sword of the Spirit"

1. How can we take up the sword of the Spirit? (263)
2. What are the three benefits of regularly reading through the Word? (264-265)
3. What is your plan for reading and studying the Word? What can you do to keep you consistent in your reading?

Part 8

Essential, Lifelong Practices

CHAPTER 30

Meditation

Truth #11: Biblical Meditation Transforms Us

I have previously mentioned attending a Bill Gothard seminar and how helpful it was. The first time I went, he impacted me in two ways. First was how he took Scripture as truth, accepting what it had to say at face value. That may seem like a statement of the obvious to believers, but I found that I was picking and choosing what to really believe — that is, to implement in my life. I was convicted specifically that when it came to forgiving and asking forgiveness, I wasn't applying God's directions one bit. When I obeyed Scripture in this area, however, there was release and a new freedom.

The second powerful application was meditation. Bill's presentation of this and the illustrations from his own life impressed me greatly, and I determined to apply it in my own life. Bill gave us a list of ten chapters to begin with and offered us a free book if we completed these. That incentive, however, had no motivating effect on me compared with the desire to cooperate with God in learning His Word.

Meditation is essentially cooperating with God in the transformation of our souls. As we have mentioned, the three major parts of our souls are our mind, our will, and our emotions. Meditation is working with the Holy Spirit to bring change in each of these areas.

Psalm 1 gives some insights into meditation. Interestingly, it begins by telling us three sins to avoid, which correspond basically to the first three parts of the armor:

> "Blessed is the man who does not walk in the counsel of the wicked. . . ."
> Those who are blessed reject ungodly advice, taking instead the counsel of God, thereby protecting their relationship with God, keeping on the *belt of truth.*
> ". . . or stand in the way of sinners . . ." They reject the way of sinners, knowing that this will lead to great inner conflict with themselves, thus keeping on the *breastplate of righteousness.*
> ". . . or sit in the seat of mockers." Instead of mocking and attacking verbally those the godly don't like or agree with, they forgive them, putting on the *shoes of peace.*

Then the second verse gives us two positive things the godly person does:

> "But his delight is in the law of the LORD, . . ." God's Word is what this person revels in, rejoices in, delights in. This means that when his or her mind is free, what comes to it is God's Word. It is a great source of joy to this one. We can tell when we delight in something or someone by noticing how we spontaneously think and talk about them. Think sports, think work, think about when you first met your spouse.
>
> ". . . and on his law he meditates day and night." Second, godly people meditate on God's Word regularly, frequently, continually. It means that they have memorized it so they can think on it at any time, and they refer to it often.

The outcome of avoiding the three sins and implementing the two positives is laid out in verse 3:

> "He is like a tree planted by streams of water. . . ." The roots of this person have grown deep down into the water of God's Word, drawing refreshment, sustenance, strength, and vitality from it all the time.
>
> ". . . which yields its fruit in season. . . ." The result of the continual watering is that whatever fruit the godly person needs to bear will come forth. Consider the fruit of the Spirit: if the situation calls for patience, it will be there; if faith is needed, that will be there.
>
> ". . . and whose leaf does not wither." No matter what the circumstances around him or her may be, the godly person will remain fresh and vital. I have seen in the Middle East two trees not far apart. One twisted and dried without a single leaf, for it grew fifty yards from the stream; when a drought came, it died. Another tree grew next to the small stream, getting its roots down into the wet soil, deep into the earth. When all else was brown, its leaves were still a rich green, making it stand out from its surroundings.
>
> "Whatever he does prospers." This is the astounding outcome: *whatever* godly persons do will prosper. Not just some things, but whatever they do. This is true, not because they are wise or talented or diligent. It is true because in meditation they have learned to think like God and to trust Him fully and thereby to obey His direction. They have internalized the truths needed for life.

I have witnessed such fruitfulness in the lives of those I know who practice meditation. It is not that meditation is magic, but that meditation is cooperation with God in bringing transformation that allows Him to empower, guide, and protect in a greater way than for those who fail to take

Meditation

the time to meditate. The meditator is then going to make decisions in line with God's will, using the wisdom of God's Word to avoid things that will prevent prospering.

The "How to" of Meditation

Meditation has three parts. The first is to memorize the passage. This is co-operating with the Holy Spirit in the *transformation of our minds.* It is learning to think God's thoughts. This is the mechanical part, but it is necessary to begin the internalization of truth.

Second is to personalize it, putting personal pronouns in where you can. This is cooperating with the Holy Spirit in the *transformation of our emotions.* Personalizing Psalm 1 would be to say, "Blessed am I when I don't walk in the counsel of the wicked, when I don't stand in the way of sinners, when I don't sit in the seat of the scornful."

When I read Scripture, it is like looking at a powerful river flowing by. When I personalize the passage, it is like that river flows over me, bringing its power and cleansing into my life.

The third part is to pray through it. This is cooperating with the Holy Spirit in the *transformation of our will.* Praying Psalm 1:1 would be to say, "Blessed am I when I don't walk in the counsel of the wicked. Lord, help me to recognize the counsel of the wicked and then to reject it. Help me to recognize your counsel and to implement it." This is a surrender to God's will, giving Him your will and taking His in its place. Since you are praying for exactly what God wants — praying Scripture, after all, is asking for the clear will of God — He is going to answer that prayer.

Such meditation brings powerful, deep, foundational change in us. I can honestly say that meditation has been the most important source of spiritual, intellectual, and emotional growth in my life.

If I hadn't known how to meditate, I never would have made it for thirty years in the Middle East; I would have been chewed up and spit out by the forces of evil. Meditation has resulted in exactly the opposite happening: all that the Lord has put my hand to has prospered — not immediately, but in the long run. This is the Lord being faithful to His Word, not my being successful in my talents and strengths. All glory must go to Him for fulfilling His promises and purposes.

Illustrations. In an analogy illustrating meditation, think of a piece of tough beef. We can eat it as is, but it is difficult to chew and get it down. This is like reading the Word; there are some difficult things in the Bible and much that we don't know how to implement.

If we dip the meat into a bowl of marinating sauce for five minutes, it will change the taste but not the texture of the meat. This is like study. We still have a lot of questions about how to implement it; we have an intellectual grasp but not necessarily a heart change.

However, if we put the meat into the sauce and leave it there for forty-eight hours, the sauce penetrates to the center of the meat, transforming both its texture and its taste. This is like meditation, which results in transformation of our soul, our relationship with God, our family life, and our work for Him.

Or, to use a second analogy, think about going to the beach. You spread out your towel on the sand, lie on your stomach, and watch the waves. The sunlight sparkles on the water; the waves roll in unceasingly, each one a bit different; some sea gulls fly overhead — it is an inspiring scene. This is like reading God's Word: uplifting, refreshing, edifying.

Then it gets hot, so you jump up and run into the water, enjoying the coolness. You ride the waves in, and swim out for another try. This is like studying the Word: you are really "into it." It is decidedly different than lying on the beach and watching the water.

After a while you decide to put on your mask and snorkel. As you dip below the surface and swim over a ridge, whole new worlds open up to you that could not be seen from the beach or while swimming in the waves: schools of fish, various types of seaweed, brightly colored creatures clinging to the rocks. This is like meditation; it gets you down below the surface into the depths of the Word. It reveals to us things we would probably never see in reading or study. And it provides the application of these truths in our lives through prayer.

Let me give you a simple example of how meditation helps us to see into the depths of Scripture. I memorized Psalm 23 when I was about five years old, and I have used it many times to encourage myself. Once while meditating on it (praying through it while personalizing it), a new point jumped out at me from verse 6: "Surely goodness and mercy shall follow me all the days of my life" (KJV). God promises goodness and mercy, but they *follow* us, so we often cannot see them when walking through difficulties. Later, however, as we look back, we can see how God was pouring mercy on us and working things out for good.

That was a really helpful insight, leading me to greater faith in God when in difficulty and giving more ability to praise when there is no visible reason to praise. I doubt that I ever would have noticed this detail in merely reading or studying.

Meditation

Helpful hints. Here are several practical ideas for implementing meditation in your life.

- Have a partner to encourage you. It's easy to begin well, but it's also easy to have your resolve peter out. Memorizing is hard work, and we naturally shy away from it. To make ourselves accountable to someone, however, can help keep us on track, especially if you and your partner are both memorizing the same passage.
- Memorize passages (paragraphs or whole chapters), not just verses. This gives you the context and the flow of what God is saying.
- Memorize a verse or two a day until you have the passage down well. Taking bit-sized chunks makes this a doable task. Doing it at the same time each day also helps — for example, making memorization part of your quiet time, then reviewing what you've memorized in the evening. Also, try to visualize a picture to go with the verse. That's easy with Psalm 1, as it is stated as a series of word pictures.
- When you have it memorized, meditate through it (personalizing and praying it) each day for two, three, or four weeks, letting it soak down into your soul.
- Avoid mechanical repetition; connect with the Word, think about it as you meditate, and pray creatively.
- Periodically review passages you have meditated on earlier, not because you should, but because you love God and His Word (that is, have good motives). I "cycle through" the chapters I've memorized every once in a while to keep them fresh.
- When you experience any difficulty in life, go to a passage that speaks to it and memorize and meditate on it. I find that, in the conflicts I have had with people, Psalm 37:1-10 has been a wonderful refuge, a boost, and a road map of how to respond. Meditating on it always gives me what I need to move ahead.
- When you have a difficulty, it is much easier to memorize a new passage that speaks to your situation than to memorize one that is theoretical at that point in your life.

Here are some passages to start with:

- Psalm 1: God's way to success
- Psalm 23: the all-purpose passage
- Psalm 37: how to respond to conflicts
- Psalm 46: dealing with difficulty
- Psalm 62: God's perspective on life
- Psalm 73: dealing with envy
- Psalm 86: the balance between weakness and God's power
- Matthew 5–7: thinking God's thoughts

- Ephesians 1: the eternal perspective
- Colossians 3: thinking God's values
- Hebrews 12:1-17: difficulties — why they come, what to do with them
- 1 Peter 1 and 4: purposes for suffering

Once you have memorized some of these, you will see other passages in Scripture that you would like to meditate on. As you memorize, give them a title, as that will help you in the process.

Once you have memorized and meditated on a passage, you will have a "gift" to give to others who are struggling with something. You can turn to a relevant passage and share from the treasures you have gleaned in your meditation.

The Healing Power of Meditation

When I was twenty-three, I fell into a deep depression. It had been slowly coming on for years, and now I had fallen over the edge. I was sleeping twenty-three hours a day, getting up only to eat.

My mother said, "I think there is something wrong with you. You'd better go see the doctor." So I did. He put me into the hospital for three days of tests. After reviewing the tests, he came and sat on my bed, looking at the results.

"Son, you are as healthy as a horse," he said. "I think the problem is that your religious ideas don't line up with everyday life!" He prescribed an antidepressant, and after some small talk, he got up and left.

I was devastated. Here I was trying to live for God — including witnessing to the doctor — and this was the outcome?! "What should I do?" I prayed.

At that moment the mailman came and brought me a card from a woman in our church. She apologized for sending me a card that really was designed for an old woman, with pink and blue sparkle on the front. As I opened it, however, I found printed on the inside just the verse I needed: "O taste and see that the LORD is good: blessed is the man that trusteth in him" (Ps. 34:8 KJV).

"OK, Lord, I will trust in you," I said. "Show me what to do." Immediately Hebrews 12:1-17 came to mind, one of the sections that Bill Gothard had recommended. It is about difficulties: where they come from, and what to do with them. So I began to memorize and meditate on this rich and powerful passage.

In it were all the answers I needed. The first big insights came from verses 5 and 6:

> And you have forgotten that word of encouragement that addresses you as sons:

Meditation

> "My son, do not make light of the Lord's discipline,
>   and do not lose heart when he rebukes you,
> because *the Lord disciplines those he loves,*
>   and he punishes everyone he accepts as a son."

The astounding conclusion that came to mind was that this depression was really proof that God loves me! He was doing something in my life, bringing my attention to a problem and training me for good through it. Therefore I could and should look at this depression as something for good, although I certainly didn't feel it was.

From this insight came the idea that difficulties are like lights blinking on the dashboard of life — they are not the real problem but indicate that something more serious is wrong. If I don't pay attention to the blinking light and find what is causing it, a lot of avoidable damage may be done. For years I'd not been paying attention to my blinking lights, and now I was in this deep depression.

Further verses revealed what God was actually doing in my life. Verse 9 says, "Moreover, we have all had human fathers who disciplined us and we respected them for it. How much more should we submit to the Father of our spirits and live!" The key point here is the word "live." According to what Jesus said in John 10:10, I am his sheep and can expect not only to have life but to have life abundantly — "to the full"! So God was at work showing me what in my life was standing in the way of my really living — that is, of having the abundant life. I wasn't understanding the message yet, but this is what He was in the process of showing me.

Verse 10 goes on to say, "Our fathers disciplined us for a little while as they thought best; but God disciplines us *for our good,* that we may share in his holiness." So in this discipline of depression God was seeking to teach me how to live out His holiness in a practical way. I just had to understand what that meant.

Verse 11 became my favorite in this trio of reasons for discipline. "No discipline seems pleasant at the time, but painful." God understood the pain I felt! "Later on, however, it produces a harvest of righteousness and peace for those who have been trained by it." God has a goal to bring righteousness and peace into my life, and He was working on training me.

Another thing stood out to me: not those who simply pass through discipline get this harvest but those who actually have been trained by it. I had to actively cooperate with God and apply what He was teaching me!

Now that God had given me the reasons for the discipline of depression, next came how I could cooperate with Him in the process. Verses 12 and 13 said, "Therefore, strengthen your feeble arms and weak knees. 'Make level paths for your feet' [quoting Prov. 4:26], so that the lame may not be disabled, but rather healed."

It was clear that the path I was on was causing me to get worse, so I had to take a new one. I obviously had to take the step of lifting up my feeble arms and weak knees, so I determined to go back to work, no matter how I felt.

I got out of bed and literally had to pry open my eyes with my fingers, the lids were so heavy from depression, in spite of the antidepressant I was taking. (It probably helped some in the beginning but actually hampered me later on, as it was addictive. It was not a cure but simply something that covered over some of the symptoms of my depression.) I got dressed and went back to work in my father's tire shop.

God's faithfulness was immediately apparent. Within two days, three people unknowingly told me what my problem was: my perfectionistic standards were so high that I was constantly causing myself to fail.

For instance, I had wanted to redo the woodshed on my grandmother's house. It was a task I could do and did it — and thirty-five years later it is still standing strong and in good shape. But in my own eyes I failed. Why? Because I wanted to complete the task in four days, when a professional carpenter working with a crew would have taken two weeks! I was trying to prove to myself that I had worth by performing way above a realistic standard. The resulting continual perception of failure subconsciously drove me into sleep as an escape.

Now, knowing this, I began to set small, achievable goals, like "jack up this car," then "remove this wheel," "dismount this tire," "mount another," "put it back on the car." In this way, I was moved out of the land of lies into the land of reality. God was helping me move toward "really living."

After three months of setting and achieving these tiny goals, my emotional state had come from minus 15 up to 0. That was almost worse: to have no emotions, positive or negative, was like being empty. But as I kept on in faith, positive emotions began to come, and after another three months I was back to normal. Actually, I was now operating *above* normal because the wrong ideas and values that had been eating away at my soul were removed, and I was healing. God was at work and bringing a new harvest in my life.

The key He used was meditation: thinking, praying, obeying His Word, taking what it says seriously. This initial healing through meditation has been repeated many times in other areas of my life, each step forward being initiated by meditation on Scripture. This cooperation with the Spirit in being transformed has been the most powerful source of growth in my life — and can be in yours too!

Meditation

Dave Gets into the Word

Jack opened the door for Dave and they walked together to the study.

"So, how was your week, Dave?" asked Jack as they settled into their chairs.

"Full and good," replied Dave. I had some exams this week and a term paper was due. But I made sure to spend time in the Word every day. These last two chapters really showed me the importance of this."

"Good," replied Jack. "What did you think about the chapter on meditation?"

"Well," said Dave, "that was touched on earlier in the book. I looked back there and found it in chapter 10. However, chapter 30 really gave a lot more information. I was impressed with how the Lord used meditation to bring the author out of his depression."

"I agree, that is a good illustration of the transforming power of the Word when we are willing to do the work to internalize it," commented Jack.

"I want to start doing some mediation and think I'll start with Psalm 1." Dave said. "I'll review the hints given of how to do this and see how I can apply them."

"Psalm 1 is definitely a great place to start," replied Jack.

Dave went on, "I am thankful, Jack, that right in the beginning you got me to read every day in the New Testament. I'm now going to add reading a chapter each evening from the OT. What struck me is how little time this actually takes in a day and how big the benefits are from it."

Jack smiled at the enthusiasm of his disciple. "The next two chapter will give you deeper insights on intercession. So read 31before our next session," he said.

Study Guide questions for Chapter 30: "Meditation"

1. What is meditation as we are defining it? (269)
2. According to Psalm1, what are the benefits of meditation? (270)
3. What are the three parts of mediation, and which part of our soul does each influence? (271)
4. Which of these helpful hints will you use? (273)
5. Which of these suggested passages will you start with? Why? (273)
6. How does the story on pages 258-260 influence you?

CHAPTER 31

Prayer for Others

Truth # 12: Intercession is God's Invitation to Join Him in What He's Doing

After putting on the spiritual armor, then what? Once a soldier has been fully equipped, you would expect the first order to be "Forward!" But God has a different idea. His first order is, "Pray in the Spirit" (Eph. 6:18).

Prayer is God's invitation to join Him in His plan for the universe. Contrary to popular thought, prayer is not our chance to convince God that He should give us what we would like.

As we join Him in prayer, God gives us power over situations in His world: when we pray, things happen; if we don't, things don't happen. Pascal said that one reason God established prayer was "to communicate to His creatures the dignity of causality."[47]

God considers prayer a priority. Look at Ephesians 6:18 and notice how many "alls" there are:

> And pray in the Spirit on *all* occasions with *all* kinds of prayers and requests. With this in mind, be alert and *always* keep on praying for *all* the saints.

Pray all the time, using all kinds of prayers, always praying for all saints. That's pretty comprehensive! This emphasizes how *very* important prayer is to God. He desires that prayer be the foundation of all we do.

Intercession

Prayer is the way we enter the throne room of grace (see Heb. 4:16). We have talked about prayers of worship, confession, and thanksgiving; now we will focus on intercessory prayer.

Intercession is hard work; it is opposed by everything around us and much in us. The devil uses the world system and our flesh to fight against our obeying God, especially in prayer. The devil is not much threatened by our being busy for God, going to meetings, doing good, even having a quiet time, as long as we are not giving prayer priority. But once we are on our knees and asking God to do His will, then Satan gets worried and does all he can to break this up.

---

47. Blaise Pascal, *Thoughts,* trans. W. F. Trotter (New York: Collier & Son, 1910), #513.

Prayer for Others

I can have a pretty quiet morning, but once I begin to have my intercessory prayer time, lots of interruptions tend to come, both from without (phone calls, requests from family members, visitors) and from within (pressure to get on with "the work," projects that pop into my mind, ideas of what I should be doing).

One significant obstacle to prayer for me is the feeling that prayer is "doing nothing." This is a wrong application of a good work ethic; it is listening to the lie that busyness is more important than prayer. In fact there is nothing more important than prayer once we have the armor on. Prayer is like shooting missiles into the enemy's territory, preparing things before we are actually involved.

God's call to prayer is for all of us, not just a special few; it is part of the battle all believers find themselves in. When we have the armor on, with our relationships in place, practicing praise, resting in the security Christ gives, and knowing the Word, then we can pray more effectively, standing against the attacks of the enemy, recognizing his wiles, and using the proper weapons to oppose them.

Perspective from Above

Jesus knew that we would struggle with prayer, especially long-term prayer, so He gave us a parable about this in Luke 18:1-8. It is the only parable where the lesson is given before the story: "Then Jesus told his disciples a parable to show them that they should always pray and not give up" (v. 1). I believe that putting this explanation at the beginning indicates that Jesus thought the subject was very important. In effect He was saying, "Heads up! Pay attention to what I'm going to tell you!"

> He said, "In a certain town there was a judge who neither feared God nor cared about men. And there was a widow in that town who kept coming to him with the plea, 'Grant me justice against my adversary.'
>
> "For some time he refused. But finally he said to himself, 'Even though I don't fear God or care about men, yet because this widow keeps bothering me, I will see that she gets justice, so that she won't eventually wear me out with her coming!'"
>
> And the Lord said, "Listen to what the unjust judge says. And will not God bring about justice for his chosen ones, who cry out to him day and night? Will he keep putting them off? I tell you, he will see that they get justice, and quickly. However, when the Son of Man comes, will he find faith on the earth?"

This is an interesting parable because the main characters are the antithesis of those they represent. The widow, representing praying believers, is weak, undefended, and without influence. The only thing she has is a persistent will.

In contrast, we are children of the King, with the right to enter His very throne room any time we desire. In Him we are strong, by Him we are protected, and with Him we can win in the battle. He is our rock, our salvation, and our high tower. When we pray, He hears.

The judge is a godless man who has no interest in justice but only in being comfortable. In contrast to the judge, our God, Yahweh, is the righteous, holy One who hates sin and will punish it, while at the same time loving the sinner and providing salvation for all. He is Adonai, the Lord, who has the right to demand obedience and who promises complete provision so we can obey Him. He is the heavenly Father who thought up prayer, the One who calls us to prayer, the One who promises to answer prayer. And He always answers our prayers with one of four possibilities: "Yes," "No," "Wait," or "Keep on praying."

God's timing and wisdom are perfect. We must wait for His chosen time and His way of answering. He has a much higher plan than we do. If He says wait, then He is making preparations, both in us and in those we are praying for. And in this process, our responsibility in cooperating with Him is to keep on praying, to persist when nothing seems to be happening.

In contrast to the judge, who viewed the widow's persistence as pestering, our God is delighted that we keep coming to Him, declaring our dependence on His wisdom, His power, His timing, and His love. We honor God by persistent prayer. It is a demonstration of faith to all around.

Spiritual Responsibilities

Our Lord gives each of us spiritual responsibilities — people, events, and things we should pray for. And He wants us to pray until He says, "Enough," or until He gives us what we have been praying for. Our part is to "pray and not give up" (Luke 18:1).

For whom, then, do we have spiritual responsibility? We can answer this question in terms of five categories. First for ourselves, asking God to work in us, to conform us to Christ, to provide our needs, to guide, protect, and use us.

Jesus gives us an example of this prayer focus both in His own prayers for Himself in John 17 ("And now, Father, glorify me in your presence with the glory I had with you before the world began," v. 5) and in the Lord's prayer ("Give *us* today our daily bread . . . lead *us* not into temptation, but deliver *us* from evil," Matt. 6:11, 13 NIV margin). Paul affirms this principle in asking for prayer for himself (for example, Col. 4:3-4).

Praying for ourselves first is like putting on our own oxygen mask in a plane before helping our children with theirs. If we first try to help our child, we may faint from lack of oxygen. If we are not attending to our own spiritual needs in prayer, then we will be that much less effective in praying for others. But we don't stop with ourselves.

Second is prayer for our immediate family. If we are married, our spouses and children are our primary responsibilities in life. Our prayers should reflect that. Then others in our family: parents, siblings, and so on.

Third are those to whom we are called to minister. This would include people in our church, those we disciple/mentor, neighbors, people at work, and so forth.

Fourth is for those in authority, starting with the leaders of our church, our bosses at work, and those in government.

Fifth is for unbelievers, starting with those we have witnessed to and those we want to share with, including our extended, unbelieving family, and moving on to include the whole world. Within that should be prayer for missionaries carrying the gospel to places far from us.

God may put other people and categories on our hearts, which then become our responsibility until He removes them, which He does at times. One way that God removes people from our prayer responsibility is when we move or He moves us to a new area of ministry. Then previous responsibilities (people or things) may drop to a lower level of importance or be dropped entirely from our list.

Structure in Intercession

When God gives us spiritual responsibility for people and things, automatically a prayer list is formed. It may not be written; it may be just in your head, but nonetheless it still is a list.

If you are like me, it is difficult to remember all the people and things I believe I should be praying for regularly, so I need a written one. My prayer list reminds me of all I have spiritual responsibility for and keeps me focused as I intercede for them.

Some people abhor prayer lists, seeing them as legalistic and deadening to prayer. And they can be. It all depends on *how* we use a list, mental or written, not *whether* we have one. We can serve them, or they can serve us.

If we are listening to the Spirit, are open to His direction in prayer, we can use a prayer list as a tool that the Spirit will expand on, rather than the list being our master. If we use lists as a tool in our wonderful, warm work of intercession, then they are positive.

Motives come into play here, too. If we use a list to make ourselves feel successful, or to bolster our sense of being spiritual, or to make others think we are a great prayer warrior, then we are going to be caught in legalism, which is deadly to our prayer life. We must purify our motives before God, getting rid of those that lead to legalism.

I work at keeping my list fresh by praying through it in different ways: forward, backward, from the middle out. Sometimes I will go through it and just praise God for what He is doing for each person. Sometimes I will spend three hours praying through the list (especially when I am traveling or find that I have empty time slots during the day, such as riding on a bus, walking, waiting in line at the grocery store or in an office). And sometimes, when I am pressed for time, I spend only half an hour going through it. The list is my servant. I do not have to pray through it. I do so because I want to join God in what He is doing in the lives of the people He has given me for responsibility.

An Example of Prayer Organization

In the first dozen years of working in the Middle East, my wife and I served as field leaders. As we interviewed each family every month, I got a pretty good idea of the needs of each person. I used a notebook with a page for each of the families on our field. (Toward the end of this time, there were about twenty-five families.) Each page was divided into five days, with different requests each day.

You might ask, "Why only five days? Why not seven?" Intercessory prayer is hard work, and I found that doing this seven days a week was too much. A Sabbath is needed. And the sixth day could be used for open, more spontaneous prayer times.

After these pages in my notebook for my teammates came other pages with people and events that were not such a high priority. Some I prayed for once a week, some once every two weeks, some once a month.

There was also a page for my own family, and each of my sons had a page. As they grew and God answered prayer in their lives, I began to add other children to that part of my list. Now there are about fifty young people that get prayed for regularly along with my sons. This was an expansion of ministry that came through prayer.

When my responsibilities changed, so did my list. When I became responsible for oversight of work in several countries, I passed on the daily intercession responsibility for each worker in our country to the new field leader. I then

Prayer for Others

took up a new list with all the country leaders and team leaders now in my care.

The results? As I look back over the years, it is clear that all but a couple of the people on the original team for whom I prayed daily were changed in just the way I prayed for them. What does that mean? That I am a wonderful prayer warrior? Hardly; I have plenty of faults in praying and have much to learn. But I do see three principles to note. First, by His grace I was listening to God concerning whom I should pray for. Second, I was praying biblical prayers. And third, in His strength He made me persistent.

Jack's Prayers for His Wife

Dave looked up from his note-taking and raised an eyebrow. "Those points on prayer sound good, but I'd like some examples. Tell me, Jack, how you organize your prayers."

"I'll be glad to tell you," replied Jack. "Let me use my intercession for my wife as an example. Since I'm a husband, I need to "husband" my wife — that word is an agriculture term meaning to protect and care for living things. So this means I need to make sure she has what she needs to prosper and grow, and to have whatever weeds she has in the "garden of her life" removed. My primary responsibility for this is to pray for her.

"So here's my list of what I pray for. You can see that I have a different list for each day." He handed Dave his opened notebook. Dave took it and read the following:

> *Mon.* Good QT each day — protect from pressure; grace; remove discontent; joy in you; growing unity; heal teeth and blood pressure, eyes
> *Tues.* Lift soul, dump junk stress, let go; praise, not complain; speak truth to self
> *Wed.* Find rest in God alone; think truth; forgive; get agendas out; me to serve her with joy
> *Thurs.* Deal with worry and tension; confess in layers; wisdom; sense of usefulness; me provide joy and refreshment
> *Fri.* Freedom: from fear, jealousy, self-pity, and discontent; patience with each other; wisdom in communication; joy in her relationships with: God, us, friends

Jack waited until Dave had read down through it. "As you can imagine, these requests have come out of knowing her needs and desires better and better.

"As I've prayed for her concerning these things, God has worked to change both her and me. I've prayed a long time for some of these items and will continue in this, as there's room for more growth. I want to be joining God in this work of intercession, for as God guides in prayer, so He answers. Now for our next session, read chapter 32."

Study Guide questions for Chapter 31: "Prayer for Others"

1. What is our definition of prayer here, and what happens when we pray? (278)
2. Why is intercessory prayer so difficult? What's your experience with it? (278-279)
3. What is there in God's character that encourages us to pray? (279-280)
4. How do you decide who to pray for? (280-281)
5. What are some ways to structure your intercessory prayer to make you effective? (281-283)
6. What changes will you make to your intercessory prayer life now?

CHAPTER 32

Prayer as Powerful — and Personal

Truth # 12: Intercession is God's Invitation to Join Him in What He's Doing

In thinking about the parable in Luke 18, two pictures came to mind. First is how praying is like chopping down trees. (See fig. 32.1.) The ax is in God's hands, and when we pray, He swings the ax.

Fig. 32.1. Prayer: like using an ax

The things we pray about are like trees, some very small, some huge. The small trees are like little requests: a parking place, courage for the moment, help in finding lost keys. God swings the ax, that little tree goes down, and the prayer is answered.

The larger trees represent bigger requests, like the salvation of someone, the starting of a church, a change in a country's condition. For this we must often pray week after week, year after year either until the prayer is answered or until the Lord indicates we should stop.

In the 1800s the famous prayer warrior George Müller ran large orphanages in England entirely on prayer. He did not ask anyone for help other than God, and God supplied so abundantly and faithfully that Müller was able to raise over 10,000 children in the orphanages.

After Müller had been a believer for about a decade, he began praying for two friends to come to Christ — but neither made any response for sixty years! One of these two was finally converted shortly before Müller's death (in 1898, at age ninety-two), and the other turned to Christ within a year after Müller's death! George Müller had cooperated over the years with God, faithfully chopping away at the tree of these friends' resistance for six decades, and eventually it fell.

My own father, who was not a believer when I was growing up, took me to a good church where I made my first commitment to Christ at age six. I began praying for my father and continued on praying for him for fifty-two years until he came to Christ at age eighty-six! As with Jacob, God had to take away everything my father valued before he began to pay attention. And then came the surrender.

Many in our family were slow to come, with my mother accepting Christ at eighty-three, her sister at eighty-seven, and my grandfather at seventy-three. Persistent prayer prepares the way!

A second picture of persistent prayer is a modern variation on the first parable.

Fig. 32.2. Prayer: like using a ray gun

God gives us the "ray gun" of prayer to train on a person or event. We need to keep pressing the trigger and letting the power of God work in the situation until He says, "Stop!"

What Prayer Accomplishes

Intercessory prayer is not just about asking God for things. Rather, it is the means

Prayer as Powerful — and Personal

God chooses for making changes in the world, and also for making changes in us.

Prayer is first of all God's way of involving us in changing the world. As has been said, it is His invitation to us to join Him in what He is doing. I like this quote from S. D. Gordon: "Prayer is striking the winning blow at the concealed enemy. Service is gathering up the results of that blow among the [people] we see and touch."[48]

This approach to God's work is not what comes naturally to us; we like to just get on with it and do something! However, God's way is far higher than ours.

It is as though God says to us, "Dig a tunnel through this mountain and carry the gospel to the other side." We immediately get out picks and shovels and start digging through the dirt. Then we come up against the solid rock of the mountain and can do little.

At this point God presents us with a pneumatic drilling machine and says, "Use this!" Such a machine makes a lot of noise and dust, but in the end all there is to show for it is a small hole in the rock. However, when we pack dynamite into the hole and set it off, the result is a very big hole with lots of small rock pieces we are able to carry off. Continual repetition of drilling and dynamiting will in the end result in us making it through the mountain.

Our prayers are like that drill; they penetrate resistant situations, but not much of a result can be seen until God drops in the dynamite of the Holy Spirit. Then things suddenly start to shake and move, blowing the situation wide open. Then we have lots of ministry to do among the people whom the Spirit has touched.

J. O. Fraser, missionary to the Lisu people in southwestern China, learned about the importance of prayer the hard way. He was a very talented, energetic evangelist who traveled to the remote villages in the high mountains of the Lisu. These were an animistic, pagan people who worshipped demons. As Fraser preached, some Lisu came to Christ, but they all eventually fell back into their pagan ways.

Then Fraser decided to change his strategy, putting prayer before preaching. He enlisted his mother back in England to set up prayer bands there, and he kept them well informed of the needs.

Then he committed himself to praying for hours in the morning before going out to do his work in the afternoon and evenings. He commented that after praying at length for a particular village, when he arrived, it was like half the work was done. That is because it *was* done, by prayer.

As Frasier proceeded with prayer, by 1918 there were 60,000 baptized

---

48. S. D. Gordon, *Quiet Talks on Prayer* (New York: Revell, 1904), p. 19.

believers. These grew in their faith and sent out members of their churches to other Lisu groups beyond their own mountains, eventually reaching far more than Fraser could have done himself.[49]

What to Pray For

In 1 John 5:14-15 we have a wonderful promise of answered prayer:

> This is the confidence we have in approaching God: that if we ask anything *according to his will,* he hears us. And if we know that he hears us — whatever we ask — we know that we have what we asked of him.

The question is, What is the will of God in this situation I'm praying about? In many cases we don't know; we can't know in ourselves because we are too small and limited. However, we can follow biblical examples and utilize two means to pray wisely.

First is to pray the general truths of Scripture. In John 17:1 Jesus prayed for what was predicted about Himself in Scripture, turning prophesy into prayer. He "looked toward heaven and prayed: 'Father, the time has come. Glorify your Son, that your Son may glorify you.'" And God answered that prayer.

We can follow in His steps by praying what we know to be God's desire, "Lord help me to act in a way today that will bring glory to your name." We may not know what that way of acting is yet, but we can have confidence that God will stand behind such a prayer and will guide us in fulfilling it.

The second way to pray according to God's will is to directly use the prayers written in the Bible. Many of the psalms are prayers, asking for things that are the will of God. For instance, in Psalm 25:2-5 David prays:

> In you I trust, O my God. . . .
> Show me your ways, O LORD,
>   teach me your paths;
> guide me in your truth and teach me,
>   for you are God my Savior,
>   and my hope is in you all day long.

We know that God answered David's prayer, and answered it often, for time and again God showed David His ways and helped him walk in them. It was

---

49. You can read the inspiring story of James O. Fraser in two biographies: *Behind the Ranges: Fraser of Lisuland,* by Mrs. Howard Taylor (London: Lutterworth Press and China Inland Mission, 1944); and *Mountain Rain,* by Eileen Crossman (Sevenoaks, Eng.: Overseas Missionary Fellowship, 1982).

when David was not seeking God that he fell into sin.

If we pray for God to guide and teach us, He will. But we must be willing to walk in His ways and paths when He shows us! This is part of the work of prayer in our lives, coming to a greater submission in Him.

The New Testament has numerous prayers for us to use. For instance, the Lord's Prayer is given both as a prayer and as an example of the elements we should include in our prayers. If we pray this prayer, realizing what we are saying, God will certainly change us and answer us.

> Our Father in heaven,
> hallowed be your name, [worship]
> your kingdom come, [intercession, asking for God's rule in the world and
>   in my heart]
> your will be done on earth as it is in heaven. [surrender]
> Give us today our daily bread. [prayer for personal daily needs]
> Forgive us our debts, as we also have forgiven our debtors. [confession,
>   asking for forgiveness, a commitment to forgive]
> And lead us not into temptation, [asking for victory in walking with him]
> but deliver us from the evil one. [asking for protection from Satan]
>   (Matt 6:10-13)

Paul has prayers in all of his epistles. I often use these, both for myself and for others. For instance, in Philippians 1:9-11 Paul writes:

> And this is my prayer: that your love may abound more and more in knowledge and depth of insight, so that you may be able to discern what is best and may be pure and blameless until the day of Christ, filled with the fruit of righteousness that comes through Jesus Christ — to the glory and praise of God.

This is a powerful prayer with a number of specific requests, all of which are the will of God for every believer. We should be praying such things regularly for the believers around us, as well as for ourselves.

I have a dozen or so of these prayers from the New Testament that I use as "blanket prayers" for those on my list. Most of these I have memorized, so praying them is also meditating. Each week I take the next scriptural prayer on my list and pray it each morning of that week for myself and all on the lists.

While praying this way, thinking about what I'm praying, the Holy Spirit often brings me face to face with sin, with lacks, and with new insights, which I must then apply. He is changing me as I pray for others. In that sense my intercession for others often does more for me than for them!

Here is a list of prayers in other passages that are outstanding for personal use:

- Psalm 19:14: pleasing God
- Psalm 143:8: living for God
- Romans 15:5-7: unity in Christ
- Romans 15:13: hope and contentment in Christ
- Ephesians 1:17-21: seeing with God's eyes, being equipped.
- Ephesians 3:16-19: growing in faith, grasping love, being filled
- Philippians 1:9-11: abounding in love, discerning the best
- Colossians 1:9-14: living a life worthy of God

Other passages state other aspects of the will of God and are excellent for making into prayers, asking Him to work these qualities into your life:

- Psalm 1:1-3: being a person after God's own heart
- Psalm 34:11-14: fearing God
- Mark 12:30-31: loving God and others
- 1 Corinthians 13:4-8a: qualities of love
- 2 Corinthians 12:9-10: delighting in weaknesses, being made strong.
- Galatians 5:22-23: fruit of the Spirit
- Philippians 4:4-7: trusting God through prayer
- Philippians 4:8: thinking truth
- 1 Timothy 4:12: how to set an example
- 1 Timothy 6:11-12: how to live a godly life.
- James 3:17: the qualities of heavenly wisdom
- 2 Peter 1:5-7: cooperating with God in transformation

As you practice praying Scripture, you will find many more such passages in the Bible you can use.

Praying When We Don't Know What to Pray For

When we don't know what the will of God is in a situation, then we need to follow the principles of prayer He's laid out for us: praise, promises, practice.

Praise Him for our dependence on Him in this uncomfortable situation.

Remember His *promises* and act on them, such as, "If any of you lacks wisdom, he should ask God, who gives generously to all without finding fault, and it will be given to him" (James 1:5). As we ask God for wisdom, He will give it to us, whether we sense it or not. I can remember times when, after asking for wisdom, I didn't have any sense of guidance or wisdom but had to make a decision anyway. Afterward, I could see in the outworking of things how the Lord had answered my prayer for wisdom.

In this asking we need to *practice* surrendering our will to God. My spiritual father, Dave Shinen, Wycliffe Bible Translator for the Yupik Eskimos, told me something in the beginning of my spiritual life that has been so helpful. He said that if I wanted the will of God in my life, I should tell Him what I wanted, but then tell Him that I am willing to accept the exact opposite of my desire, if that should be God's will. That leaves everything open between these two extremes, with my having agreed to accept whatever He chooses to give from all those possibilities.

Jesus prayed exactly this way in the garden. He told His Father that He did not want to go through with the torture, beatings, crucifixion, the very rending of the intimacy of the Trinity, the decent to hell, and the fight with the devil and death. But then He told God He was willing to do those things. His exact words were, "Not my will, but yours be done" (Luke 22:42).

When we are faced with a situation where we would like a certain outcome but don't know the will of God, we can pray this way. For instance, "Lord, I pray that you will heal my little girl, but do what you know is best. Not my will but yours. If you chose not to heal her but take her, I will praise you, for you are Lord!"

"Lord, provide this need, if it be your will. It seems to me this is the right thing for you to do, but I surrender this desire to you. Not my will but yours."

This is being conformed to the will of God. This is living the truth that we don't know, but He does. This is the opposite of "name it and claim it," telling God what He should do. In praying such prayers of surrender, we join Him in His plans, and we are transformed.

In my twenties I wanted to get married and prayed about it. "Lord, you know I would like to have a wife, and I ask that you give me one, a good one. But if it is your will to remain single all my life, I will accept that, too."

In praying this way, two things came out: I had a lot of anxiety about remaining single, and I had a lot of anxiety about getting married! Those fears had been hidden below the surface until I prayed that prayer of surrender, and then they came out, and I was able to confess them to God and process them biblically. That set me free from these fears so I could better listen to and obey the direction that God was giving. And He gave me wonderful direction!

Understanding What God Is Doing

So many of our prayers have to do with sickness. Look at the list of requests for any church prayer meeting, and health needs will make up the majority. We definitely should pray for healing and health, but we should pray in line with what God may be doing because we know the way He works.

He has reasons for allowing or sending sickness. It may be to chasten. Perhaps the person needs to be brought up short in an area where he or she is sinning or perhaps holding a grudge or trying to cover over inner pain with wrong activities. As mentioned in the section on meditation, God allowed me to be depressed to bring out my wrong value system.

Or God may be calling the person aside to teach something to him or her.

Or perhaps the person needs to live more wisely, learning to be disciplined, sleeping adequately, eating better. This was true for me. At one period in my life I had sinusitis several times a year. I prayed for God to heal me, but first He taught me about keeping hydrated, praying more, and working less — and He led us to move to an area with less pollution. From these ways of cooperating with Him, He brought me health. Since then I've not had sinusitis once.

Or it could be because He wants the person to be still and spend more time with Him. Several times when I've been sick, God has used the time to move me forward in my walk with Him, pointing out areas for focus and growth or giving ideas or answering prayer for more time in the Word.

Or the sickness will give the person a platform to demonstrate God's grace.

Or it is God's means of bringing someone into contact with those He wants that person to share with. This happened to me recently, as my heart problems were the means of meeting a fellow who was very ready to hear the gospel.

Or it may not be His will to heal the person because he or she is more useful not cured. I think of Joni Eareckson Tada, who has been a quadriplegic and confined to a wheelchair since she was seventeen — and who is now over sixty. She has been prayed over for healing by some but remains mostly paralyzed. She has stated clearly that she is a much better instrument in God's hands that way than if she were fully well.

Or it may be God's will to heal the person very slowly or to perform an immediate miracle. We can't know unless God reveals it directly to us.

Or, finally, it may be God's way of taking that person home. When it is time for the person to go, no matter how much we pray, he or she is still going to die.

Knowing all these possibilities, we can ask God for wisdom in how to pray, asking the Holy Spirit to help us and to pray through us. Then we can pray biblically for the person. Here's an example of how to apply all this:

> Lord, as you know, Aunt Annie is sick and has been for a week now. Lord, you know why she is sick and what you are doing in her life. I pray that you will give her strength and grace to endure the pain and difficulties of her ill-

Prayer as Powerful — and Personal

ness. I pray that she will take the opportunity to spend more time in your Word and prayer. May she learn the lessons you have for her. May she demonstrate to those around her your grace and give you glory in that. May she take opportunities to witness to those who help her in her sickness. And at the right time and in the right way, we ask that you heal her. Whatever you decide to do, Lord, we will praise you. Amen.

As we pray like this, we will become more and more aware of what God is doing with and through the events in our own lives as well as in others. This will make us more and more able to join God in what He's doing, rather than just praying blindly for what may come to our minds.

Praying for Others' Salvation

When working in church planting, we prayed a lot for people to come to the Lord. Realizing that God knows all, including who will become believers, one thing we prayed was, "Lord, bring to us those who will believe." And He answered those prayers.

In thinking more about this, I began to look at what God says He will do to draw people to Himself. Using that knowledge, here is what I now consistently pray for those I've shared the gospel with. I pray for:

1. *Sight:* "The god of this age has blinded the minds of unbelievers, so that they cannot see the light of the gospel of the glory of Christ, who is the image of God" (2 Cor. 4:4).

> Lord, give them spiritual sight! Take away their blindness!

2. *Light:* "But the way of the wicked is like deep darkness; they do not know what makes them stumble" (Prov. 4:19); "For God, who said, 'Let light shine out of darkness,' made his light shine in our hearts to give us the light of the knowledge of the glory of God in the face of Christ" (2 Cor. 4:6).

> Lord, shine the light of the knowledge of the gospel deeply into their heart!

3. *Conviction:* The Holy Spirit "will convict the world of guilt in regard to sin . . . because men do not believe in me; in regard to righteousness, because I am going to the Father . . . and in regard to judgment, because the prince of this world now stands condemned" (John 16:8-11).

Lord, may they see their guilt because of their unbelief, because of your righteousness and the judgment to come, and may they come to you for forgiveness and surrender!

4. *Revelation:* "I, when I am lifted up . . . , will draw all men to myself" (John 12:32); "I keep asking that the God of our Lord Jesus Christ, the glorious Father, may give you the Spirit of wisdom and revelation, so that you may know him better" (Eph. 1:17).

Lord, reveal yourself to these people; give them whatever you know is necessary to move them to seek you, whether it be dreams, visions, blessings, tragedies, fears, longings, experiences, relationships, or whatever!

5. *Repentance:* "Those who oppose him he must gently instruct, in the hope that God will grant them repentance leading them to a knowledge of the truth, and that they will come to their senses and escape from the trap of the devil, who has taken them captive to do his will" (2 Tim. 2:25-26).

Lord, grant them repentance and lead them to a knowledge of the truth, that they may come to their senses and escape from the trap of the devil!

Joining God in what He is doing — that's what intercession is all about. Otherwise we are just thinking human thoughts, working toward human goals with human power, which will end in failure to accomplish anything for eternity. As Jesus said in John 15:5b, "Apart from me you can do nothing."

Let's keep on the armor and diligently pray with all kinds of prayer for all the saints all the time!

Dave and Prayer

Dave shook his head. "It is just such a struggle for me to be consistent in intercessory prayer, Jack. Every day there are interruptions, and once I get into the stream of events, then I forget about it. In the evening there are other things to do, and when it's time for bed, I'm too tired. If I try to pray then, I fall asleep. I get my quiet time in, but not prayer." He paused, "As I say these things, I see that I'd rather get with it and do things than pray."

Jack smiled. "What is the one word that we've used over and over as we've talked together these past weeks?"

"Joy?" asked Dave.

"Yes, joy, but more foundationally, warfare," replied Jack.

"Ah, I see what you are driving at," said Dave. "Prayer is hard because it is part of the battle!"

Prayer as Powerful — and Personal

"Right!" Jack said. "As we mentioned, everything works against prayer: the world, the flesh, and the devil. There is nothing natural about it. Prayer is a demonstration of faith, it is powered by faith. Therefore it is hard."

"So what's the answer to my dilemma, my inability to be disciplined in this?" asked Dave.

"Unbelief," replied Jack.

"Unbelief? You mean if I really believed God's Word, I would pray?"

"Correct," said Jack.

"So I need to confess down through the layers to unbelief, repent, and then practically find a way to express belief in prayer," Dave said sheepishly.

"Again correct. What are the layers of sin here?" asked Jack.

"Hmmm," Dave was visibly connecting with previous lessons. He replied slowly, thinking it through, "Well if we start at the top, the evident sin is prayerlessness. Then lack of commitment . . . laziness . . . .then selfishness (wanting my way, not God's priorities), under that pride (thinking I know better), and at the bottom unbelief and rebellion."

"Well done," said Jack. "Now what are you going to do with this? How are you going to proceed?"

Again Dave hesitated, thinking through what Jack had taught him. "Well, after confessing, I need to make a realistic commitment to intercessory prayer, say fifteen minutes a day. Then I need to pick a time for it, along with the commitment to do it later if that time proves impossible."

"That will start you off well," said Jack. "You might commit yourself to praying for a certain number of people or subjects rather than a period of time. That will keep you focused on the prayer rather than the passage of time."

"Yes, I can see the wisdom of that," relied Dave. "I will make a commitment to that and also make myself accountable to you. I'll tell you next week how I do with it."

"I like that: understanding, commitment, a workable plan, accountability. God will work in that!" Jack said enthusiastically. "One other thing you might add is a record of the answers to your prayers; that will encourage you to pray more."

"Agreed," Dave replied. "Pray for me that I'll follow through!"

Study Guide questions for Chapter 32: "Prayer as Powerful and Personal"

1. Why do we have to keep on praying for a long time for some things? (285)
2. What does prayer accomplish? (288-287)
3. What are the two ways we can be praying for God's will? (288-289)
4. What are God's principles of prayer? How can we use them to intercede when we are unsure of what wants in this situation? (290-291)
5. How can we join God in what He's doing in praying for the sick? (291-293)
6. How can I cooperate with God in praying for others' salvation? (293-294)

A Final Word

Truth #2: We Can Win by Putting On and Using the Armor of God

It's been quite a journey, learning what it means that knowing Jesus is enough for joy, period! And learning how to put on and use the armor of God. Now that you have just about finished this book, it would be easy and natural to put it up on the shelf and let the insights and guidance in it fade into forgetfulness.

In order to avoid this and to help you keep on using the basic principles presented, let me encourage you to do just one thing that will help you apply many of the disciplines/tools presented in this book. This one thing is to *daily pray through putting on the armor of God*. To begin with, you could use as a model the following prayer, which prays through Ephesians 6:10-18. If you have memorized this passage, then it is pretty easy to pray through it.

When I do this, it keeps the Lord Jesus before my eyes, it keeps the whole gospel in my mind, it keeps His principles in my thoughts, and it helps me to implement them each day, which brings continual growth. So here's what I pray:

> Lord Jesus, help me today to be strong in you and the power of your might. I confess to you my sinful tendencies to [you can add your own list here]:
> - be selfish (help me to be Christ-centered instead)
> - be critical (help me to reject such thoughts and words before speaking)
> - be unloving (help me to be a channel of your love)
> - think lustful thoughts (help me to flee from them to you immediately)
> - rely on myself rather than praying to you about all things (help me to pray even in the midst of conversations so I may be joining you in what you are doing).
>
> Forgive me for these tendencies. Fill me with your Spirit in a way that He overflows my life, so that those who meet me today will meet him too. I make you the Captain and Navigator of my life.
>
> Fill me with your Spirit so I will follow your direction throughout the day. Here are the things that are on the docket for me today: help me to.... [list out what you have planned for the day]
>
> Help me, Lord, to put on the whole armor of God that I may be able to stand against the wiles and evil schemes of the devil. May I be aware of his traps before I fall into them, may I fight them with the whole armor on.

A Final Word

Help me, Lord, to remember that I am not fighting against flesh and blood but against powerful spiritual powers of evil. Help me to fight them with praise, prayer, and persistence in obedience to you.

Help me, Lord, to put on the whole armor of God so I can stand in the evil day, whenever it comes — and to be able to do all your will, whatever that may be.

Help me, Lord, to stand having on the belt of truth, remembering that in my flesh I am a child of wrath, deserving only hell, that in my flesh there dwells no good thing. But you, in your great love, chose me before the foundation of the world, you called me to yourself, cleansing and transforming me, claiming me as your son, and I stand before you now, delighted in and dearly loved.

Help me, Lord, to put on the breastplate of righteousness, forgiving myself as you have forgiven me.

Help me, Lord, to put on the shoes of peace, forgiving others as you have forgiven me.

Help me to, above all these things, having my relationships in place, to lift up the shield of faith, with which I can quench all the flaming arrows of the evil one. Help me to praise you in and for all things, trusting you to be ordering my life and all that is in it. Help me to give you honor before all the unseen hosts by trusting you through praise.

Help me to put on the helmet of salvation, believing that you have given me all the security and significance I need, and to minister out of them with your grace.

Help me to take up the sword of the Spirit, reading, thinking, and acting out of what your Word has to say.

And help me to pray with all prayer and supplication for all saints. Guide me as I intercede for those you have given me responsibility for. Praise be to you, Lord Jesus, for this equipping you have given me!

You have permission to photocopy this prayer. May you have great growth and joy as you walk in His way!

Study Guide Questions for: "A Final Word"

1. How will "praying on the armor" every day help you internalize the truths of this book? (296)
2. Why is it important to "preach the gospel" to yourself every day, using a "liturgy" like this prayer? (296-297)
3. What am I going to do to get started on this? Did you notice that you have permission to photocopy this prayer if you'd like?

Index of Subjects

Adam, spiritual defeat of, 56, 120n.28
Adonai ("Lord"), 15, 280
adultery, and discerning ahead, 147-49
arrows, flaming, 73-77, 238-43
Arterburn, Stephen, 129n.30
Asaph, 46, 162-64, 246-47

balance, in grasping truth, 27-32, 69-70, 111, 206-9, 227
Baxter, J. Sidlow, 31-32
believe in Christ, how to, 15-18
belt of truth, 68-70, 86, 206-14
Bible reading, plan of, 79-80, 94, 263-65, 271-74
blindness, spiritual, 82-83, 293
breastplate of righteousness, 70-71, 215-22
Breedlove, Steve and Sally, 70n.17, 211n.39
Bridges, Jerry, 69n.16, 211

Cain and Abel, 56
care-fronting. See confrontation
Carothers, Merlin, 244
celebration aversion, 181-82
cells, as revealing God's creativity, 103-4
character of God, 41, 56, 77; as basis of salvation, 250-52; as central in worship, 90-105, 109-11, 154, 185, 187
China, believers in, 45, 287-88
Christ. See Jesus Christ
cleansing, 271; and forgiveness, 124, 225, 253; and transformation, 80, 253, 297
complaining, 10, 23, 75-76, 90, 162, 180, 239, 242, 248
compulsive behavior, 85, 255

confessing: ahead of time, 142-50, 196; in layers, 117-26, 130-31, 135, 193, 196, 217-18, 252; and motives, 135-41; pornography, 127-34
confrontation, 41, 172, 227, 233-34
context, importance of, 10-156, 264; of truth, 19-26
creation, as displaying God's character, 12, 33-34, 95-96, 99-101, 210-11

darts, fiery. See arrows, flaming
"Dave" and "Jack", 4, 7-8, 24-25, 37-38, 48-49, 66-67, 85-86, 105-6, 112, 125-26, 133-34, 139-41, 149-50, 167-68, 177-78, 188-89, 203-4, 213-14, 219-22, 235-36, 248-49, 261-62, 277, 283-84, 294-95
David, 9, 99, 153-54, 206, 248-49, 288
Dean, William Allen, 11n.6, 13n.7, 15n.9, 94
demon possession, 53-54, 82-84
dependence, on God, 70, 280, 290
depression, xv, 69, 158, 216-17, 239; and meditation, 274-77
destruction, as goal of Satan, 54, 56, 58, 73, 127
devil: as enemy, 40-42, 84, 129, 278, 291, 294; schemes of, 64, 77, 80, 142, 193-97, 279, 296
discerning ahead, 147-49, 193
discipline: by God, 251, 253n.46, 264, 275; worship as, 89-90, 94, 97, 108, 248
Disciplines of a Godly Man (Hughes), 31

Elohim (the powerful and faithful One), 12-14, 95-96, 99

INDEX OF SUBJECTS

enemies, true and false, 59, 64-65, 197
Ennis, Ralph and Jennifer, 70n.17, 211n.39
Eve, tempted by Satan, 54-56, 120n.28, 220-21
Every Man's Battle (Arterburn, Stoker, and Yorkey), 129n.30
expanded view of God, as purpose of worship, 108-9

faith: balanced, 27-30; as condition for relationship with God, 16-18
fear: of events, 22, 27, 118, 180-81, 243, 256; of God, 13, 97; of man, 74, 131, 136, 138, 144-46, 161, 211, 216, 220, 258; as Satan's weapon, 54, 56, 58, 76, 243
filling of the Spirit, 185, 188; how to have, 171-78; and spiritual freedom, 85
first love, for Jesus, 4, 111-12, 131; and filling with the Spirit, 185-88; nurtured, 111-12, 131, 164
flesh, the: as enemy, 40-44, 54, 147, 278; as principle of self-centeredness, 2-3, 68-69, 71, 80, 110, 140, 177, 207, 209, 297
forgiveness, 10, 68, 73, 197, 230, 235-36, 289; as God's gift to us, 17, 23, 70-72, 84, 111, 117, 124, 160, 211, 215; of ourselves, 71-72, 146, 148, 160, 215-21, 241; principles of, 224-27; and rewriting, 230-32; and violence, 199-201
Fraser, J. O., 287-88
freedom: and filling with the Holy Spirit, 180-82; from Satan's control, 84-86; from sin, 18, 118, 283

glory, giving of, to God, 12, 23-24, 62, 89-100, 107-10, 120, 129, 196, 226-27, 260, 288. See also worship
glory, of God: as basis for worship, 11, 62, 89; in His holiness, 11, 95-96, 112; revealed in His acts, 11-12, 245, 288
glory, of Jesus Christ, 33, 83, 174, 187, 293
"God is moving history to a conclusion and taking us with him," 44-49, 89
Gordon, S. D., 287
gospel, summary of, 68-69, 206, 211-13
Gothard, Bill, xvi, 244, 269, 274
grace, 14-15, 33-34; as essential trait of God, 23, 210, 278; as God's provision to us, 33-34, 70, 79, 93; needs to be appropriated, 200, 251; for trials, 19, 21, 157, 199-201, 244, 292
greatness, of God, 12-14, 24-25, 33-34, 90, 176, 179
grieving: God, 60, 92, 117, 130-31, 148, 221; the Holy Spirit, 62, 129, 172, 183-84, 264
guidance: of God, 62, 105, 153, 159; of God's Word, 43, 153, 157, 243; of the Holy Spirit, 158, 183; of Jesus, 35
guilt, 15-17, 71, 293-94

Habakkuk, 19-22, 24, 27, 30
happiness, secrets of, 186-87
Harris, Josh, 129-30
Hayford, Jack ("Majesty"), 101
helmet of salvation, 77-79, 250-62, 297
holiness: of God, 11, 95-96, 112, 133, 220; as personal goal, 202, 253, 275
Holy Spirit: being filled with, 62, 171-89; guidance of, 158, 183
Hughes, R. Kent, 31
humility, 13, 70, 107, 207-10, 213, 259

idols, personal, 36, 42, 45, 119, 121, 195, 246
Illustra Media, 103
impatience, layers of sin underlying, 121-23
Instruments in the Redeemer's Hands (Tripp), 3
intercession, 31, 62, 286-88; of Jesus, 4;

Index of Subjects

practice of, 176, 212, 261, 278-84, 294-95
Iran, believers in, 45

"Jack." See "Dave" and "Jack"
Jesus Christ: as Creator, 34, 96; prayers of, 280, 289, 291; sacrifice of, 17, 111, 216-20, 250, 253; as Savior, 3, 12, 16-18, 77, 99, 226; worship of, 101, 107, 110
Job, 239-43, 246
Joseph (Old Testament), 14, 136-38, 230-31
journal entries (author's), 98-99, 148, 159-60, 164-65, 212-13, 218, 226
journaling, 75, 98, 153-61, 167-68, 196, 226, 243; and lifting our souls, 36, 154-61, 177, 196, 217-18
Journeys to the Edge of Creation (Moody Science Film), 102
joy: God, as source of, 30, 154-58, 246; in knowing Jesus, 8, 10-11, 33-37, 41, 53, 72, 74, 76, 90, 245, 256, 296; in trials, 11, 53, 122, 168; as we trust God, 3, 9, 21, 23-24, 30, 35, 39-47, 53
judo, spiritual, 61-62, 66
"junk stress," 161, 283

Kingston, Peter, 117
Knowing God (Packer), 9, 10n.5, 211n.40

law of God, purpose of, 16
"Let go, hold on, rise above," 39-44, 48, 160, 195-96, 234, 248
lies: to be rejected, 10, 43, 130; as Satan's weapon, 54-56, 124, 129, 241-42; vs. the truth, 53-57
lifting our souls, 151-68, 193, 196, 217-18, 226
Lord's Prayer, 72, 280, 289
love: from God, 17, 71, 94-95, 153-54, 211-13, 254-55; from God, not from performance, 77, 108, 111, 209, 215; for Jesus, 111, 146, 185-86; from Jesus, 34, 42, 44, 65, 175, 260-61; as spiritual weapon, 57, 83

"Majesty" (Hayford), 101
majesty, of God, 11, 99-102
marriage, and the devil's schemes, 127, 194-95
McGee, Robert S., 252n.45
meditation, 78, 269-77; and journaling, 153-61; and lifting our souls, 153-58, 165. See also Scripture
memorizing, of Scripture, xv, 64, 78, 97, 156, 200, 270-74, 296
Moses, 11, 108
motives: and layers, 135-41; weighing of, 119, 135-41, 260
Müller, George, 285-86

Names of God, The (Dean), 11n.6, 13n.7, 15n.9, 94
Not Even a Hint (Harris), 129-30

obedience, as a benefit of lifting our souls, 164-67; faith flowing from, 30; faith resulting in, 174; and forgiveness, 224, 233
occult, sins of the, 84-85

Packer, J. I., 9-10, 21, 24, 211
Pascal, Blaise, 278
Paul, 9-10, 58, 83, 174, 187-88, 244-46, 289
perfectionism, 71, 217-21, 276
Peter, 10, 110, 208, 228
poetry, as aid in worship, 99-101
pornography, layers of sin underlying, 127-34
power, from the Holy Spirit, 174-76, 182-85
praise: of God's character, 93-106; and holding up the shield of faith, 73-77; learning to offer, 242-48. See also worship

INDEX OF SUBJECTS

prayer, 64, 79-80, 176, 288-91; as focus of worship, 91-92; for others, 31, 62, 278-84; for personal freedom, 84-85; for putting on the armor, 79-80, 296-97; and the will of God, 271, 288-91. See also intercession

prayer letters, 144-46, 158-59, 164-67, 259-60

Prison to Praise (Carothers), 244

Psalms, use of: in meditation, 8-9, 35-36, 75, 146-47, 156-57, 269-73, 277; in private worship, 78-79, 94, 96-97, 109, 160, 166, 264

public worship, as enriched by private worship, 109

quenching: the devil's flaming arrows, 74, 80, 242, 297; the Holy Spirit, 62, 129, 172, 183-84

quiet time, daily, 28, 45, 57, 62, 78, 84, 91, 97-98, 105-6, 158, 173-74, 181, 264, 273, 278

rebellion, as root sin, 76, 118-29, 149, 167, 178, 185, 195, 217-18, 221, 252, 295

Recapture the Wonder (Zacharias), 89

Respectable Sins (Bridges), 69n.16, 211

revival: and filling with the Holy Spirit, 179-83; prayers for, 130-31, 142

rewriting, 226, 230-32, 235

"right-side-up-ness" of God's kingdom, 107, 146, 177, 185, 245

Rogers, Adrian, 265

Roman soldiers, 73, 206, 215, 237-38

salvation: offered to all by God, 14, 18, 77, 95-96, 206, 250; prayer for, 18, 285, 293-94; and security and significance, 35, 77, 251-56, 297. See also helmet of salvation

Satan, weapons of, 53-58, 76, 124, 129, 199-201, 241-43

schemes of the devil, 64, 77, 80, 142, 193-97, 279, 296

science, as aid in worship, 101-4

Scripture, as guide for living, 15, 104, 138, 157, 242, 253, 264-65, 269, 271; internalized by meditation, xvi, 78, 166, 244-45, 269-76; as praise aid, 62, 75, 85, 94-96, 247. See also meditation

Search for Significance, The (McGee), 252n.45

security: as part of salvation, 35, 77, 255-56; personal, 41, 77-79, 118-24, 142, 159, 181, 220, 258-61, 297

self-pity, 21, 44, 74, 76, 194-96, 241-42

Sex Is Not the Problem (Lust Is) (Harris), 129-30

shame, 70, 92, 148, 211

Shame Exchange, The (Breedloves and Ennises), 70n.17, 211n.39

shield of faith, 60, 73-80, 237-48

shoes of peace, 71-72, 80, 86, 223-36, 269

sickness, prayers about, 291-93

significance, as part of salvation, 35, 77, 251-55; personal, 44, 77-79, 118-29, 136-37, 143, 159, 165, 183, 195-96, 218, 257-62, 297

sin: in layers, 117-41, 149, 177-78, 193-96, 217-18, 221, 252, 283, 295; worship reveals, 110-11, 117

soldiers, Roman, 73, 206, 215, 237-38

soul, as mind, will, and emotions, 27, 154, 269

spiritual armor, 58-61, 68-80; to be put on daily, 63-64, 203, 211-13, 249, 296-97

Stoker, Fred, 129n.30

Strong's Concordance, 265

suffering: of Christ, 99, 111, 226; dealing with, 11, 14, 46-47, 231; as means of growth, 23, 207, 240-41; purposes of, 53, 200, 240, 274

Swenson, Richard, 102

sword of the Spirit, 43, 78-80, 263-65

Index of Subjects

Tada, Joni Eareckson, 23, 292
"thumb theology," 36-37
transformation, 3, 89, 108, 124, 177, 251; as fruit of worship, 174-85; meditation as leading to, 78, 269-72
transparency, 154, 162-68, 213-14
Tripp, Paul David, 3
truth: and lies, 54-57; living in the context of, 19-26; negative and positive sides of, 68-70, 206-14

unbelief, as root sin, 76, 119-29, 167, 178, 195, 216-18, 221, 252, 294-95
universe, as revealing: God's greatness, 12-13; God's majesty, 101-4
Unlocking the Mystery of Life (Illustra Media), 103
violence, as Satan's weapon, 53-58, 199-201

wiles. See schemes, of the devil
wisdom, heavenly, 118, 135, 290
world, as enemy, 40-43, 140, 182, 242, 248
worldview, biblical vs. natural, 9-18, 24-25, 66, 86
worry, layers of sin underlying, 118-20
worship, 62; as thanksgiving + praise, 89-92; purposes of, 107-12. See also praise

Yahweh ("I Am"), 8, 10-12, 95-96, 99, 280
Yorkey, Mike, 129n.30

Zacharias, Ravi, 89, 109

Index of Scriptures

OLD TESTAMENT

Genesis
1:1	12
1:26	253
2:15-17	120n28
3	54
3:1	55
3:2-4	55
3:4	120n28
3:5	55
3:6	56, 120n28
3:15	250
37:5-11	136
37:17-20	136
37:24	136
39:2-4	230
50:20	14, 231

Exodus
3:13-14	95
15:11	11
20:11	95
33:18-19	11

Numbers
11:1	76

Judges
2:20	264

1 Samuel
30:6	249
30:8	249

1 Kings
11:9	264

2 Kings
6:15-17	198

Job
1	239
1:20-21	239
2:9-10	240
42:3	240

Psalms
1	269, 273, 277
1:1	269, 271
1:1-3	290
1:2	270
1:3	270
14:1	11
19:8	254
19:14	290
23	75, 272, 273
23:1	139
23:6	231, 272
25:2-5	288
27	166
34	36
34:1	73
34:7	13
34:8	274
34:9	108
34:11-14	290
37	273
37:1-2	197
37:1-10	273
37:3-4	198
37:4	41, 166, 187
37:5-6	198
37:9-13	184-85
39:7	15
40:16	166
40:17	15
43	154-57
46	36, 273
50:1	94, 96
50:23	47, 140, 245, 248
54:4	15
62	8, 9, 256, 273
62:1	8, 35, 77
62:2	196
62:5	9, 145, 195
62:5-6	256
68:4-6	12
73	46, 162, 246, 273
73:3-6	162
73:13-14	162-63
73:16	46
73:16-17	163
73:21-26	246-47
73:22	163
73:23-25	163
78:72	22
81	45-46
81:10-12	46
81:11-16	64
84:11-12	64
86	36, 273
86:1-2	206
86:4-5	154
91:1	243
91:4	245
103:4	254
106:25-26	76
107	45
132:2	160
132:5	160
143	153

Index of Scriptures

143:8	153, 290	18:23-25	228	**Romans**	
147:3-6	13	18:23-35	72	1–3	135
147:4	103	18:26-28	228	3:9-18	15-16
		18:29-34	229	3:10	207
Proverbs		18:34-35	226	3:19-20	16
4:18	182, 194	18:35	229	3:21	16
4:19	194, 293			3:22	17
4:26	276	**Mark**		3:22-24	17
12:16	196n36, 259	12:30-31	290	3:23	207, 209
16:2	119, 135	12:31	71	3:25	17
21:30	13			3:26	17
29:11	196n36	**Luke**		3:27-28	17
29:25	145, 146	5:8	110	5:3-5	200
		5:34-35	4	5:10	207, 209
Isaiah		6:27-28	233	6:6	2n3, 3n3
29:13	135	7:41-42	111	6:23	207, 209
40:26	103	7:43	111	7:18	110, 207, 209
47:6	264	15	182	8:7	207, 209
		18	285	8:9	173, 209
Habakkuk		18:1	279, 280	8:12-13	3n3
3:2-15	19-20	18:1-8	279	8:13	3n3, 251
3:16	20	22:42	157, 291	8:34	4
3:17	20-21	22:44	157	8:35-37	65
3:18	21	23:34	197	8:37	15
3:19	21			12:17-19	227
		John		12:17-21	225, 232
NEW TESTAMENT		1:12	209, 253	12:19	232
		1:29	253	12:19-20	14
Matthew		8:32	57	15:5	122
5–7	273	8:44	241	15:5-7	290
5:44	233	10:10	275	15:13	3, 9, 290
6:10-13	289	12:32	294		
6:11	280	13:3-5	259	**1 Corinthians**	
6:12	72	15:5	171, 294	1:30	209
6:13	280	16	188	10:12	147
6:14-15	226, 230	16:8-11	293	10:13	193
6:15	72	16:13-14	188	13:4	121
6:33	13	16:14	4, 187	13:4-8	290
13:44-46	xiii	17	280		
18:15-17	227, 233, 234	17:1	288	**2 Corinthians**	
18:21-22	228	17:5	280	3:18	108
18:21-35	227			4:4	83, 293
18:22	225	**Acts**		4:4-6	4
		4:12	4	4:6	293

5:7	74	3:20	176	3:2	49
12	245	4:22	2n3	3:3-4	47
12:9	217	4:24	3n3	3:5	3n3
12:9-10	244-45, 290	4:27	84	3:9	3n3
		4:30	172, 264	3:10	3n3
Galatians		5	229	3:12	70, 209, 210, 213, 253, 257
5:1	180	5:3	130		
5:13	180	5:16	177	3:13	71, 72, 216, 220, 225
5:17	2n3	5:18	173		
5:19	84	5:21	177	3:17	244
5:19-21	84	6	194	4:3-4	281
5:20	84	6:10	62, 173, 182		
5:21	84	6:10-18	58, 61, 62, 79, 89, 145, 182, 296	**1 Thessalonians**	
5:22-23	290			4:3	61
5:24	3n3			4:7	61
6:1-2	227	6:11	64, 77, 193	5:18	226, 244
6:7-8	3n3	6:12	64, 146, 197, 200, 201	5:19	172
Ephesians		6:13	65, 201	**1 Timothy**	
1	212, 274	6:14	68, 206, 215	2:4-6	250
1:3-8	69	6:15	71, 223	2:6	253
1:4	77, 253	6:16	xiv, 73, 74, 77, 238	4:12	290
1:4-5	215			6:11-12	290
1:7	253	6:17	77, 78		
1:17	187-88, 294	6:18	79, 278	**2 Timothy**	
1:17-21	290			2:25-26	294
1:22	4	**Philippians**		3:12	33
1:23	103	1:9-11	289, 290		
2	212	2:13	209	**Titus**	
2:1	2n3	3:8	10	3:3-7	17-18
2:2	207, 209	4:4	246		
2:3	110, 207, 209	4:4-7	290	**Hebrews**	
2:3-4	212	4:8	290	1	82, 83
2:4-5	111			1:3	4
2:8-10	17n10	**Colossians**		3:1	4
2:10	77, 209, 253	1:9-14	290	4:16	278
2:19	253	1:10-12	129	5:8	226
3:10	92	1:11	122n29	7:25	4
3:14-19	174, 176	1:12-13	209	11:6	90
3:16-17	174	1:16	4	12	264
3:16-19	290	1:18	4	12:1-17	274
3:17-19	174, 260	3	48, 274	12:2	4
3:18	4	3:1	49	12:4-11	251
3:19	175	3:1-2	39	12:5-6	274-75

Index of Scriptures

12:7-11	253n46	4:1-3	251	1:13	208
12:9	275	4:3	119, 135	1:15	208
12:10	253n46, 275	4:6	226		
12:11	275			**1 John**	
12:12-13	276	**1 Peter**		1:9	84, 117, 118
12:14	251	1	274	2:1	4
		1:2	209	2:2	12, 209, 253
James		1:7	90	2:15-16	54
1:2-3	122	1:8	10	3:1	211
1:2-4	53	4	274	5:14-15	288
1:5	122, 290				
1:6-8	28	**2 Peter**		**Revelation**	
1:22	28	1:3	122, 176	2:4	4
1:22-25	182	1:5-7	110, 118, 208, 290	2:4-5	185
1:23-24	29			4:8	93
1:25	30	1:6	108	4:11	93-94
2:13	12	1:9	110	9:20-21	45
3:14-16	135	1:12	208	12:10	241
3:17	118, 135, 290	1:12-15	193, 208	19	4

S.M Wibberley's next book,
to be available soon at www.edifyingservices.com.

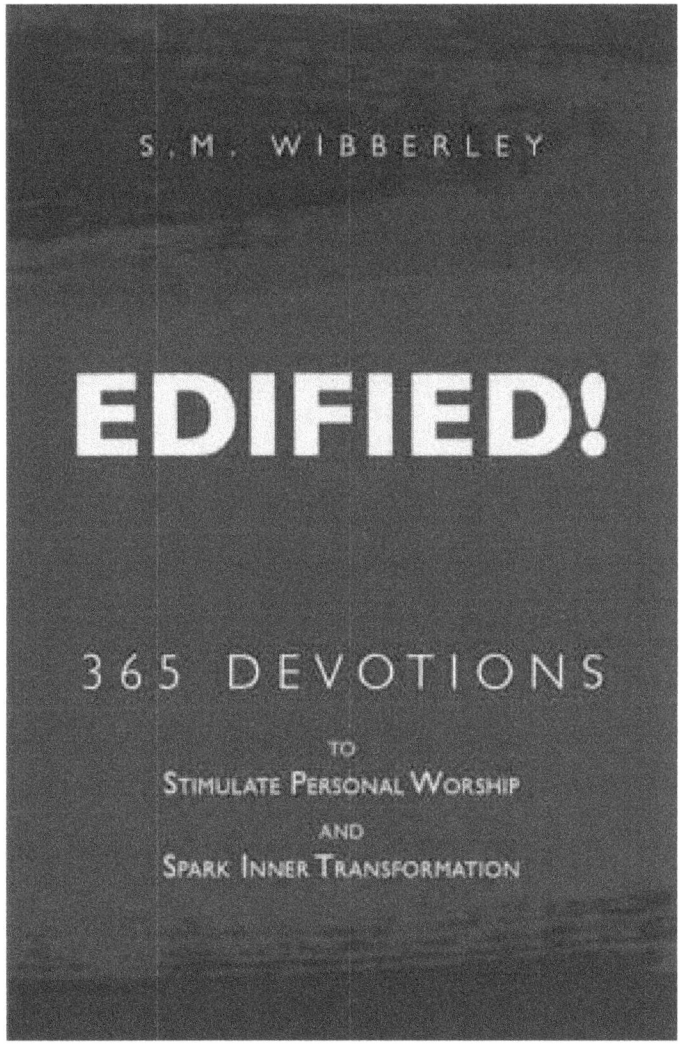

One reader's comment: "Started reading through this daily devotional. Very good stuff!…I know I will benefit from it and am already compiling a mental list of folks I would love to send it to."

www.ingramcontent.com/pod-product-compliance
Lightning Source LLC
Chambersburg PA
CBHW071649090426
42738CB00009B/1468